✓ "first put aside dynasties, king lists, + battles, + sought what is essential in history, namely culture, as it is manifest in customs, in beliefs + in forms of government."

Russia
under Peter the Great

Russia
under Peter the Great

VOLTAIRE

Translated by M. F. O. Jenkins

RUTHERFORD ● MADISON ● TEANECK
FAIRLEIGH DICKINSON UNIVERSITY PRESS
LONDON AND TORONTO: ASSOCIATED UNIVERSITY PRESSES

Associated University Presses, Inc.
440 Forsgate Drive
Cranbury, NJ 08512

Associated University Presses Ltd
25 Sicilian Avenue
London WC1A 2QH, England

Associated University Presses
2133 Royal Windsor Drive
Unit 1
Mississauga, Ontario
Canada L5J 1K5

Library of Congress Cataloging in Publication Data

Voltaire, 1694–1778.
  Russia under Peter the Great.

  Translation of: Histoire de l'empire de Russie sous
Pierre le Grand.
  Includes index.
  1. Soviet Union—History—Peter I, 1689–1725.
2. Peter I, Emperor of Russia, 1672–1725. I. Jenkins,
Michael F. O. II. Title.
DK131.V913   1983   947'.05   81-72050
ISBN 0-8386-3148-7

Printed in the United States of America

The preparation of this volume was made possible (in part) by a grant from the Translations Program of the National Endowment for the Humanities, an independent federal agency.

Contents

Part II

Translator's Introduction

Peter the Great, as we all know, was the czar who almost singlehandedly re-created his nation in the image of eighteenth-century Western Europe, substituted modern *Russia* for archaic *Muscovy* in European consciousness, and remains to this day perhaps the most successful of all Russian rulers. It might therefore seem rather paradoxical that his earliest—and, in many respects, best—biographer should be a Westerner, a Frenchman.[1] And yet all things considered, it is peculiarly appropriate that the life of so remarkable a man should be chronicled by Voltaire, the most articulate and effective spokesman for the Enlightenment and an unabashed admirer of reason, progress, and civilization.

The predominant theme in Voltaire's *Russia Under Peter the Great* is Peter's astonishing twofold achievement, first, in overcoming every obstacle to educate himself in the broadest possible sense of the term, and second, in fulfilling his ambition to transform his immense, ramshackle, feudal empire into a modern nation-state on the Western European model.

In both spheres he was extraordinarily successful, thanks to his own restless, driving energy and to his singleminded, ruthless subordination of everything—including, on at least one occasion, his own happiness (witness the trial and death of his son Alexei)—to the supreme goal that Russia was to become a great modern power in Peter's own lifetime and that his work was to be carried on by his successors. Hence Voltaire's ceaseless harping on the theme of Peter the polymath, the man who was at one and the same time shipbuilder, navigator, and creator of Russia's first navy, reorganizer of an undisciplined feudal militia into a formidable modern army that was to defeat the "invincible" Charles XII at Poltava, founder of academies, builder of cities (Saint Petersburg being the most celebrated example), mapmaker and geographer, religious reformer, astute statesman, supreme creator of modern Russia, and, in a word, its father, a title that Voltaire rightly asserts to be far superior to the merely honorific *emperor*. Hence also the incessant repetition in the Life of such terms as *founder, lawgiver, innovator, builder, creator, reformer,* etc., and Voltaire's insistence on Peter's virtually nonstop travels to every corner of his vast domains in order to see everything for himself, and, if need be, to work on his grandiose projects in person—which at one point included wielding a pick, shovel, and wheelbarrow to demonstrate the art of canal-digging to his workmen.

11

The History of the Russian Empire under Peter the Great, to give the work its original, unabridged title, was published in two parts. The first volume was printed in Geneva in 1759, but not released until 1760, after it had been reviewed in Saint Petersburg. The second volume, also printed in Geneva, appeared in 1763. Six English versions of the work were published in the eighteenth century,[2] the most notable being that in the edition of Voltaire's collected works by Tobias Smollett and his colleagues; I have been able to find no new translation later than 1812.

Russia under Peter the Great is the third of Voltaire's major historical studies, and was preceded by *The Age of Louis XIV* (1751), his acknowledged masterpiece in the genre, and by the much earlier *History of Charles XII King of Sweden* (1731).[3] *The Concise History of the Age of Louis XV* was published in 1768. In many respects, *Peter the Great* both completes and complements *Charles XII,* a portrait of the youthful Swedish warrior-king who was Peter's chief adversary during the Great Northern War of 1700–1721. Voltaire regarded his subjects as the two "most remarkable men to have appeared in over two thousand years,"[4] and it is apparent even in the earlier book that he believes the Russian to be by far the greater man. In both works, frequent comparisons, very much in the manner of Plutarch's *Parallel Lives,* are drawn between the two rivals. For example, just before his description of the crucial Battle of Poltava, Voltaire writes this brilliantly concise summation: "Charles was styled 'the Invincible,' a title that a moment could take from him; the nations had already given Peter Alexeevich the name of 'the Great,' which one defeat could not take from him, since he did not owe it to victories."[5]

The thirty years that elapsed between *Charles XII* and *Peter the Great* gave their author the necessary distance and perspective to approach his life of the czar with a vigor and freshness that might well have been lacking had the two works been composed at the same period of his career. Moreover, Voltaire at sixty-six was, if anything, even more convinced than he had been in his youth that Charles's reign, devoted solely to the pursuit of military glory, was vastly inferior to Peter's, since—at least in theory, and in Voltaire's opinion—the czar made war only to secure the peace essential to his dream of establishing a modern Russia, prosperous and enlightened. Historically, this favorite viewpoint is simplistic, not to say a trifle disingenuous. In the opening chapters of *Charles XII* we are shown the apparently defenseless Charles (then no more than a boy of seventeen) being threatened by a coalition of three would-be conquerors: the king of Denmark, the elector of Saxony, and Peter himself. However, it was Charles who subsequently became intoxicated with visions of excelling Alexander and Julius Caesar, and Peter who did in fact to a great extent realize his own dreams for Russian greatness. The colossal sacrifices in both men and treasure were viewed by Peter and his biographer alike as the tragic price that had to be paid in order to achieve the final goal.

It is surely no coincidence that we find chapter 18 of Part I—which, in sharp contrast to many of the elaborately titled chapters of the rest of the work, is introduced with the laconic heading "Battle of Poltava"—at the exact center of *Peter the Great*. It was Poltava that destroyed Charles XII's predominance in the North and reduced Sweden to the status of a second-rate power; by the same token, it was Poltava that at last enabled Peter to turn his attention and energies to consolidating his vast territorial gains and to the reorganization of his empire. Poltava is the climax of Peter's career, a fact brought into sharp focus by the haste with which Peter's fellow sovereigns began to style him "Emperor" after his victory, whereas before the event only his admirers in Holland had awarded him the title.

Voltaire rarely if ever misses an opportunity to praise Peter's indefatigable efforts to import into Russia all those useful arts and crafts, the modern technology and thriving commerce capable of transforming his backward nation into a power to be reckoned with. Posterity was to reap the benefits of the often agonizing birth pangs of Peter's new state. The task Peter had set himself was gigantic, and if even his apparently larger-than-life endeavors could not solve in one short generation the countless problems created over the centuries, nevertheless his enthusiastic biographer may perhaps be excused for what certainly strikes the twentieth-century reader as excessive optimism.

At all events, the moral of the life is clear enough: a wise, farsighted, and, all things considered, beneficent ruler like Peter genuinely deserves to be called "the Great," whereas Charles XII, despite his indomitable courage and personal heroism, succeeded only in wrecking forever Swedish hegemony in the North. It is most fitting that absolute monarchy in Sweden, which reached its apogee with Charles XII, did not survive him.

Voltaire, who holds Peter up as the undoubted prodigy of the age, the *stupor mundi* of the Enlightenment, attributes almost all his hero's shortcomings to circumstances over which he had no control. Voltaire blames in particular Peter's early environment and upbringing in the half-medieval, half-Asiatic court of Muscovy, where at the age of ten he suffered the horrible experience of witnessing the murder of a favorite uncle at the hands of the barbarous Streltsi militia. The psychological scars inflicted by this incident, as well as the rumored attempts to poison the young czar during his sister Sophia's regency, for Voltaire explain the terrifying convulsions to which Peter was subject for the rest of his life, particularly at moments of severe emotional stress (at the Pruth, for example). The czar is lauded to the skies for having overcome so many insurmountable barriers and triumphed over handicaps that would have destroyed a lesser man. One illustration of this is the fact that the father of the Russian navy and its victorious admiral was as a young man possessed of an overwhelming dread of water.

In addition to the unstinted praise showered upon him by his great biographer, Peter almost invariably receives the benefit of the doubt whenever his conduct strikes the modern reader as, to say the least, questionable. In the *History of Charles XII,* Voltaire does not fail to ridicule the preposterously feeble grounds for Russia's joining with Poland-Saxony and Denmark in a cynical attempt to crush and despoil the seventeen-year-old Charles (in 1700)—i.e., Peter had not been treated with the respect due a reigning monarch when passing incognito through the city of Riga, then a Swedish possession. The same incident is glossed over with somewhat unseemly haste in *Peter the Great.*

And yet there is one question on which Voltaire finds himself manifestly, and most untypically, at a loss to justify Peter's conduct, though he certainly does his utmost to vindicate his hero. I refer to the "tragic episode"—to use Voltaire's own words—of the arrest, trial, conviction, and death, under extremely suspicious circumstances, of Peter's hapless son, the Czarevich Alexei. It is painfully obvious that Voltaire hates this affair, even though he does his valiant best to conceal the fact. The chapter dealing with it (Part II, chapter 10) is the longest in the entire work (only the episode of the Pruth Campaign at the beginning of Part II comes anywhere near it in length), mainly because it is crammed with interminable explanations and rather unsatisfactory rationalizations of Peter's handling of the incident. Is he an unhappy father compelled by reasons of state to sacrifice his own flesh and blood or simply a ruthless and bloodthirsty tyrant, an unnatural and parricidal monster whose blatant perversions of justice are rendered all the more horrible in that the victim *is* his own flesh and blood? The reader is left with an uneasy impression that he has not been given a complete and accurate account of what really occurred. This is hardly surprising, because Voltaire himself is all too clearly left languishing in the same unhappy state of uncertainty, as is evidenced by his constantly referring back to "this catastrophe" in the succeeding chapters of the book, when he cites this or that tremendous achievement or triumph as occurring at about the same time as the czarevich's trial. If this is indeed an attempt to excuse Peter by demonstrating that his performance in behalf of the common weal far outweighs the injustice done Alexei, it must be admitted that it fails singularly of its purpose. However, it seems more likely that Voltaire has become to a certain degree obsessed with the whole sorry business and is in effect simply incapable of either dropping it or forgetting it.

His unfeigned and virtually unbounded enthusiasm for his subject might well have led a lesser writer to commit those very excesses of adulation we are sternly warned against in the Historical and Critical Preface to *Peter the Great*, and there are to be sure occasional flights of hyperbole to be found in the work, but these are more a matter of literary convention than anything else; the association of the encomiastic style and the biographical genre goes back to the Greco-Roman rhetorical tradition. *Peter the Great* is nonetheless an authentic life in the strictest sense of James Boswell's definition,[6] a true portrait, "warts and all," subject only to the proprieties. It is in no sense a hagiographical whitewash. Indeed, Voltaire's eulogy of Peter, for all its sincerity, is not without a trace of condescension. He takes pride in being one of the very few Westerners perceptive enough to glimpse the great man occasionally hidden by uncouthness and gross buffoonery, but he has far too sharp an eye to miss the crude and unpolished aspects of Peter's character and conduct. The Life concludes with a passage that could be considered slightly patronizing: "The sovereigns of nations long civilized will say to themselves: 'If, in the frozen regions of ancient Scythia, one man, by his own unaided genius, has accomplished such great things, what should not we achieve, in kingdoms where the accumulated labors of several centuries have made everything easy for us?' "

As in his other historical works, Voltaire makes much of the fact that he is a serious historian, far removed from the "penurious scribblers" and hoaxers like the "self-styled Boyar Nestesuranov," who churn out scurrilous items of gossip in order to titillate the idle and frivolous reader of "gazettes" (and, needless to say, to earn their daily bread). Even writers of the highest repute, such as Lamberti, have been known to fall into the trap of retailing such ludicrous tidbits as the tale of Peter's jotting down a memo to himself to the effect that "I must remember to have my wife locked up in a convent." Not so Voltaire, who seldom if ever fails to produce with a flourish his distinguished sources and authorities. Thus the frequent interjection of phrases of the following kind: "As my sources in Saint Petersburg inform me," "according to the archives entrusted to me by Count Shuvalov," "The following is cited from the journal of Peter the Great," "Count Poniatowski has told me more than once," "His Majesty King Stanislas has been gracious enough to confirm my version of the incident in question," etc., etc. And in his description of Baron von Görtz's shuttle diplomacy during the years 1716 and 1717, Voltaire cannot resist a little oneupmanship. "The author of this present history," he writes somewhat smugly, "is particularly well informed about his subject matter, since Görtz proposed that he accompany him on his travels, and since, despite his extreme youth at the time, he was one of the earliest eyewitnesses of a major part of these intrigues."[7]

On the other hand, by no means all of the author's claims to precision and accuracy are to be taken as seriously as he would have us take them. For example, in one section of the Life (Part II, chapter 3), Voltaire, the very embodiment of enlightened skepticism, gives free rein to the powers of wishful thinking latent in all of us, not to mention the urge to tell a good story for its own sake. I refer to the highly implausible scene where the Empress Catherine is reunited with her long-lost brother, one Karl Skavronsky, an episode that serves to provide the empress—whose own story is in all conscience as improbable as it is historic—with a respectable family background in the person of her father, the ruined Lithuanian nobleman of the tale. I personally suspect that Voltaire, despite his protestations to the contrary, no more believes in this little melodrama than we do, but rather endearingly yields to the impulse of the moment. And if events did not occur as he tells them, then they *should* have done, which is precisely why Aristotle, in his *Poetics*, rates literature above history.

Similarly, the geographical "Grand Tour" of Russia in the first chapter of the work, where the reader, "map in hand, must first of all get a clear idea of this empire," contains some rather startling lapses, e.g., the city of Orenburg's location some 750 miles from its actual site. And even when we make every allowance for the changes in place names that are only to be expected after two centuries, there are several little puzzles which this reader at least has found to be insoluble. Voltaire's insouciance (one might almost say his cavalier attitude) with regard to the spelling of non-French proper names is of course a typically Gallic phenomenon. *Charles XII* has its Dr. Areskines, M. Couk, and Colonel Bère (Erskine, Cook, and Baer), while *Peter the Great*'s Véronise, Kiovie, and Jean Basilides conceal the more familiar Voronezh (River), Kiev, and Ivan Vasilievich (the Terrible). Contemporary Russian objections to such liberties provoked the studied and exquisite courtesy of the Letter to Ivan Shuvalov, where the author's ill-concealed irascibility is highly reminiscent of Samuel Johnson's indignant "And is it thus, Sir, that you presume to controvert my arguments?" Criticism, it must be confessed, was never taken lightly by Voltaire. "Can such observations have possibly been made?" he rhetorically inquires of Shuvalov on the subject of some relatively minor disagreement over the first draft of *Peter the Great*.[8]

At sixty-five, the author of *Peter the Great* retains all those qualities considered uniquely Voltairean; the life of the Russian emperor was in fact published within a year of the appearance of Voltaire's best-known work, *Candide* (1759). The irony has lost none of its bite,[9] and his wonderful prose, so effortless and so eminently *readable*, remains as sprightly as ever. The gift for the lapidary phrase is still much in evidence too.

Writing as he is about a country that to the vast majority of his

European contemporaries was strictly terra incognita, Voltaire of necessity makes frequent comparisons between Russia—or rather the Russias—and the West. These are as often as not quite unflattering to Europe, and Voltaire deliberately goes out of his way to justify or excuse customs and manners somewhat bizarre or primitive when viewed from Paris, Vienna, or London. The concluding paragraphs of chapter 14, Part II, describe the grotesque buffoonery of a wedding arranged by Peter between the octogenarian jester Zotov and a bride as old as himself. Anticipating the superior smiles of European sophisticates, Voltaire pounces on equally absurd aspects of the French carnival. "Is it a finer thing to see five hundred persons wearing hideous masks and ridiculous garments capering all night long in a large room without speaking to one another?" The same tolerant attitude (or possibly pure bloodymindedness) is displayed toward other cultures, e.g., the Turks and Chinese.[10] Furthermore, in the lengthy chapter dealing with the trial and death of the Czarevich Alexei, Voltaire warns us sternly that "we must not form an opinion of the customs and laws of one nation by comparing them with those of others." This is in reference to the powers of life and death possessed by any Russian paterfamilias over his children, and more especially so in the case of the czar. And yet there can be no doubt whatsoever that, for all his genuine approval of certain praiseworthy aspects of non-Western civilizations that we should do well to imitate, etc., despite his undeniable broadmindedness and tolerance, Voltaire is thoroughly persuaded that the norm, the ideal after which mankind should be striving, is that of the enlightened European *philosophe*. The first chapter of the work closes with an interesting reflection on the long and painful emergence from the melting pot of every human society and nation, and the fragility of all cultures. ". . . The only real cause of wonder is that most nations do not live like Tartars."

The hiatus of some thirty years between the publication of what are in effect companion volumes of history has in no way diminished Voltaire's superb self-assurance or the relish with which he makes statements of the most highly provocative and controversial nature on every subject imaginable. *Peter the Great,* like *Charles XII* before it, abounds in pronouncements such as: ". . . the Dnieper, named Borysthenes by the Greeks. The contrast between these two names, the former hard to pronounce, the latter melodious, serves to demonstrate, along with a hundred other proofs, both the uncouthness of all the ancient peoples of the North and the refinement of the Greek language."[11] It is precisely this total lack of diffidence and contempt for objectivity that gives rise to the occasional outburst from a Voltaire impatient of what strikes him as nitpicking criticism, the petty cavilings of Shuvalov's commentator, for instance. And I must not omit the running battle of the footnotes—

already begun in Charles XII—directed against the unfortunate Chaplain Nordberg, "confessor" to the king of Sweden and author of a life of his royal master in which he has the temerity to disagree, from time to time, with Voltaire. The latter loses no opportunity to cite Nordberg, either to rebut his arguments with withering scorn or else maliciously to turn his own words against him. Actually, Nordberg is disposed of, so to speak, very early in the work: "Nordberg has been rebutted in those passages which seemed most important, but in minor matters has been given license to be wrong with impunity."[12]

To a certain extent we may say that *Peter the Great* is a work of uneven excellence. Voltaire is a dedicated apostle of the Enlightenment; contrary views simply do not interest him, and criticism, is, as we have seen, absolute anathema to him. Moreover, the book as a whole lacks the organizational tautness and density of *Charles XII*. There are examples of this in the author's occasional repetitiousness, notably in the apocryphal anecdote of Ivan the Terrible's nailing the English ambassador's hat to his head, which crops up no less than three times, as is also the case with Peter's remark to the effect that the arts have traveled all around the world. Voltaire is the first to reject the authenticity of the ambassador's hat episode, and yet seems to be either fascinated by it or, more probably, simply forgot that he had already mentioned it. One is tempted to believe that Voltaire, perhaps exasperated by the carping comments of Shuvalov's "German" critic in Saint Petersburg, never thoroughly proofread his book. Be that as it may, even when nodding Voltaire is still Voltaire, i.e. (as I have said before), one of the most *readable* of historians. This alone, I venture to hope, justifies my translation into English of a work perennially in print in the language in which it was written. As Professor Ian Grey observes in his own excellent study of Peter the Great, ". . . while Voltaire could be misled at times into making wrong judgments, mainly due to limitations on the materials available to him, his biographies of Peter and of Charles XII remain among the most readable and sound studies available."[13]

This translation is based on the text of the Kehl edition of Voltaire's *Oeuvres Complètes*, published at Kehl in Baden, Germany, between 1784 and 1790. Before his death in 1778, Voltaire had been revising his works and is known to have completed, among others, the histories, including *Peter the Great*.

I have throughout followed Voltaire's practice of lightening the text by leaving most dates in parentheses. For the same reason I have relegated biographical details concerning the more minor figures, as well as geographical information about relatively unimportant places, to the index. In the interest of clarity and simplification I have consistently used those spellings of proper names most easily recognizable to the present-day reader, *Kiev* for Voltaire's *Kiovie*, *K'ang Hsi* for *Cam Hi*,

Don for *Tanaïs,* etc., putting the author's original version in a footnote only when that version is so idiosyncratic or unusual as to call for comment. For example, in the section devoted to Peter's ancestors Voltaire identifies the mother of Czar Mikhail Romanov as "Sheremeto," whereas her actual name was Xenia (sometimes known as "Marta the Nun"). Since he occasionally uses this orthography for the name of Marshal Sheremeteyev, I presume that the lady's surname was actually Sheremeteyeva.

Certain names, both of characters and places, have escaped me altogether. However, these are almost invariably of minor importance, and even should the mystery be solved, I suspect that the result would scarcely justify the effort.

My deepest thanks are due to the National Endowment for the Humanities, whose generous financial support enabled me to spend the summers of 1979 and 1980 on this project, and to Angelo State University for a Faculty Research Grant awarded during the summer of 1978. On a more personal level, I would like to single out two individuals from among the many of whose services I have freely availed myself. These are Dr. Bernard T. Young, dean of the Graduate School of Angelo State University, whose warm encouragement and unfailing moral support have been of inestimable assistance to me, and my long-suffering wife Georgia, the unpaid heroine of this translation, typist, secretary, copy editor and proofreader, and above all first critic.

MICHAEL JENKINS

San Angelo, Texas

Russia
under Peter the Great

Historical and Critical Preface

I

When, at the turn of the present century, Czar Peter was laying the foundations of Saint Petersburg,[1] or rather of his empire, nobody foresaw a happy outcome. Had anyone in those days imagined that a Russian sovereign would be able to send victorious fleets into the Dardanelles, subjugate the Crimea, expel the Turks from four vast provinces, control the Black Sea, found the most brilliant court in Europe, and make all the arts[2] flourish in the midst of war, he would have been considered a mere visionary.

But a more openly avowed visionary is the writer who predicted in 1762, in some *Social*—or anti-social—*Contract* or other[3] that the Russian empire was about to collapse. He says in so many words: "The Tartars, his subjects or neighbors, will become his masters and ours too; this strikes me as a certainty."

It is a curious sort of derangement when a rascal speaks with authority to monarchs and unerringly prophesies the impending fall of empires from the interior of the tub in which he preaches, and which he believes to have once belonged to Diogenes. The astounding achievements of the Empress Catherine II and the Russian nation are sufficiently convincing evidence that Peter the Great built on a solid and enduring foundation.

Of all the lawgivers since Mohammed, he is the one whose people have distinguished themselves the most after his death. The Romuluses and Theseuses come nowhere near him.

A rather splendid demonstration that Russia owes everything to Peter the Great took place during the ceremony of thanksgiving to God performed, in accordance with custom, in Saint Petersburg's cathedral for the victory of Count Orlov, who burned the entire Ottoman fleet in 1770. In the middle of his sermon, the preacher, who was called Plato and who was worthy of that name, came down from the pulpit where he was speaking to the tomb of Peter the Great and, embracing the founder's statue, said: "*You* won this victory, *you* built our first ship, etc., etc." This act, which we have reported elsewhere and which will delight our most distant posterity, is, like the behavior of more than one Russian official, an example of the sublime.

In 1759 a certain Count Shuvalov, chamberlain to the Empress Elizabeth[4] and possibly the most learned man in the Russian empire,

23

was good enough to communicate to Peter's historian[5] those essential and authentic documents that he has scrupulously followed.

II

The public possesses several so-called histories of Peter the Great, most of them based on news sheets. The one published in Amsterdam in four volumes, under the name of the boyar Nestesuranov, is one of these all-too-common typographical frauds. Such are *The Memorials of Spain* ascribed to Don Juan de Colmenar; the *History of Louis XIV* composed by the Jesuit La Motte, based upon the bogus memoirs of a minister of state, and attributed to La Martinière; such are the histories of the emperor Charles VI, of Prince Eugene, and of so many others.

In this way the noble art of printing has been forced to serve the most contemptible trafficking. A Dutch bookseller orders a book as a manufacturer does cloth, and there unfortunately exist writers driven by necessity to sell their services to these merchants like workmen for their pay. This is the origin of all those insipid panegyrics and scurrilous slanders with which the public is inundated. It is one of the most disgraceful blemishes of our time.

Never did history have a greater need of authenticated evidence than today, when there exists such an impudent traffic in falsehood. The author who offers the public *The History of the Russian Empire under Peter the Great* is the same who, thirty years ago, wrote *The History of Charles XII,* following the memoirs of several public personages who had lived for a long time in that monarch's company. The present history both corroborates and complements the former one.

At this point I believe I owe it to the public and the truth to bring to light an unassailable piece of evidence which will validate the credibility of *The History of Charles XII.*

Not long ago, the king of Poland and duke of Lorraine[6] had the work reread to him at Commercy. He was so struck by the truth of many of the incidents that he had personally witnessed, and so outraged by the audacity with which they have been contradicted in several scandal sheets and journals, that he desired to confirm by the seal of his own testimony the credence merited by the historian. Accordingly, being unable to write in person, he commanded one of his court officials to draw up a certified document.

The receipt of this document occasioned the author a surprise which was all the more agreeable in that it came from a king who was as well informed of all these affairs as Charles XII himself, and who is moreover as famous throughout Europe for his love of the truth as he is for his beneficence.

We possess a host of equally irrefutable witnesses for the history of the age of Louis XIV, a work of no less veracity and no less importance than *Charles XII*, imbued with patriotism, yet in which love of country in no way detracts from the truth, never exaggerates the good nor disguises the bad, a work written with no axe to grind, without fear or favor, by a man whose circumstances free him from the necessity of flattering anyone.[7]

There are few quotations in *The Age of Louis XIV*,[8] because the events of the earlier years, which are well known to all, required only to be put into perspective, and because the author himself witnessed those of the later period. In *The History of the Russian Empire*, on the other hand, I invariably cite my authorities, the first of whom is Peter the Great himself.

III

I have not wearied myself in this *History of Peter the Great* with vain inquiries into the origins of most of the peoples who comprise the immense Russian empire, from Kamchatka to the Baltic Sea. It is a strange business to try to prove by means of authenticated documents that the Huns originally came to Siberia from northern China, and that the Chinese themselves are an Egyptian colony. I am aware that excellent scholars have believed that they could discern some similarities between these races, but their doubts have been excessively imposed upon, and attempts have been made to transform their conjectures into certainty.

For example, this is how one sets about nowadays to prove that the Egyptians are the ancestors of the Chinese. An ancient writer relates that the Egyptian Sesostris traveled to the Ganges, and that if he went to the Ganges, he could have gone to China, which is very far from the Ganges; therefore, he *did* go to China. Now at that time China was uninhabited, so it is clear that Sesostris peopled it. During their festivities, the Egyptians lit candles; the Chinese have lanterns: accordingly, it cannot be doubted that the Chinese are an Egyptian colony. Moreover, the Egyptians have a mighty river, and so do the Chinese. In conclusion, it is evident that the first kings of China bore the same names as the ancient kings of Egypt, for in the name of the Yu dynasty may be found characters which, when arranged in a different order, form the word *Menes*. It is thus not to be doubted that the Emperor Yu took his name from King Menes of Egypt, and that the Emperor Ki is manifestly King Atoës if you change *K* to *A* and *i* to *toës*.

However, if a scholar from Tobolsk or Peking had read some of *our* books, he would be able to prove much more conclusively that *we* are descended from the Trojans. Here is how he could go about it, and how he would astonish his countrymen by his profound investigations. The most ancient and most respected books, he would say, in the little Occidental country named France are romances. These were written in a pure language derived from the ancient Romans, who never told lies. Now, over a score of these authentic books testify that Francus, founder of the Frankish monarchy, was Hector's son. The name Hector has been preserved ever since in that land, and in this very century one of its greatest generals was called Hector de Villars.

This truth has been so unanimously recognized by France's neighbors that Ariosto, one of the most learned of Italians, acknowledges in his *Orlando Furioso* that Charlemagne's knights fought over Hector's helmet. In conclusion, an unanswerable argument is the fact that the ancient Franks, in order to perpetuate the memory their Trojan forebears, built a new city of Troy[9] in Champagne, and that these modern Trojans have always retained so great an aversion to their Greek enemies that in our day there are not four inhabitants of Champagne willing to learn Greek. They have never even wanted Jesuits among them, which is probably because they have heard that certain Jesuits used once to expound Homer to youthful scholars.

Such reasoning would surely produce a great effect in Peking and Tobolsk; and yet another learned man could overthrow the entire edifice by proving that the Parisians are descended from the Greeks. For, he would say, the senior magistrate of a law court in Paris was called Achille de Harlai. Achille obviously comes from the Greek Achilles, and Harlai from Aristos, if you change *istos* to *lai*. The Champs-Elysées, which are still to be found at the city gate,[10] and Mount Olympus, which may be seen to this day near Mézières,[11] are historical relics impervious to the most resolute skepticism. What is more, every Athenian custom is preserved in Paris: tragedies and comedies are criticized as frivolously as they were by the Athenians, generals are crowned with laurel in the theaters just as in Athens, and, finally, the Maréchal de Saxe received publicly from an actress[12] a wreath which would not have been bestowed upon him in the cathedral. The Parisians have academies which come from those of Athens, also a church,[13] a liturgy, parishes, dioceses, all of them Greek inventions, all words derived from the Greek. Parisian illnesses are Greek: apoplexy, phthisis, peripneumonia, cachexy, dysentery, jealousy, etc.

One must confess that this opinion would do much to counter the authority of the learned gentleman who has just demonstrated that France is a Trojan colony. Furthermore, both theories would be attacked by other erudite antiquaries. Some would show that we are Egyptians, since the cult of Isis was established in the village of Issy, between Paris and Versailles. Others would prove that we are Arabs, as evidenced by the terms almanac, alembic, algebra, and admiral. The scholars of China and Siberia would be hard put to it to make up their minds, and would eventually leave us as we are.

It would seem that we must rest content with this uncertainty regarding the origins of every nation. What is true of families is true of peoples: several German barons claim direct descent from Arminius,[14] and a genealogy was drawn up for Mohammed according to which he sprang from Abraham and Hagar.

And so the house of the old czars of Russia came down from Bela, king of Hungary; Bela himself from Attila; Attila from Turk, progenitor of the Huns; and Turk was the son of Japhet. His brother Rus had founded the Russian dynasty, and a second brother called Camari established his own power near the Volga.

Japhet's sons were all, as everyone knows, the grandsons of Noah, who was unknown to the whole world except to a little nation which itself remained unknown for a very long while. Noah's three sons lost no time in settling down thousands of miles apart, for fear they might be of mutual assistance, and fathered, probably with their own sisters, millions of people in no time at all.

Several grave persons have scrupulously traced these bloodlines just as perceptively as they have discovered that the Japanese colonized Peru. This type of history, which is not to the taste of President de Thou or of Rapin de Thoyras,[15] was long in vogue.

IV

If we should be somewhat wary of historians who go back to the Tower of Babel and the Flood, we must be equally suspicious of those who give particulars for the whole of modern history, who let us into the secrets of cabinet ministers, and who brazenly give an exact account of battles that the commanding generals would have found extremely hard to describe.

Since the beginning of the century,[16] nearly two hundred major battles—most of them bloodier than the Battles of Arbela and Pharsalia[17]—have been fought in Europe; but since very few of these actions had any significant aftermath, they have been lost to posterity. Had there been but one book in all the world, children would know every line of it by heart, its every syllable would be numbered. Had there been only one battle, every soldier's name would be famous, and his genealogy would pass down to the remotest posterity; but in the long, almost uninterrupted series of bloody wars waged among themselves by the Christian princes, old interests—which have all changed—are obliterated by new ones. Battles fought twenty years ago are forgotten for those fought in our own time, just as in Paris yesterday's news is stifled by today's, which in turn will be stifled by tomorrow's; and nearly all events are cast into eternal oblivion by those following. This is a reflection upon which it is impossible to dwell too much. It serves as a consolation for misfortunes suffered and demonstrates the vanity of human affairs. The sole remaining topic worthy of the attention of mankind is those striking upheavals which have changed the customs and laws of great nations. This is what renders the history of Peter the Great worthy of acclaim.

If I have dwelt excessively on certain details of battles and the capture of cities that resemble other engagements and other sieges, I crave the enlightened reader's indulgence, and my only excuse is that these minor facts, being linked to the major ones, follow inevitably in their train.

Nordberg[18] has been rebutted in those passages which seemed most important, but in minor matters has been given license to be wrong with impunity.

V

I have kept the *History of Peter the Great* as brief, yet as complete as possible. There are chronicles of small provinces, of small towns, even of abbeys, which fill several folio volumes. The memoirs of an ecclesiastic who retired for some years to Spain, where he did hardly anything, comprise eight tomes, whereas one sufficed for the life of Alexander.

It may be that there still exist child-men who prefer the fables about the Osirises, Bacchuses, Herculeses, and Theseuses hallowed by antiquity to the true history of a contemporary ruler, either because the ancient names of Osiris and Hercules are more pleasing to the ear than than of Peter, or because tales of giants and lions laid low are more gratifying to a feeble imagination than valuable laws and endeavors. Nevertheless, it must be conceded that the defeat of the giant of Epidaurus and of Sinis the Thief and the fight against the Crommyonian Sow[19] are not to be compared with the exploits of the conqueror of Charles XII, the founder of Saint Petersburg, and the lawgiver of a formidable empire.

It is true that the ancients taught us how to think, but it would be very odd to prefer Anacharsis the Scythian, simply because he was ancient, to the modern Scythian[20] who has brought orderly government to so many peoples.

The present history contains the czar's public life, which was beneficial, and not his private life, about which we merely possess a few fairly well-known anecdotes. The secrets of his study, his bedchamber, and his table may not and should not be disclosed by a foreigner. Had anyone been capable of writing such memoirs, it would have been a Prince Menshikov or a General Sheremeteyev, who for so long were privy to his domestic affairs. They have not written such memoirs, and anything based solely on current hearsay would be unworthy of credence. Wiser heads would rather see a great man work for twenty-five years for the welfare of a vast empire than learn from highly unreliable sources what that great man might have in common with the ordinary people of his country. Suetonius[21] reports the most intimate secrets of the first Roman emperors, but had he lived on intimate terms with twelve Caesars?

VI

When it is merely a question of style, criticism, or minor authorial concerns, the petty pamphleteers must be permitted to bark. One would become almost as ridiculous as they by wasting time answering them or even reading them. But when important matters are at stake, truth must occasionally condescend to refute these men and their despicable lies. Their infamy must no more prevent truth from having its say than the vile conduct of a criminal from the dregs of the populace prevents justice from taking action against him. It is for this twofold reason that I have been compelled to silence the ignorant wretch who corrupted *The History of the Age of Louis XIV*[22] by notes that are as absurd as they are libelous, in which he savagely insults one branch of the French royal family, the entire Imperial House of Austria, and a hundred illustrious European families whose antechambers were as unknown to him as the facts which he had the audacity to falsify.

The unfortunate facility with which impostures and slanders may be published is a great disadvantage attached to the noble art of printing.

The Oratorian priest Levassor and the Jesuit La Motte, the former a beggar in England, the latter a beggar in Holland, both wrote histories to earn their bread. The one chose King Louis XIII of France as subject of his satire; the other's target was Louis XIV. Their credentials as apostate monks ought not to have won them the public's trust. It is a pleasure, however, to see with what confidence they both proclaim themselves to be the repository of truth. They constantly reiterate the maxim that one must dare to tell the whole truth; they should add that one must begin by knowing what it is.

They stand condemned by their own maxim, which in itself is nonetheless well worthy of examination, since it has become the pretext for every kind of satire.

There is no question but that any public, significant, and useful truth must be told, but if there exists some hateful anecdote about a prince,[23] if in his private life he has indulged, like so many ordinary citizens, in human frailties known possibly to one or two confidants, who has authorized you to reveal to the public what these two confidants ought not to have disclosed to anyone? I grant that you have penetrated the mystery, but why do you rend the veil with which every man has the right to cover himself in the privacy of his own home? What is your reason for publishing this scandal? To gratify the curiosity of mankind, you reply, to pander to their spite, and to sell my book, which but for this would not be read. You are therefore no historian, but a mere lampoonist, a scandalmonger, and a pedlar of gossip.

If a public figure's shortcomings, if the hidden vice which you are seeking to divulge has influenced affairs of state, caused a battle to be lost, unbalanced the national economy, and made the citizens miserable, then you must speak of it. Your duty is to discern the tiny hidden cause that has produced great events; beyond that you must keep silence.

Let no truth remain hidden: this is a dictum to which there may be a few exceptions. But here is one which never suffers any exception: "Only tell posterity what is worthy of posterity."

VII

Over and above lying with respect to facts there is lying with respect to portraits.[24] The frenzy for encumbering a history with portraits began in France with the novel. It was *Clélie*[25] that made this craze fashionable. Sarrasin, in the dawn of the era of good taste, wrote a *History of Wallenstein's Conspiracy,* though Wallenstein had never conspired.[26] Sarrasin, while describing Wallenstein, whom he had never seen, did not fail to transcribe nearly everything that Sallust says about Catilina, whom Sallust had often seen. This is history written as an intellectual exercise; and whoever wishes to make an excessive display of his wit merely succeeds in flaunting it, which does not amount to very much.

It was fitting for Cardinal de Retz[27] to depict the principal figures of his time, since he had been well acquainted with all of them, friend and foe alike. Doubtless he did not paint them in those insipid hues with which—in his historical romances—Maimbourg[28] illuminates the princes of a bygone era. But was he a faithful painter? Did not enthusiasm and a fondness for the unconventional misdirect his brush? Should he, for example, have spoken of the Queen Mother[29] in the following terms: "She had the type of mind necessary not to appear stupid to those unacquainted with her; she possessed more acerbity than haughtiness, more haughtiness than greatness, more affectation than substance, more avarice than liberality, more liberality than self-interest, more self-interest than impartiality, more affection than passion, more severity than pride, more will to be pious than actual piety, more obstinacy than steadfastness, and more incompetence than all of the above"?

It cannot be denied that the obscurity of these expressions, this mass of antitheses and comparisons, and the burlesque quality of a painting so unfit for history are not destined to gratify the judicious mind. Lovers of truth suspect the truth of this portrait when comparing it with the queen's actual behavior, and virtuous souls are as disgusted by the bitter contempt displayed by the historian speaking of a princess who had heaped kindnesses upon him as they are outraged to see an archbishop waging civil war, as he himself admits, simply for the pleasure of the thing.

If we are obliged to mistrust portraits created by those so well qualified to paint them, how seriously can we take a historian with pretensions to divulge everything about a prince who lived two thousand miles away? Such a prince must be depicted through his actions, while all the rest must be revealed by those who have been long in his company.

Another kind of rhetorical falsehood in which historians formerly indulged is the fictitious speech, where one's heroes were made to speak words they could not possibly have uttered. These liberties in particular could be taken with characters from remote antiquity, but nowadays such fabrications are no longer tolerated. Much more is demanded, for if a speech that a monarch had not actually made were to be put into his mouth, the historian would be considered a mere rhetorician.

A third type of deception, the crudest of all yet long the most seductive, is the supernatural, which is preponderant in every ancient history without exception.

Even today a few predictions may be found in Nordberg's *History of Charles XII,* but there are none to be seen in any of our rational historians writing in this day and age. Signs, prodigies, and apparitions have been banished to fairy tales. History needed to be enlightened by philosophy.

VIII

There is an important point which may be of concern to the dignity of crowned heads. Olearius, who in 1634 accompanied the emissaries from Holstein to Russia and Persia, tells us in the third book of his history that Czar Ivan Vasilievich[30] banished an Imperial ambassador to

Siberia. This is a fact that no other historian, to the best of my knowledge, has ever mentioned. It is unlikely that the Emperor[31] would have
tolerated so extraordinary and so outrageous a violation of the *ius gen-
tium.*[32]

This same Olearius says elsewhere: "We set off on February 13, 1634,
in the company of a certain French ambassador named Charles de Talleyrand, Prince de Chalais, etc. Louis[33] had sent him and Jacques Roussel on an embassy to Turkey and Muscovy, but his colleague did him
such disservice with the Patriarch that the Grand Duke banished him to
Siberia."

In his third book he writes that this ambassador, the prince de
Chalais, and the man Roussel, his colleague, who was a merchant, were
Henry IV's envoys. It is not very likely that Henry IV, who died in
1610, sent any missions to Muscovy in 1634. If Louis XIII had dispatched as his ambassador a member of so illustrious a family as the
Talleyrands, he would never have assigned him a merchant as a colleague. Europe would have been informed about the embassy, and the
remarkable affront to the king of France would have caused even more
of a sensation.

Having challenged this implausible statement, and seeing that
Olearius's fiction had gained some credence, I felt that it was incumbent
upon me to request information from the archives of the French Minis-
try of Foreign Affairs. Here is what gave rise to Olearius's blunder.

There was indeed a member of the house of Talleyrand who, being
passionately fond of travel, went all the way to Turkey without telling
his family or asking for letters of recommendation. He encountered a
Dutch merchant named Roussel, the representative of a business firm,
who had connections with the French government. The marquis de
Talleyrand joined him on a trip to Persia, and, having quarreled with his
traveling companion during the journey, Roussel maligned him to the
Patriarch of Moscow. He was indeed sent to Siberia, but found a way to
inform his family, and three years later Monsieur Desnoyers, then secretary of state, obtained his release from the court of Moscow.

That is the truth of the matter, which is worthy of inclusion in this
history only inasmuch as it serves to put us on our guard against the
prodigious quantity of travelers' tales of this kind.

There are historical errors and there are historical falsehoods.
Olearius's report is merely erroneous, but when we are told that a czar
had an ambassador's hat nailed to his head, that is a lie. If a mistake is
made concerning the number and strength of the vessels in a fleet, if one
attributes a larger or smaller area to a country, it is only an error, and a
very pardonable one at that. Those who repeat ancient fables in which
the origins of every nation are shrouded may well be accused of a failing

common to all the writers of antiquity, but this is not lying. Strictly speaking, it is simply a matter of transcribing tales.

Inadvertence also makes us liable to many lapses which cannot be termed lies. If in Hubner's new geography[34] we find that the boundaries of Europe are located at the spot where the Ob River[35] flows into the Black Sea and that Europe has a population of thirty million, these are slips that any educated reader will rectify. This atlas often shows as great, populous, and fortified cities townships which nowadays are almost deserted. It is therefore easy to perceive that time has changed everything. The author has consulted the ancients, and what was true in their day is no longer so in ours.

It is also possible to make mistakes through jumping to conclusions. Peter the Great abolished the patriarchate. Hubner adds that he proclaimed himself Patriarch. Stories supposedly originating in Russia go even further and say that Peter personally officiated as Patriarch. Thus from an avowed fact erroneous conclusions are drawn, which is an all-too-common occurrence.

What I have termed historical falsehood is still more common, and is due to the inventions of flattery, satire, or a foolish love of the supernatural. The historian who praises a tyrant in order to please a powerful dynasty is pusillanimous, the man who desires to besmirch the memory of a good prince is a monster, and the writer of fiction who passes off his inventions as the truth is contemptible. An author who once caused entire nations to believe in fables would not now be read by the lowest of mankind.

There are critics who are even greater liars, those who falsify passages or who do not understand them and those who, prompted by envy, ignorantly criticize useful works. They are serpents gnawing the file; they are best left alone.

PART I

Foreword

In the opening years of the present century, the only Northern hero known to ordinary people was Charles XII. His personal valor, far more appropriate to a soldier than to a king, the glamor of his victories and even of his misfortunes dazzled all those who can easily see great events but fail to perceive prolonged and useful labors. At that time, foreigners even doubted whether Czar Peter I's ventures could endure. They have survived and been successfully concluded under the Empresses Anna and Elizabeth, but especially under Catherine II,[1] who has raised Russia's prestige to such heights. The empire is now numbered among the most flourishing of states, and Peter ranks with the greatest of lawgivers. Although in the eyes of the judicious his endeavors had no need to be crowned with success, their fulfillment has forever enhanced his glory. The contemporary view is that Charles XII should have been Peter the Great's first general. The former left behind him nothing but ruins, the latter was a founder in every domain. I ventured to make more or less the same pronouncement thirty years ago while writing the history of Charles.[2] The documents about Russia with which I am now provided enable me to make better known this empire whose people are so ancient yet whose laws, customs, and arts are of recent creation. The history of Charles XII was entertaining; that of Peter the Great is edifying.

Chapter 1
Description of Russia.

The Russian empire is the vastest in our hemisphere. From east to west it extends for more than two thousand common French leagues,[1] and from north to south more than eight hundred leagues at its deepest point. It borders upon Poland and the White Sea; it touches both Sweden and China. Its length, from Dago Island west of Livonia to its easternmost frontier, comprises nearly one hundred and seventy degrees of longitude, so that when it is noon in the west of the empire it is nearly midnight in the east. From north to south it measures three thousand six hundred versts, or eight hundred and fifty leagues.

In the last century, we knew so little about the extent of this country that when, in 1689, we learned that the Chinese and Russians were at war and that the Emperor K'ang-hsi, on the one hand, and Czars Ivan and Peter,[2] on the other, were sending diplomatic missions to put an end to their dispute three hundred leagues from Peking on the limits of the two empires, we at first called the whole thing nonsense.

Today, what is comprised under the name of Russia or the Russias is more immense than all the rest of Europe put together, more immense than the Roman Empire ever was, or Darius's empire which was conquered by Alexander, for it is more than eleven hundred thousand square leagues in area. The Roman and Alexandrian empires contained only some five hundred and fifty thousand square leagues apiece, and there is no kingdom in Europe one twelfth the size of the Roman Empire. To make Russia as populous, as affluent, and as rich in cities as our southern lands will require centuries, as well as more czars like Peter the Great.

A British ambassador resident in Saint Petersburg in 1733—and who had previously been in Madrid—tells us in his written account that in Spain, which is the least densely populated kingdom in Europe, there are forty people per square mile, whereas in Russia there were only five. We shall see in chapter 2 whether or not this minister was mistaken. It is said in *The Tithe*, falsely attributed to the maréchal de Vauban,[3] that every square mile of France contains, on the average, two hundred persons. Such estimates are never precise, but they do serve to demonstrate the enormous disparity between the population of one country and that of another.

At this point I will make the observation that from Saint Petersburg to Peking there is scarcely a single high mountain along the caravan route through independent Tartary, by way of the Kalmuck Plains and the Great Gobi Desert, and it is noteworthy that from Archangel to Saint Petersburg, and from Saint Petersburg to the tip of northern France, via Danzig, Hamburg, and Amsterdam, there is not so much as one fairly high hill to be seen. This remark may cast doubt on the theory according to which mountains were formed simply by the action of the sea, assuming that all of today's dry land was submerged for ages. But why did not the waves, which according to this supposition formed the Alps, the Pyrenees, and the Taurus Mountains, also form some high hill between Normandy and China along a tortuous route three thousand leagues in length? Thus considered, geography could shed some light on physics, or at least raise some questions.

We used to call Russia by the name of Muscovy, because the city of Moscow, capital of the empire, was the residence of the Grand Dukes of Russia, but nowadays the ancient name of Russia has reasserted itself.

It is no part of my task to find out why the lands from Smolensk to beyond Moscow are called White Russia—and why Hubner calls it Black Russia—nor the reason why the Ukraine[4] is supposed to be Red Russia.

Again, it may be true that Madyes the Scythian,[5] who invaded Asia nearly seven centuries before the Christian era, led his armies into this region, like Genghis Khan and Tamerlane after him, and as others had probably done long before him. Not all of the ancient world merits our investigations. The ancient civilizations of China, India, Persia, and Egypt are conspicuous by their renowned and interesting remains, which presuppose others of a much earlier period, since a great number of centuries are needed simply to invent the art of transmitting thoughts by means of durable signs, and since aeons must previously have elapsed in order to form a regular language. And yet we possess no such remains in our own Europe, which is so civilized today. The art of writing was long unknown throughout the North; in Russia, the Patriarch Constantine, who wrote the history of Kiev, admits that the use of writing was nonexistent there in the fifth century.

Let others examine whether Huns, Slavs, and Tartars once led their wandering and hungry families toward the source of the Dnieper.[6] My intent is to reveal what Czar Peter has created, rather than vainly to disentangle the ancient chaos. It must always be remembered that no family on earth knows its first ancestor, and that consequently no people can know its earliest origins.

I use the name *Russes* to designate the inhabitants of this great empire.[7] That of *Roxolani*, by which they used to be known, would be more euphonious, but one must conform to the usage of the language in which one is writing. The gazettes and other memorials have for some time now been employing the term *Russians*, but as this is too close to

Prussians, I shall retain *Russes,* which nearly all our writers have applied to them. It seems to me that the most widely scattered people on earth should be known by a term which distinguishes them unmistakably from other nations.

The reader, map in hand, must first of all get a clear idea of this empire, nowadays divided into sixteen great administrative territories, which, when the northern and eastern territories have a larger population, will ultimately be further subdivided.

Here then follow the sixteen territories, several of which contain immense provinces.

Livonia

The province nearest to ourselves is Livonia, one of the most fertile in the North. In the twelfth century it was still pagan. Merchants from Bremen and Lübeck traded there, and crusading monks called sword-bearers, who subsequently joined together in the Teutonic Order,[8] seized Livonia in the thirteenth century, when the frenzy of the Crusades armed Christians against all who were not of their faith. Albert, margrave of Brandenburg and Grand Master of these conquering monks, made himself overlord of Livonia and Brandenburger Prussia in about the year 1514. After that, the Russians and Poles fought over the province. Soon the Swedes invaded, and Livonia was long ravaged by all these powers. King Gustavus Adolphus of Sweden conquered it, and it was awarded to Sweden in 1660 by the famous Peace of Oliva. Eventually, Peter the Great won it from the Swedes, as we shall see in the course of this history.

Courland, which borders on Livonia, is still a Polish dominion, but heavily dependent on Russia. These are the western boundaries of the empire in Christian Europe.

Territories of Reval, Saint Petersburg, and Viborg

The territories of Reval and Estonia are farther north. Reval was built by the Danes in the thirteenth century. Estonia was a Swedish possession from 1561 on, when the country placed itself under Swedish protection. It is yet another of Peter's conquests.

Off the coast of Estonia is the Gulf of Finland. East of this sea, at the mouth of the Neva and Lake Ladoga, is Saint Petersburg, the newest and most beautiful city in the empire, built by Peter in the teeth of all the combined obstacles to its foundation.

Saint Petersburg stands on the Gulf of Kronstadt, in the middle of nine river branches dividing it into zones. A citadel occupies the center of the city, which is on an island formed by the main stream of the Neva; seven canals drawn from these rivers bathe the walls of a palace, the Admiralty, the shipyard where galleys are built, and several industries. Thirty-five large churches embellish the city, and among them there are five for foreigners, Catholics, Protestants, or Lutherans. They are five temples to tolerance, and, as such, examples to other nations. There are five palaces: the oldest, the so-called Summer Palace, on the Neva, has an immense balustrade of fine stone all along the river bank. The new Summer Palace near the triumphal arch is one of the finest pieces of architecture in Europe. The buildings erected for the Admiralty, the Imperial Cadets, the Imperial Colleges, the Academy of Sciences, the Stock Exchange, the warehouses, and shipyards are all magnificent structures. The administrative complex, the public pharmacy, where all the jars are of porcelain, the court repository, the foundry, arsenal, bridges, marketplaces, city squares, the barracks for the horse guards and foot guards all contribute as much to the beauty of the city as they do to its protection. At the present time it has a population of four hundred thousand. On the outskirts of the city there are country houses whose magnificence amazes foreigners. One of them has fountains far superior to those of Versailles. In 1702, there was nothing here but an impassable swamp. Saint Petersburg is regarded as the capital of Ingria, a little province captured by Peter I. Viborg, another of his conquests, together with that part of Finland lost and surrendered by Sweden in 1742, forms a separate territory.

Archangel

Still farther north is the province of Archangel, whose landscape is utterly unfamiliar to southern Europeans. It derives its name from Saint Michael the Archangel, under whose protection it was placed long after the conversion of the Russians to Christianity, which occurred as recently as the beginning of the eleventh century. It was not until the middle of the sixteenth that this land became known to other nations. In 1533, the English were looking for the Northeast Passage in order to reach the East Indies. Chancellor, captain of one of the vessels outfitted for this expedition, discovered the port of Archangel in the White Sea. There was nothing in this wilderness but a monastery attached to the little church of Saint Michael the Archangel.

Having sailed inland up the Dvina, the English reached the hinterland and finally the city of Moscow. They easily gained a monopoly of the Russian trade, which, from the city of Novgorod, where it was carried out over land, was transfered to the seaport. Archangel, to be sure, is inaccessible for seven months of the year; nevertheless it proved far more practical than the fairs of Novgorod the Great, which had declined since the Swedish wars. The English obtained the privilege of duty-free trading, which is doubtless the way all countries should conduct their affairs with one another. Soon the Dutch took a hand in the Archangel trade, which remained unknown to the rest of Europe.

Long before, the Genoese and Venetians had established trade with the Russians at the mouth of the Don, where they had built a town called Tana, but since the havoc wrought by Tamerlane in that part of the world, this branch of Italian commerce had been destroyed. The Archangel trade survived, with numerous benefits for the English and Dutch, until Peter the Great gained access to the Baltic Sea for his own domains.

Russian Lapland: The Territory of Archangel

To the west of Archangel, and within its purview, lies Russian Lapland, which comprises one third of the region; the other two thirds of Lapland belong to Sweden and Denmark. It is a very big country, occupying approximately eight degrees of longitude and extending in latitude from the Arctic Circle to the North Cape.[9] Its natives were known vaguely to the ancients by the name of Northern Troglodytes or Northern Pygmies. Such names were in effect appropriate for men the majority of whom were only three cubits tall and who lived in caves. They remain now what they were then: tanned, though other Northern tribes are white. Nearly all of them are short, though their neighbors and the Icelanders near the Arctic Circle are of lofty stature. They seem to have been created for their hilly environment, being agile, stocky, and robust. Their skin is tough, the better to resist the cold; their thighs and legs are supple and their feet are tiny, enabling them to run more nimbly among the rocks with which their land is completely covered. They love their homeland passionately, and are the only ones who could love it. They are unable even to exist anywhere else. It has been claimed, on the authority of Olaüs, that these people originated in Finland and withdrew to Lapland, where their height retrogressed. But why would they not have chosen a less northerly territory, where life would have been more comfortable? Why are their faces, their shape, and their color totally different from those of their alleged ancestors? It would perhaps be as appropriate to say that the grass which grows in Lapland comes from the grass of Denmark, and that the fish indigenous to their lakes are descended from Swedish fish. There is every reason to believe that the Lapps are aborigines—just as their animals are a product of their land—and that nature has made them for one another.

Those who live near Finland have adopted some of their neighbors' modes of speech, as happens in every culture; but when two nations call everyday objects in constant view by utterly different names, there are very good grounds for believing that one of these peoples is not an offshoot of the other. The Finns call a bear *karu,* the Lapps call it *muriet;* in Finnish the sun is named *auringa,* in Laplandish, *beve.* There is no analogy whatsoever. Both the natives of Finland and those of Swedish Lapland once adored an idol called *Iumalac,* and since the time of Gustavus Adolphus, to whom they owe their Lutheran faith, they have called Jesus Christ the son of Iumalac. The Muscovite Lapps are nowadays supposedly Orthodox, but those of them who roam in the area of the northern peaks of the North Cape are content to worship a god in the form of some crude idol or other, which is the ancient custom of all nomadic peoples.

This sparse race of men possesses very few concepts, and is fortunate to have no more than it does, for then the Laplanders would have new wants impossible to satisfy. They are content and free from disease, drinking hardly anything but water in the coldest of climates, and they live to a ripe old age. The custom once imputed to them, namely, that of begging strangers to do their wives and daughters the honor of sleeping with them, was doubtless due to the superiority which they sensed in these strangers, who, they hoped, would amend the imperfections of their race. This was an established practice among the virtuous Lacedemonians. A husband would beg a comely youth to give him handsome children whom he might adopt as his own. Jealousy and the law forbid other men to give their wives in this manner, but laws were practically unknown to the Lapps, and they were probably not in the least jealous.

Moscow

When one travels inland along the Dvina, from north to south, one reaches Moscow, the capital of the empire.[10] This city was long the center of the Russian territories, before they expanded toward China and Persia.

Moscow, situated fifty-five degrees thirty minutes north, in a warmer and more fertile area than Saint Petersburg, is surrounded by a vast and beautiful plain. It lies on the river Moska[11] and two smaller rivers, which all flow into the Oka and ultimately swell the Volga. In the thirteenth century this city was a mere collection of hutments occupied by unfortunates oppressed by the race of Genghis Khan.

The Kremlin,[12] former residence of the Grand Dukes, was only built in the fourteenth century, for of such recent origin are the cities of this part of the world. The Kremlin was constructed by Italian architects, as were several churches, in the Gothic style that was then prevalent throughout Europe; there are two by the famous Aristotle of Bologna, who flourished in the fifteenth century. But the houses of private citizens were simple wooden huts.

The earliest writer to inform us about Moscow is Olearius, who, in 1633, accompanied a diplomatic mission sent by a duke of Holstein. Its pomp was as vain as its mission was fruitless. One might expect a Holsteiner to be impressed by Moscow's immensity, its five walls, the enormous palace of the czars, and the Asiatic splendor then predominant at the court. There was nothing like it in Germany, no city anywhere near so vast or so populous.

On the other hand, Lord Carlisle, Charles II's ambassador to Czar Alexei in 1663, complains in his report of having found no amenities in Moscow, no hostelry along the way, or assistance of any kind. One was judging like a North German, the other like an Englishman, and both by comparison. The Englishman was disgusted to see that most of the boyars slept on boards or benches over which were thrown furs or blankets, the primordial practice of every race. The houses, most of which were wooden, lacked furniture; nearly all the dinner tables were without linen. The streets were not paved,[13] there were no amusements or conveniences, very few craftsmen, and even those were unskilled and worked only on indispensable projects. These people would have resembled Spartans, had they been sober.

But on ceremonial occasions, the court resembled a Persian king's. Lord Carlisle says that he saw nothing but gold and precious stones on the robes of the czar and his courtiers. These garments had not been made in Russia; and yet it was obviously possible to make the people exert themselves, since long before, during the reign of Czar Boris Godunov, the greatest bell in Europe had been cast in Moscow, and in the metropolitan church could be seen silver ornaments which had demanded much painstaking work. These projects, supervised by Germans and Italians, were short-lived efforts; it is ceaseless application and the constant exercise of a host of arts and crafts that make a nation flourish. Contemporary Poland, like all of Russia's neighbors, was no more advanced than Russia. Craftsmanship was no further developed in North Germany, where the fine arts were scarcely better known in the middle of the seventeenth century than they were in Muscovy.

Although at that time Moscow had none of the magnificence and the amenities of our great European cities, nevertheless its circumference of twenty thousand paces, the section known as the Chinese City, where the curiosities of China were displayed, the immense area of the Kremlin—the site of the czar's palace—several gilded domes, lofty and distinctive towers, and finally its enormous population of nearly five hundred thousand all contributed to making Moscow one of the most notable cities in the world.

Theodore or Feodor, Peter the Great's elder brother,[14] was the first to bring order to Moscow. He had several large stone houses built, though none displayed harmonious architectural proportions. He encouraged the leading courtiers to build, advancing them money and furnishing them with materials. It is to him that we owe the first fine stud-farms, as well as several other useful embellishments. Peter, who accomplished everything, paid attention to Moscow even while he was building Saint Petersburg. He had it paved, beautified, and enriched with public buildings and industries. And finally, a chamberlain[15] to the Empress Elizabeth, Peter's daughter, founded a university in Moscow some years ago. It is he who has provided me with all the materials on which I base my writings. He was far more capable than I of composing this history, even in French; all his letters to me testify that it is only through modesty that he has left the task to me.

Smolensk

West of the Duchy of Moscow is the Duchy of Smolensk, a part of ancient European Sarmatia.[16] The two duchies constituted White Russia, in the strict sense of the term. Smolensk, which originally belonged to the Grand Dukes of Russia, was conquered by the Grand Duke of Lithuania at the beginning of the fifteenth century, and recaptured a hundred years later by its former masters. King Sigismund III of Poland seized it in 1611. Czar Alexei, Peter's father, recovered it in 1654, since which date it has belonged to the Russian empire. It was stated in the eulogy of Czar Peter delivered to the Academy of Sciences in Paris that before his time the Russians had conquered nothing to the west or the south. It is obvious that this was incorrect.

The Territories of Novgorod and of Kiev, or the Ukraine

Between Saint Petersburg and Smolensk lies the province of Novgorod. The ancient Slavs, or Sarmatians, are said to have originally settled in this region. But where did these Slavs—whose language has spread throughout northeastern Europe—come from? *Sla* means both a chieftain, and a slave belonging to the chieftain. All that is known about these ancestral Slavs is that they were conquerors. They built the city of Novgorod the Great on a river that is navigable right from its source,[17] and for a long while it enjoyed a flourishing commerce and was a powerful ally of the Hanseatic League. Czar Ivan Vasilievich[18] captured

it in 1467 and carried off all its treasures, which contributed to the
magnificence of the court of Moscow, until that time virtually unknown.

To the south of the province of Smolensk, you find the province of
Kiev,[19] known as Little Russia, Red Russia, or the Ukraine, through
which flows the Dnieper, named Borysthenes by the Greeks. The contrast between these two names, the former hard to pronounce, the latter
melodious, serves to demonstrate, along with a hundred other proofs,
both the uncouthness of all the ancient peoples of the North and the
refinement of the Greek language.[20] The capital, Kiev, formerly
Kisovia, was built as a colony by the Byzantine emperors; one may still
see twelve-hundred-year-old Greek inscriptions there. It is the only city
with some claim to antiquity in this land where men have lived for so
many centuries without erecting city walls. Here it was that the Grand
Dukes of Russia resided during the eleventh century, before the Tartars
enslaved Russia.

The Ukrainians, who are called Cossacks, are a motley pack of former Roxolani, Sarmatians, and Tartars. This territory formed part of
ancient Scythia. Rome and Constantinople, which held sway over so
many lands, fall far short of the Ukraine with respect to fertility of soil.
Nature strives to benefit the Ukrainians, but they have not responded to
her. Existing on the fruits of a land that is as little cultivated as it is
productive, dependent even more on rapine, excessively fond of a possession far superior to anything else—namely, their liberty—and yet
having served in turn both Poland and Turkey, they eventually gave
themselves to Russia in 1654, without conceding too much in actual
fact, but Peter subjugated them.

Other peoples can be distinguished by their cities and larger villages.
The Ukraine is divided into ten regiments. Leading these ten regiments
there was a chief elected by majority vote, named the *hetman* or *itman*.
This captain of the nation did not possess supreme power. Nowadays
the rulers of Russia appoint a nobleman from the court as their hetman.
He is a true provincial governor, similar to our governors in regions
which still enjoy certain privileges.

At first there were only pagans and Muslims in the land. When they
belonged to Poland, they were baptized as Christians of the Catholic
persuasion; today—and ever since they have belonged to Russia—they
are Orthodox.

Among them are to be found some Zaporozhsky Cossacks, who are
more or less like our old-time freebooters, i.e., courageous brigands.
What set them apart from all other peoples was the fact that they never
allowed women in their tribes, as the Amazons are claimed never to
have admitted men. The women who served them for breeding purposes lived on separate islands in the river. There was no marriage

among them, and no family life; they enrolled the boys in their armed bands and left the girls with their mothers. Frequently the brother had children by his sister and the father by his daughter. The only other laws among them were usages dictated by their wants. They did have some priests of the Greek rite with them, however. Some time since, Fort Saint Elizabeth was built on the Dnieper in order to keep them in check. They serve in the Russian army as irregular troops, and woe betide anyone who falls into their hands.

The Territories of Belgorod, Voronezh, and Nizhny-Novgorod

If you travel to the northeast of the province of Kiev, between the Dnieper and the Don, you will come upon the territory of Belgorod. It is as big as the Ukraine and is one of the most fertile provinces of Russia. It is Belgorod which supplies Poland with a tremendous quantity of those big steers known as Ukrainian oxen. Both provinces are sheltered from raids from Little Tartary[21] by lines reaching between the Dnieper and the Don and strengthened by forts and redoubts.

Go still further north and cross the Don. You now enter the territory of Voronezh, which extends as far as the banks of the Sea of Azov.[22] Near its capital, which we call Voronezh,[23] at the mouth of the river of the same name which empties into the Don, Peter the Great constructed his first fleet. This was an undertaking the mere thought of which had never previously occurred to anyone in all those vast domains. You will then find the territory of Nizhny Novgorod, rich in grain, through which flows the Volga.

Astrakhan

From this province you enter the kingdom of Astrakhan to the south. The country begins in the most beautiful climate, at forty-three degrees thirty minutes of latitude, and ends near the fiftieth degree, comprising almost as many degrees of longitude. On one side it is bounded by the Caspian Sea, on the other by the Circassian Mountains,[24] and it extends along the Caucasus beyond the Caspian, into which pour the waters of the mighty Volga, the Yaik, and several other rivers.[25] According to the English engineer Perry, it is possible to link these rivers by digging canals that, by serving as flood-control channels, would produce the same effect as the canals of the Nile, and increase the fertility of the soil. But to the left and right of the Volga and the Yaik, this lovely country was infested, rather than inhabited, by Tartars who have never cultivated anything, and who have always lived like strangers on the land.

Perry,[26] who was working for Peter the Great in this part of the world, found vast empty spaces covered with pastures, vegetables, and cherry and almond trees. Wild sheep of excellent stock were grazing in the bush. A start had to be made by taming and civilizing the men of the region so as to lend a helping hand to nature, which in the vicinity of Saint Petersburg had actually to be coerced.

The kingdom of Astrakhan is a part of the ancient Kipchak,[27] conquered by Genghis Khan and then by Tamerlane. These Tartars ruled as far afield as Moscow. Czar Ivan Vasilievich, grandson of Ivan Vasilievich[28] and the greatest of the Russian conquerors, delivered his country from the Tartar yoke in the sixteenth century and added the kingdom of Astrakhan to his other conquests in 1554.

Astrakhan is the boundary between Asia and Europe, and thus is able to act as middleman between them, by ferrying merchandise brought across the Caspian Sea up the Volga. This was yet another of Peter the Great's grandiose designs, which has been carried out in part. An entire suburb of Astrakhan is inhabited by East Indians.

Orenburg

Southeast of the kingdom of Astrakhan there lies a small, recently created country called Orenburg. The city of the same name was founded in 1734 on the banks of the Yaik River.[29] Over this land extend the foothills of Mount Caucasus. Fortresses erected at intervals defend the mountain passes and the rivers that flow down from them. It is to this formerly uninhabited region that the Persians of our own day come to deposit and hide from rapacious brigands the possessions they have saved from their civil wars. The city of Orenburg has become a haven for the Persians and their wealth, and has grown as a result of their misfortunes. Indians and the peoples of Greater Bukhara[30] come to traffic there; it is becoming the emporium of Asia.

The Territories of Kazan and Greater Permia

Northward, beyond the Volga and the Yaik, is the kingdom of Kazan, which, like Astrakhan, was inherited by one of Genghis Khan's sons and later by one of Tamerlane's sons, and was finally conquered by Ivan the Terrible. It is still inhabited by many Muslim Tartars. This huge land stretches as far as Siberia. It is an established fact that it was once flourishing and prosperous; it still retains some opulence. A province of this kingdom, called Greater Permia, later Solikamsk, was the emporium for merchandise from Persia and furs from Tartary. A great quantity of money coined by the earliest caliphs and a few golden Tartar idols have been found in Permia,[31] but these relics of ancient riches were discovered in the middle of a poverty-stricken wilderness. There was no longer any trace of commerce. Such drastic changes occur only too swiftly and too readily in barren lands, since they have also occurred in the most fertile ones.

The famous Swedish prisoner of war Strahlenberg,[32] who turned his misfortune to such good account and who examined all of these vast territories so painstakingly, was the first to give credibility to a fact which no one had been able to believe. It concerns the commerce carried on in this region in ancient times. Both Pliny and Pomponius Mela state that in the Augustan age a king of the Suebi presented Metellus Celer with some Indians who had been shipwrecked on the coast near the Elbe. How could natives of India have been sailing in German waters? This adventure seemed apocryphal to all our moderns, especially since the discovery of the Cape of Good Hope has altered the trade routes of our hemisphere; but in the old days it was no more peculiar to see an Indian trading in the northern lands of the Occident than it was to see a Roman travel to India by way of Arabia. The Indians went to Persia, embarked on the Caspian Sea,[33] sailed up the Rha, which is the Volga, and went as far as Greater Permia on the Kama River. There they could take ship on the Northern Sea[34] or on the Baltic. There have been men of initiative in every age. The voyages of the men of Tyre were even more surprising.

If, having cast an eye over all these immense domains, you then turn your attention to the East, the confines of Europe and Asia are once again indefinite. There should have been a new name for this enormous territory. The ancients divided up the known world into Europe, Asia, and Africa, of which they had not seen one tenth. That is why when we have passed the Sea of Azov, we no longer know where Europe ends and Asia begins. Everything beyond the Taurus Mountains[35] was designated by the vague name of Scythia, and later by that of Tartary or Tatary. Perhaps it would be more appropriate to term everything between the Baltic and the Chinese frontier Arctic or Northern Lands, just as the name Southern Lands[36] is applied to the no less enormous area around the South Pole, which forms the globe's counterweight.

The Territories of Siberia, the Samoyeds and the Ostiaks

Siberia, together with the lands beyond, stretches from the frontiers of the provinces of Archangel, Ryazan, and Astrakhan, as far as the Sea of Japan. It touches southern Russia at the Caucasus mountains, the distance from there to the land of Kamchatka being some twelve hundred French leagues, and from northern Tartary—which serves as its limit—to the White Sea, about four hundred leagues. This is the narrowest part of the empire.[37] Siberia produces the finest furs, which is what brought about its discovery in 1563. It was not under Czar Feodor Ivanovich,[38] but during the reign of Ivan the Terrible in the sixteenth century, that a private citizen from the Archangel region, named Anika[39]—a wealthy man for one of his social standing and part of the world—became aware that men dressed in a style hitherto unknown in his district, and speaking a language that no one could understand, were making annual trips down a river that flows into the Dvina[40] and bringing to market the pelts of sables and black foxes, which they bartered for nails and bits of glass, just as the first American Indians gave their gold to the Spaniards. Anika had his children and servants follow them back to their own land. They were Samoyeds, people who resemble the Laplanders but who are not of the same stock. Like the Lapps, they are ignorant of the use of bread; they are also similar in that they use Rangifers, or reindeer, to pull their sleighs. They live in caves or huts in the snow,[41] but in other respects nature has sharply distinguished between this breed of men and the Laplanders. I am assured that their upper jaw protrudes further at the level of the nose, and that their ears are set higher. Neither the men nor the women have body hair; their nipples are ebony in color. Male and female Lapps have none of these characteristics. I have been informed in documents sent from these little-known lands of an error in the beautiful *Natural History* published by the Royal Botanical Gardens,[42] in which, during the discussion of many curious facts relative to human nature, the Lapps have been confused with the Samoyeds. There are far more races of men than is generally supposed. The Samoyeds and Hottentots appear to be the two extremes of our continent [*sic*], and if one takes into consideration the black nipples of Samoyed women and the natural apron of the Hottentots, which is said to come halfway down their thighs, one will have some notion of the variety of our animal species,[43] varieties which are unknown in our cities, where almost everything *is* unknown except our immediate surroundings.

The moral makeup of the Samoyeds is as singular as their physique. They do not worship any supreme being. In one respect only they come close to Manicheism—or rather to the ancient religion of the Magi—in that they acknowledge the existence of good and evil principles. Their horrible abode seems in some sort to justify this belief, so venerable among many races, and so natural to the ignorant and unfortunate.

One hears no mention of theft or murder among them; being virtually devoid of passions, they are without injustice. There are no words in their language for virtue and vice. Their extreme simplicity has not as yet permitted them to form abstract ideas; their feelings are their only guide, which is perhaps an irrefutable demonstration that men love justice instinctively when they are not blinded by their fatal passions.

The Russians persuaded some of these primitives to let themselves be taken to Moscow, where everything filled them with admiration. They regarded the emperor as their god and bound themselves to give him an annual tribute of two sables per man. Several colonies were soon established beyond the Ob and the Irtysh.[44] Forts were even built there. In 1595 a Cossack, sent into the country with a few soldiers and some artillery, conquered it for the czars, just as Cortez subjugated Mexico, but he conquered little more than a wilderness.

On their journey up the Ob, at the confluence of the Irtysh River with the Tobol, they came upon a small settlement which they turned into the now-important city of Tobolsk,[45] capital of Siberia. Who would believe that this land was long the abode of those same Huns who, under Attila, ravaged everything as far afield as Rome, and that these Huns came from northern China? The Uzbek Tartars succeeded the Huns, and the Russians the Uzbeks. Men have fought over these wild lands just as they have destroyed one another for the most fertile ones. Siberia was once far more populous than it is today, expecially in the south, as is evidenced by tombs and ruins.

This entire part of the world, from approximately the sixtieth degree to the eternally frozen mountains that line the northern seas, bears not the slightest resemblance to the temperate zone. The plants are not the same, neither are the animals nor the fish in the lakes and rivers.

South of the land of the Samoyeds, the country of the Ostiaks lies along the Ob River. They have nothing in common with the Samoyeds except that, like them and like all primitive peoples, they are hunters, fishermen, and shepherds. The Samoyeds have no religion, because they are dispersed; the Ostiaks, who are grouped in hordes, do have a form of worship, making vows to the principal object of their needs. They are said to adore a fleece, because nothing is so essential to them as their livestock. Similarly, ancient Egyptian farmers selected an ox, in order to venerate in the image of the animal the god who had created it for mankind. Some writers claim that the Ostiaks worship a bearskin, seeing that it is warmer than sheepskin. It is quite possible that they worship neither.

In addition, the Ostiaks have other idols, whose origins and cult are no more deserving of our attention than their worshippers. A few of them were converted to Christianity in about the year 1712. They are Christians in the manner of our most brutish peasants, i.e., without knowing what they are. Several authors maintain that these people are natives of Greater Permia, but Greater Permia is practically deserted. Why would its population have picked such a distant and wretched place in which to settle? Obscurities of this kind are not worth inquiring about. Any people which has not cultivated the arts must be condemned to remain unknown.

It is above all among the Ostiaks, the Buryats, and the neighboring Yakuts that a kind of ivory of as yet unknown origin is often found in the earth. Some think it a fossilized ivory, others the tusks of a now extinct species of elephant.[46] In what land do we not discover products of nature which astound and confute philosophy?

Several mountains in this vicinity are full of asbestos, an incombustible flax which is sometimes used to make cloth and sometimes a type of paper.

South of the Ostiaks live the Buryats, another tribe as yet unconverted to Christianity. Eastward, there are several hordes which have not so far been completely subjugated. Not one of these tribes has the slightest knowledge of the calendar. They reckon time by snows, not by the visible progress of the sun. Since the snowfalls each winter are regular and sustained, they say, "I am so many snows old," where we would say, "I am so many *years* old."

At this point I must transmit the account given by the Swedish officer Strahlenberg, who, having been captured at Poltava, spent fifteen years in Siberia and traveled the length and breadth of it. He says that there are still some survivors of an ancient race whose skin is mottled and speckled,[47] and that he himself has seen members of this race. This fact has been corroborated by Russians born in Tobolsk. It would appear that the variety of human types has greatly diminished. We find few of these peculiar races, which have no doubt been exterminated by others. For example, there are very few white Moors or Albinos, one of whom was presented to the Academy of Sciences in Paris, and seen by myself. The same is true of several very rare species of animals.

As for the Borandians, of whom there is much talk in the learned *History* of the Royal Botanical Gardens, my sources inform me that this people is absolutely unknown.

The entire southern portion of these lands is inhabited by numerous Tartar hordes. The ancient Turks set off from Tartary to overcome all the countries that now belong to them. The Kalmucks and Mongols are those same Scythians who, under the leadership of Madyes, seized Upper Asia and defeated Cyaxares, king of the Medes. It is they whom Genghis Khan and his sons later led into Germany,[48] and who formed the Mogul empire under Tamerlane. These people are a striking instance of the changes which occur in all nations. Some of their hordes, so far from being redoubtable, have now become Russian tributaries.

Such is a Kalmuck tribe living between Siberia and the Caspian Sea, where, in 1720, a subterranean house built of stone was discovered, as well as urns, lamps, ear pendants, an equestrian statue of an oriental prince wearing a diadem, two women sitting on thrones, and a roll of manuscripts later sent by Peter the Great to the Academy of Paleography in Paris,[49] which identified the language as Tibetan. These objects are a remarkable demonstration that the arts long sojourned in that now barbarous land, and offer enduring proofs of what Peter the Great said on more than one occasion, namely, that the arts have traveled all around the world.

Kamchatka

The last and most easterly province on the continent is Kamchatka. Its northern region is another source of beautiful furs. The natives wear them during the winter and go naked in summer. It was surprising to find men with long beards in the southern region, whereas in the north, from the Samoyed country to the mouth of the Amour or Amur, the men are as beardless as American Indians. Thus it is that in the Russian empire there are more different species, more oddities, and more divergent customs than anywhere else on earth.

Recent reports inform me that this primitive people also has its theologians, who trace the descent of the inhabitants of the peninsula from a kind of higher being named *Kouthou*. The reports say that they do not worship him in any way, and that they neither love nor fear him.

And so they apparently have mythology without religion, which might be true, yet seems unlikely, fear being the natural attribute of mankind. It is claimed that among their absurdities, they make a distinction between what is permissible and what is forbidden. It is permissible to gratify all of one's passions, but forbidden to sharpen a knife or an axe when traveling, or to save a drowning man. If it is indeed a sin for them to save their neighbor's life, they differ in this respect from all other men, who instinctively hurry to aid their fellows when neither passion nor self-interest corrupts this natural inclination. It would appear impossible to make a crime of an action so commonplace and so necessary that it is not even a virtue, except by means of a philosophy as erroneous as it is superstitious, which would argue that providence must not be opposed and that a man destined by heaven to be drowned must not be aided. Barbarians, however, are far removed from subscribing to even a false philosophy.

Nevertheless, they are said to celebrate a great feast, whose name in their language signifies purification; but of what do they purify themselves if everything is allowed? And why do they purify themselves if they neither fear nor love their god Kouthou?

There are doubtless inconsistencies in their thinking, as there are in nearly every race, but theirs are the result of a defective intelligence, while ours are due to the misuse of thought. We have many more inconsistencies than they, because we have been thinking longer.

Just as they have a kind of god, so they also have demons and, last of all, sorcerers, exactly like those there have always been among even the most civilized nations. In Kamchatka it is the old women who are the sorcerers, as they used to be with us before we became enlightened thanks to rational science. Thus it is an unfailing attribute of the human mind to conceive absurd ideas, grounded on our curiosity and frailty. The Kamchatkans also have prophets who interpret dreams; it is not so long since we had them ourselves.

Since the Russian crown subjugated these people by building five fortresses in their land, they have preached the Orthodox faith to them. A highly educated Russian nobleman tells me that one of their principal objections was that this religion could not have been intended for them, because bread and wine are indispensable for our mysteries, whereas in their region they have neither.

The Kamchatkans in any event merit few observations except the following: if we cast our eyes over three quarters of America,[50] the entire southern part of Africa, and the North from Lapland to the Sea of Japan, it is plain that half the human race ranks no higher than the people of Kamchatka.

A Cossack officer was the first to go overland from Siberia to Kamchatka, in 1701, on Peter's orders; for Peter, even after the ill-starred Battle of Narva, was still broadening the scope of his vigilance to cover the continent from one end to the other. Ultimately, in 1725, a short while before death surprised him in the midst of his grand projects, he sent the Danish Captain Bering with explicit instructions to sail to America by way of Kamchatkan waters, if such a venture were practicable. Bering's first voyage was unsuccessful. In 1733, the empress Anna sent him off again. Spangenberg, a ship's master associated with the expedition, was the first to leave Kamchatka, but was unable to put to sea until 1739, because it took so much time to reach the port of embarkation and to build, rig and outfit ships. Spangenberg sailed as far as northern Japan along a strait formed by a long chain of islands[51] and returned home having discovered nothing but this passage.

In 1741, Bering sailed these waters, accompanied by the astronomer Delisle de La Croyère,[52] a member of the Delisle family that has produced such erudite geographers. A second captain went on a voyage of discovery on his own account. He and Bering both reached the American coast at northern California. The passage[53] through the northern seas which had been sought for so long was thus finally discovered; but no relief could be found along that deserted coastline. The expedition ran short of fresh water, and a number of the crew died of scurvy. They saw a hundred miles of the northern California coast, where they observed leather boats carrying men resembling Canadians. The land was totally barren. Bering died on the island to which he gave his name. The other captain, who was closer to California, put ten of his crew ashore; they were never seen again. The captain was forced to return to Kamchatka after waiting for them in vain, and Delisle expired as soon as he left the ship.[54] Such calamities were the fate of nearly all the earliest endeavors in northern waters. It is still uncertain what benefits will be derived from such distressing and perilous discoveries.

I have described the general outlines of the entire Russian dominion from Finland to the Sea of Japan. All the great parts of this empire have been unified at different periods, as has occurred in every other kingdom throughout the world. Scythians, Huns, Massagetes, Slavonians, Cimbri, Getae, and Sarmatians all are now subject to the czar. The Russians proper are the ancient Roxolani or Slavonians.

When one thinks about it, most other states were formed in the same way. France is an assemblage of Goths, of Danes called Normans, of north Germans called Burgundians, of Franks, Allemanni,[55] and a few Romans mingled with the ancient Celts. In Rome and Italy many families are descended from the northern tribes, whereas not one is known to be descended from the ancient Romans. The Supreme Pontiff is frequently the scion of a Lombard, a Goth, a Teuton, or a Cimbrian. The Spanish are a race of Arabs, Carthaginians, Jews, Tyrians, Visigoths, and Vandals, incorporated with the aboriginal inhabitants of the land. Whenever nations emerge from this kind of melting pot, they take a long while to become civilized, or even to form their language. Some organize themselves sooner than others. Civil administration and the arts become established so painfully, and upheavals so often ruin the social edifice in its early stages, that the only real cause of wonder is that most nations do not live like Tartars.

Chapter 2
Description of Russia Continued.
Its Population, Finances, Armies, Customs, and Religion. The Status of Russia before Peter the Great.

The more highly civilized a nation is, the more populous it will be. China and India are accordingly the most densely populated of all empires, because after the countless revolutions which have changed the face of the earth, the Chinese and Indians constitute the most ancient civilizations known to man. Their governments go back more than four thousand years, which presupposes, as I have already remarked,[1] trials and exertions throughout the centuries preceding. The Russians came late on the scene, and, the arts having been introduced among them already perfected, they have consequently made more progress in fifty years than any other nation had made on its own in five hundred. The country's population is far from commensurate with its extent, but even so it has as many subjects as any state in Christendom.

Thanks to the poll-tax register and the census figures of merchants, artisans, and male peasants, I am in a position to vouch for the fact that modern Russia has at least twenty-four million inhabitants. The majority of these twenty-four million are serfs like those found in Poland, in several German states, and formerly in almost all of Europe. In Russia and Poland the wealth of a nobleman or a churchman is reckoned not according to his income, but by the number of his slaves.

Here are the figures of the 1747 census of males paying the poll tax.

Merchants	198,000
Workmen	16,500
Peasants affiliated with the merchants and workmen	1,950
Peasants called *odnovortsy*[2] who contribute to the support of the militia	430,220
Others who do not contribute to it	26,080
Workers in various trades, and of unknown parentage	1,000
Others who are not affiliated with the trade guilds	4,700
Peasants immediately dependent upon the crown, approximately	555,000
Workers in the imperial mines, Christians as well as Muslims and pagans	64,000
Other crown peasants working in privately owned mines and factories	24,200
Recent converts to the Orthodox Church	57,000
Pagan Tartars and Ostiaks	241,000

Mourses, Tartars, Mordvinians, and others, either heathen or Orthodox, employed as laborers for the Admiralty.	7,800
Taxpaying Tartars, known as *tepteris* and *bobilitz*, etc.	28,900
Serfs belonging to several merchants and other privileged persons who, without being landowners, are permitted to own slaves	9,100
Land serfs intended for the service of the court	418,000
Land serfs belonging to His Majesty in his own right, independently of the rights of the crown.	60,500
Land serfs confiscated by the crown	13,600
Noblemen's serfs	3,550,000
Serfs belonging to the Assembly of the Clergy and paying its expenses	37,500
Bishops' serfs.	116,400
Serfs belonging to the monasteries, whose numbers were greatly reduced by Peter	721,500
Serfs belonging to cathedral and parish churches	23,700
Peasants employed as laborers for the Admiralty, or other public works, approximately	4,000
Workers in privately owned mines and factories	16,000
Land serfs given to the principal manufacturers	14,500
Workers in the imperial mines	3,000
Bastards brought up by priests	40
Sectarians known as Raskolniki[3]	2,200
TOTAL	6,646,390

In round numbers, that is six million six hundred and forty thousand males paying the poll tax. Male children and old men are included in this enumeration, but women and girls are not, and neither are boys born between one survey and the next. Simply triple the number of taxable heads, include the women and girls, and you will find nearly twenty million souls.

To this total must be added the military, amounting to three hundred and fifty thousand men. Throughout the empire, neither the aristocracy nor the clergy, who number two hundred thousand, are subject to the poll tax. All foreigners in the empire are exempt, regardless of profession and nationality. The inhabitants of conquered provinces, namely Livonia, Estonia, Ingria, Carelia, and a part of Finland, the Ukrainians and the Cossacks, the Kalmucks and other Tartars, the Samoyeds, Laplanders, Ostiaks, and all the idolatrous tribes of Siberia—a country larger than China— are not included in the census.

According to this calculation, the total population of Russia could not possibly have amounted to less than twenty-four million in 1759, when these records, taken from the imperial archives, were sent to me. By this count, there are eight persons per square mile. The British ambassador whom I mentioned earlier allows only five persons per square mile, but doubtless he did not have access to records as faithful as those which have been graciously imparted to myself.

The territory of Russia is therefore—*mutatis mutandis*—exactly five times less densely populated than Spain, yet it has nearly four times as many inhabitants. It is almost as populous as France[4] and Germany, but in relation to its immense area the number of people is thirty times fewer.

There is an important comment to be made concerning this enumeration, which is that out of six million six hundred and forty thousand taxpayers, about nine hundred thousand are found to belong to the Russian clergy, not counting either the clergy of the conquered territories or that of the Ukraine and Siberia.

Thus, out of every seven taxable persons, one belongs to the clergy; but despite their one seventh, the clerics are far from enjoying the seventh part of the state's revenues (as is the case in so many other kingdoms, where they possess at least one seventh of all the wealth), for their peasants pay poll tax to the sovereign, and one must make a sizable allowance for the remaining revenues of the Russian crown, in which the clergy does not share.

This assessment differs widely from that made by every other writer on Russia. Foreign envoys who have sent reports to their sovereigns have all been mistaken in this regard. One must scrutinize the imperial archives.

It is highly probable that Russia was once much more populous than it is today, in the period when smallpox, which came from the heart of Arabia, and the other pox, which originated in America, had not yet wrought havoc in the areas where they have since become entrenched.[5] These twin scourges, a greater cause of depopulation than warfare, are due to Mohammed and Christopher Columbus, respectively. The plague, indigenous to Africa, rarely approached the countries of the north. And lastly, since the northern peoples—from the Sarmatians to the Tartars beyond the Great Wall of China—have flooded into every part of the world, this ancient seedbed of mankind must have dwindled sadly.

In all this vast expanse of territory, there are estimated to be some seven thousand four hundred monks and five thousand six hundred nuns, despite Peter the Great's endeavors to reduce their numbers, an effort worthy of a lawgiver in an empire where what is principally lacking is people. These thirteen thousand cloistered and—so far as the state is concerned—wasted persons possessed, as the reader will have noted, seven hundred and twenty thousand serfs to cultivate their lands, which is obviously far too many. This abuse, so widespread and detrimental to so many states, was finally ended by the empress Catherine II, who boldly avenged both nature and religion by depriving the secular and regular clergy of a detestable form of wealth. She reimbursed them from the public purse and tried to compel them to be useful, while at the same time preventing them from being dangerous.

I find from the imperial budget of 1725 that, including the tribute paid by the Tartars and all the taxes and duties levied in cash, the total amounted to thirteen million rubles, the equivalent of sixty-five million francs, excluding tributes paid in kind. This paltry sum was then sufficient to maintain three hundred and thirty-nine thousand five hundred soldiers and sailors. The revenues have since increased, and so have the numbers of troops.

In Russia, customs, clothes, and manners had always resembled those of Asia rather than of Christian Europe. Such was the time-honored practice of receiving the people's tributes in the form of produce, of defraying ambassadors' expenses en route and during their period of residence, and that of never appearing in church or before the throne while wearing a sword. This is an oriental practice contrary to our own ridiculous and barbarous custom of conversing with God, kings, our friends, and women with a long offensive weapon trailing at our heels. On ceremonial occasions, the long robe seemed more stately than the shorter garments of Western Europe. A fur-lined tunic with a long gown adorned with precious stones, on solemn occasions, and those lofty turbans which make one taller were more imposing to the eye than perukes and tight-fitting jackets, and more suited to cold climates; but this costume, worn by all peoples in ancient times, seems less appropriate for war and less convenient for work. Nearly all their other usages were uncouth, yet we must not imagine that their manners were as barbarous as many writers say they were. Albert Krants speaks of a czar who had an Italian ambassador's hat nailed to his head because he did not remove it during his speech to the throne. Others attribute this misadventure to a Tartar, and last of all the tale has been told about a French ambassador.[6]

Olearius claims that Czar Mikhail Feodorovich banished to Siberia a certain Marquis d'Exideuil,[7] ambassador of King Henry IV of France, but that monarch certainly never sent an ambassador to Moscow. In the same way, travelers speak of the nonexistent country of Borandia; they have trafficked with the people of Novaya Zemlya, which has scarcely any inhabitants, and have had long conversations with Samoyeds, as if they were capable of understanding them. If what is neither true nor useful were to be expunged from the enormous compilations written about voyages, both these works and the public would be the better for it.

The Russian government was similar to the Turkish with respect to the Streltsi militia, which, like the Janissaries, sometimes acted as kingmakers, disrupting the state as much as they upheld it. The Streltsi numbered forty thousand men. Those who were dispersed throughout the provinces lived on plunder, while those stationed in Moscow lived a bourgeois existence, engaged in trade, were completely useless, and carried their insolence to extremes. To establish order in Russia, the Streltsi had to be broken. Nothing was more necessary, nor more dangerous.

In the seventeenth century, the state's annual revenue was less than five million rubles (about twenty-five million francs). That was sufficient, when Peter ascended the throne, to remain in the old rut; it was not one third of what was needed to escape from it and to become a power in Europe. But on the other hand, many taxes were paid in produce, in accordance with the Turkish practice, which is far less onerous to the common people than paying in cash.

The Title of Czar

As for the title of czar, it is possible that it comes from the tsars or tchars of the kingdom of Kazan. When the Russian sovereign John or Ivan Vasilievich[8] had reconquered this realm—which had been subjugated by his grandfather but subsequently lost—in the sixteenth century, he assumed its royal title, which his successors kept. Before Ivan Vasilievich, the masters of Russia bore the name of *veliki knes* (grand prince, grand lord, grand chief), which the Christian nations translate as *grand duke*. Czar Mikhail Feodorovich, in his dealings with an embassy from Holstein, took the titles of Grand Lord and Grand Knes, Preserver of All the Russias, Prince of Vladimir, Moscow, Novgorod, etc.; Czar of Kazan, Czar of Astrakhan, and Czar of Siberia. The name *czar* was therefore the title of those oriental rulers, and was thus more plausibly derived from the Shahs of Persia than from the Roman Caesars, of whom the Siberian czars on the banks of the Ob had doubtless never heard.

A title, regardless of what it may be, is nothing if those who bear it are not great in themselves. The name *emperor*, which used to mean no more than commander, became the title of the masters of the Roman Republic.[9] It is given nowadays to the sovereigns of Russia with more justification than to any other potentate, if one considers the extent and power of their dominion.

Religion

From the eleventh century on, the state religion has always been what we call Greek, to distinguish it from the Roman, but there was more Muslim and pagan territory than Christian. Siberia was idolatrous all the way to China, and in more than one province no religion of any kind was known.

The engineer Perry and Baron von Strahlenberg, who lived in Russia for so long, both say that they found more good faith and probity among the heathen than among the others. It is not paganism which made them more virtuous, but, leading a pastoral existence, far removed from dealings with other men, and living as it were in those times which we term the first age of the world, free from violent passions, they were of necessity better men.[10]

Christianity was accepted in Russia very late, as it was in every other northern land. It is claimed that a certain Princess Olga introduced it at the end of the tenth century, just as Clotilde, the niece of an Arian prince, made it acceptable to the Franks, the wife of one Mieczylaw, duke of Poland, to the Poles, and the sister of the emperor Henry II to the Hungarians.[11] It is the destiny of women to be susceptible to the blandishments of ministers of religion, and then to persuade men to follow their example.

This Princess Olga, they add, was baptized in Constantinople, where she took the name Helena. No sooner was she a Christian than the emperor John Zimisces inevitably fell in love with her.[12] Apparently she was a widow[13] and wanted none of the emperor. Princess Olha or Olga's example did not at first make a great number of converts. Her own son, who had a long reign,[14] was not at all of his mother's way of thinking, but her grandson Vladimir, the offspring of a concubine, after murdering his brother in order to reign himself, sought an alliance with the Byzantine emperor Basil, and only obtained it on condition he became a Christian.[15] It is in fact from this period—the year 987—that the Orthodox faith began to establish itself in Russia. A Patriarch of Constantinople named Chrysoberges sent a bishop to baptize Vladimir and to add this part of the world to his patriarchate.[16]

And so Vladimir completed the task begun by his grandmother. The first Metropolitan or Patriarch of Russia was a Greek, which is why the Russians adopted an alphabet derived in part from the Greek. They would have benefited from this had not their language, which is Slavonic, always remained basically the same, with the exception of a few words concerning their liturgy and hierarchy. One of the Greek Patriarchs, named Jeremiah, who had been engaged in a lawsuit at the Divan[17] and who had come to Moscow to ask for help, finally renounced his claims over the Russian Church, and consecrated Job, archbishop of Novgorod, as Patriarch in 1588.

From that time on, the Russian Church was as independent as it was dominant in Russia. It was indeed dangerous, shameful, and ridiculous that it should be subordinate to a Greek Church enslaved by the Turks. The Patriarch of Russia was henceforth consecrated not by the Patriarch of Constantinople, but by the Russian bishops. In the Orthodox

Church he ranked after the Patriarch of Jerusalem, but in reality he was the only Patriarch both free and powerful, and consequently the only real one. Those of Jerusalem, Constantinople, Antioch, and Alexandria are merely the hired and degraded leaders of a church subservient to the Turks. Indeed, those of Antioch and Jerusalem are no longer considered to be Patriarchs, and enjoy no more prestige than do the rabbis of synagogues in Turkey.

Peter the Great was the direct descendant of a man who had become Patriarch of all the Russias.[18] Before long, these supreme prelates wished to share in the authority of the czars. It was not enough that once a year the sovereign walked bareheaded before the Patriarch, leading his horse by its bridle. Such outward tokens of respect serve only to inflame the thirst for domination, a passion that occasioned great troubles in Russia, as elsewhere.

The Patriarch Nikon[19]—regarded by the monks as a saint—who held office in the time of Peter the Great's father Alexei, tried to elevate his throne higher than the czar's. Not only did he usurp the right to sit beside the czar in the senate, but he further maintained that it was not lawful to make either peace or war without his consent. His authority, which was supported by his wealth and his scheming, by the clergy and by the people, kept his master in a kind of servitude. He had the audacity to excommunicate several senators opposed to his excesses, and Alexei, not feeling sufficiently powerful to depose him on his own authority, was eventually obliged to convene a synod of all the bishops. Nikon was accused of having received money from the Poles. He was deposed and confined in a monastery for the rest of his life, while the prelates elected a new Patriarch.

Since the advent of Christianity in Russia there had always been a few sects, as there were in other states, for sects are often just as much the fruit of ignorance as of self-styled learning.[20] And yet Russia is the only major Christian nation where religion has not fomented civil wars, although it has occasioned some turmoil.

The Raskolniki sect, which today consists of about two thousand males—and is alluded to in the census—is the oldest. It was founded early in the twelfth century[21] by zealots with a little knowledge of the New Testament. They had, and still have, the presumption of all sectarians, namely, that of following the New Testament to the letter, accusing all other Christians of falling away, refusing to permit a priest who has drunk brandy to perform baptisms, affirming with Jesus Christ that there is neither a first nor a last among the faithful, and above all that a believer may kill himself for the love of his Savior. According to them it is a very grievous sin to say "alleluia" three times; it must be said only twice, and the sign of the cross must never be made except with three fingers.[22] Furthermore, no community is more orderly or more rigorous in its life-style. They live like Quakers, but unlike them do not admit other Christians into their assemblies. That is why the others have imputed to them all the horrors of which the pagans accused the early Galileans, with which the latter charged the Gnostics, and the Catholics the Protestants. They have frequently been accused of cutting an infant's throat in order to drink its blood, and of mingling together during their clandestine ceremonies without any distinction as to kinship, age, or even sex. They have on occasion been persecuted, at which times they have shut themselves up in their villages, set fire to their houses, and cast themselves into the flames. Peter chose the only course capable of reconciling them: that of letting them live in peace.

What is more, in such an enormous empire there are only twenty-eight episcopal sees, and in Peter's time only twenty-two. So small a number was perhaps one of the reasons why the Russian Church had remained at peace. Besides, the church was so unschooled that Czar Feodor, Peter the Great's brother, was the first to introduce plainsong into it.

In their armies and their councils Feodor, and more especially Peter, admitted with no distinction those of the Greek, Catholic, Lutheran, and Calvinist persuasions. They left everyone at liberty to serve God according to his own conscience, so long as the state was well served. In all the two-thousand-league expanse of the empire there was not a single Latin church. However, when Peter set up new industries in Astrakhan, there were some sixty Catholic families under the spiritual guidance of the Capuchin friars, but when the Jesuits tried to gain access to his domains, he expelled them by edict in April, 1718. He tolerated the Capuchins as monks of no consequence, but considered the Jesuits to be dangerous politicians. They had established themselves in Russia in 1685, were driven out four years later, and came back only to be driven out again.

The Orthodox Church is delighted to see itself extending over an empire two thousand leagues in length, whereas the Roman Church does not possess half as much territory in Europe. Those of the Greek rite have at all times and above all things wanted to preserve their equality with the Latins, and have always feared the zeal of the Church of Rome, which they have taken for ambition, because the Roman Church, though very cramped in our hemisphere, calls itself Universal, and has in fact attempted to live up to that lofty title.

There never have been any Jewish institutions in Russia, as there are in so many European states from Constantinople to Rome. The Russians have always carried on their commerce themselves, with the help of foreign nationals who have settled among them. Of all the Orthodox countries, Russia is alone in having no synagogues next to its churches.

Situation of Russia before Peter the Great (Continued)

Russia, which owes its great influence on the affairs of Europe solely to Peter the Great, had enjoyed no influence at all since its conversion to Christianity. In the old days, it could be seen doing on the Black Sea what the Normans used to do on our Atlantic coasts: i.e., fitting out forty thousand small craft in the time of Heraclius, besieging Constantinople, and exacting tribute from the Greek Caesars. But the Grand Knes Vladimir, busily engaged in bringing Christianity to his people and worn out by the domestic turmoil of his own household, weakened his domains still more by dividing them among his offspring. Almost all of them fell prey to the Tartars, who reduced Russia to slavery for two hundred years. Ivan the Terrible delivered her and enlarged her territories, but after his death she was ruined by civil strife.

Before Peter the Great, Russia was far from being so powerful or having so much land under cultivation, so large a population, or such great revenues as in our day. She had no Finnish possessions, and none in Livonia either, and Livonia by itself is more valuable than the whole of Siberia was for a long time. The Cossacks had not been tamed; the tribesmen of Astrakhan were only half obedient; the paltry amount of commerce engaged in was not to Russia's advantage. The White, Baltic, and Black Seas,[23] the sea of Azov, and the Caspian were utterly useless to a nation which had no vessels and whose language even lacked a term for *fleet*. If it was merely necessary to be superior to the Tartars and the northern peoples as far away as China, Russia already enjoyed such an advantage; but she had to be the equal of the civilized nations and put herself in a position to surpass several of them one day. Such an endeavor seemed unrealistic, since the Russians had not a single ship at sea and were totally ignorant of military discipline on land; the most basic industries were receiving scarcely any encouragement, while agriculture itself, the prime mover par excellence, was neglected. Agriculture demands the attention and encouragement of the government, which is why the English have found a greater treasure in their wheat than in their wool.[24]

Their meager cultivation of the useful arts shows plainly that the Russians had no conception of the fine arts, which become necessary in their turn when one has everything else. It would have been possible to send some Russian nationals to study abroad, but the difference in language, customs, and religion discouraged this. There was even a civil and ecclesiastical law, as sacred as it was pernicious, which forbade Russians to leave their country,[25] apparently condemning them to eternal ignorance. They possessed the vastest territory in the whole world, and everything remained to be accomplished. At last Peter was born, and Russia was created.[26]

Happily, of all the world's great lawgivers, Peter is the only one whose story is well known. The histories of Theseus and Romulus, who achieved far less than he, those of the founders of all other civilized states, are compounded with absurd fables, whereas here we have the advantage of writing facts which would be considered fables had they not been authenticated.

achievements fabulous

Chapter 3
Peter the Great's Ancestors.

Peter's family had been on the throne since the year 1613, before which date Russia had undergone disturbances which further postponed any reforms and the cultivation of the arts. This is the fate of every society, but never had a kingdom suffered more cruelly than Russia. In 1597 the tyrant Boris Godunov murdered the legitimate heir Dmitry—whom we call Demetrius—and usurped the crown. A youthful monk assumed the name Dmitry, claimed to be that prince escaped from his murderers, and, with the aid of the Poles and that large faction which always opposes tyrants, drove out the usurper and usurped the crown himself. His imposture was discovered as soon as he was on the throne, because people were dissatisfied with him, and he was murdered in his turn. Three more false Dmitrys arose one after the other. This series of deceptions presupposed a country in total disarray. The less civilized men are, the easier it is to deceive them. One may judge to what an extent these frauds increased the general confusion and public misfortune. The Poles, who had begun the disturbances by setting up the first counterfeit Dmitry, were on the verge of ruling Russia. The Swedes took a share of Russian Finland, and likewise laid claim to the throne. The state was threatened with utter ruin.

In the midst of these calamities, in 1613, an assembly of the leading boyars elected as sovereign a fifteen-year-old boy, which did not appear to be a conclusive method of putting an end to the troubles. This young man was Mikhail Romanov,[1] Czar Peter's grandfather and son of the archbishop of Rostov—whose name was Filaret—and of a nun. Filaret was related on his mother's side to the old czars.

It must be realized that the archbishop was a powerful nobleman who had been forced to take holy orders by the tyrant Boris. His wife Sheremeto[2] had been obliged to take the veil, a time-honored practice among western Catholic tyrants; the custom of the Greek Christians was to put out the eyes. The tyrant Dmitry gave Filaret the archdiocese of Rostov and sent him away as ambassador to Poland. The ambassador became the prisoner of the Poles—then at war with Russia—so little was the law of nations heeded by any of these peoples. It was during the archbishop's detention that his son, the younger Romanov, was elected czar. His father was exchanged for some Polish prisoners, and the young czar created him Patriarch. The old man in actual fact ruled in his son's name.

If such a form of government appears curious to foreigners, Czar Mikhail Romanov's marriage will seem even more singular. Since 1490, Russian monarchs had no longer chosen foreign brides. It appears that after their acquisition of Kazan and Astrakhan, they followed Asiatic usage in practically everything, and especially in the matter of marrying only their own subjects.

Even closer to the customs of old Asia is the fact that when a czar was to be married, the most beautiful girls from the provinces were summoned to court. The czar would see them either openly or under an assumed name. The wedding day was set without anyone's knowing who had been selected. On the appointed day, a wedding dress was given to the girl who had been secretly chosen; different clothes were then distributed to the other candidates, who then returned home. There were four instances of such marriages.

It was in this fashion that Mikhail Romanov married Evdokiya, daughter of an impoverished nobleman named Streshnev. He and his servants were tilling his fields when chamberlains sent by the czar with presents informed him that his daughter was now on the throne. The name of this princess is still cherished in Russia. All this is most unlike our ways, but is none the less respectable for that.

It is necessary to point out that before Romanov was chosen, a strong party had elected Prince Ladislas, son of King Sigismund III of Poland.[3] The provinces adjacent to Sweden had offered the crown to a brother of Gustavus Adolphus. Russia was thus in the same situation so often experienced by Poland, where the elective monarchy has occasioned civil wars. But the Russians did not imitate the Poles, who make a contract with the king they elect. Although they had had experience of tyranny, they placed themselves in the hands of a young man without making any demands of him in return.

Russia had never had an elective monarchy, but, the male line of the old dynasty having failed and six czars or pretenders having perished miserably in the recent troubles, it became necessary, as we have seen, to elect a sovereign. The election was the cause of new wars with Sweden and Poland, who both fought for their alleged rights to the Russian throne. These claims to rule a nation against its will never stand up for very long. The Poles, on the one hand, after advancing as far as Moscow and after the pillaging that passed for warfare in those days, concluded a fourteen-year truce. By its terms Poland remained in possession of the Duchy of Smolensk, in which the Dnieper has its source. The Swedes also made peace, keeping control of Ingria and depriving the Russians of all communication with the Baltic Sea, so that the empire was now more than ever separated from the rest of Europe.

Once peace was made, Mikhail Romanov reigned undisturbed, making no changes either to corrupt or to perfect the administration of his domains. After his death in 1645, his sixteen-year-old son Alexei Mikhailovich, or Mikhail's son, reigned by right of inheritance. It may be noted that the czars were crowned by the Patriarch in accordance with the rites of Constantinople, the sole difference being that the Patriarch of Russia was seated on the same dais as the sovereign and invariably affected an air of equality, which was an affront to the supreme power.

Alexei Mikhailovich, Mikhail's Son

Alexei married as his father had done, and selected from among the girls brought to him the one who seemed the most congenial. He married one of the two daughters of the boyar Miloslavsky in 1647, and later, in 1671, a Naryshkin.[4] His favorite, Morozov, married the other Miloslavsky daughter. It is impossible to give Morozov a more appropriate title than that of vizier, since he wielded despotic powers throughout the empire, and his authority incited revolts among both the Streltsi and the common people, as has often been the case in Constantinople.

Alexei's reign was troubled by bloody insurrections and by domestic and foreign wars. A chieftain of the Don Cossacks, named Stenka Razin, tried to make himself king of Astrakhan. For a long while he inspired terror, but having been defeated and captured at last, he suffered the extreme penalty like all his fellows, for whom there is never anything but the throne or the scaffold. Some twelve thousand of his followers are said to have been hanged along the Astrakhan highway. In that part of the world men, being the least governed by principle, could only be governed by punishments, and from their frightful torments sprang both serfdom and the hidden passion for revenge.

Alexei waged war on Poland with success, obtaining a treaty which left him in secure possession of Smolensk, Kiev, and the Ukraine. However, against the Swedes he was not so fortunate, and the empire was still very restricted on the Swedish side.

The Turks were more to be feared in those days than they are now; they would fall upon Poland and threaten the lands of the czar adjoining Crimean Tartary, the ancient Chersonesus Taurica. In 1671 they seized the important city of Kamenets and all the Polish dependencies in the Ukraine. The Ukrainian Cossacks, who had never wanted any masters at all, now did not know whether they belonged to Turkey, Poland, or Russia. Sultan Mahomet IV, who had vanquished the Poles and recently exacted tribute from them, demanded with all the hauteur of a victorious Ottoman that the czar withdraw from his Ukrainian possessions. His demand was rejected with equal pride. In those days the art of concealing pride under a cloak of decorum was unknown. In his letter, the sultan called the sovereign of all the Russias a mere Christian Hospodar,[5] while styling himself "Most Glorious Majesty, King of the Entire Universe." The czar replied "that he was not the man to yield to a dog of a Muslim, and that his saber was as good as the Grand Seignior's scimitar."

Alexei then conceived a plan which seemed to foreshadow the influence Russia was one day to enjoy in Christian Europe. He sent ambassadors to the Pope and to nearly all the major European sovereigns, except the king of France—the ally of the Turks—in an attempt to form a league against the Ottoman Porte. In Rome, his ambassadors' sole success lay in not kissing the Pope's feet; elsewhere they obtained nothing but empty expressions of good will. The quarrels among the Christian kings, and the interests arising out of their disputes, always rendered them incapable of uniting against the common enemy of Christendom.

Meanwhile, the Ottomans were threatening to crush Poland for refusing to pay the tribute. Czar Alexei gave her aid on the Crimean side, and General of the Crown John Sobieski expunged his country's disgrace in Turkish blood at the famous Battle of Khotin in 1674, which cleared his way to the throne.[6] Alexei challenged his claim to the throne, and suggested uniting Poland with his own vast domains, as the Jagello dynasty had united it with Lithuania.[7] However, the more grandiose his offer, the less acceptable it was. He was eminently worthy, it is said, of ruling this new kingdom, because of the manner in which he governed his own. He was the first czar to draw up a legal code, albeit an imperfect one. He introduced textile and silk mills, which did not indeed survive, but for which he must receive the credit. He settled the wilderness around the Volga and the Kama with Lithuanian, Polish, and Tartar families captured during his wars. Previously, all prisoners had become the slaves of those to whom they were allotted; Alexei turned them into farmers. He disciplined his armies, to the best of his ability. In short, he was worthy to be Peter the Great's father, but he had no time to bring any of his enterprises to a successful conclusion, dying as he did at the early age of forty-six, at the beginning of 1677 reckoning by our calendar, which is eleven days in advance of the Russian one.

Feodor Alexeevich

After Alexei Mikhailovich, everything fell back into disorder. By his first marriage, he left two princes and six princesses. The older son, Feodor, who ascended the throne at fifteen, was delicate and sickly, but his ability was not impaired by his bodily weakness. His father Alexei had him officially acknowledged as his successor the previous year. Such had been the practice of the kings of France, from Hugh Capet down to Louis the Younger, and so many other sovereigns.[8]

Alexei's younger son was Ivan, or John, who was even more ill-used by nature than his brother Feodor, in appalling health, virtually blind and dumb, and frequently a prey to convulsions. Of the six daughters of this first marriage, the only one to become celebrated in Europe was Princess Sophia, who was of a notably superior intellect, but unfortunately even better known for the harm she tried to do Peter the Great.

From his second marriage with another of his own subjects, the boyar Naryshkin's daughter, Alexei left Peter and Princess Natalya. Peter, born on May 30, 1672 (or June 10, new style), was barely four and a half years old when he lost his father. There was no liking for the offspring of second marriages, and it was not expected that he would one day reign.

The unswerving intent of the Romanov dynasty was to bring order to the state, and such was also the will of Feodor. We have already noted, while speaking of Moscow, that he encouraged its citizens to build several stone houses. He enlarged the capital, which was indebted to him for some general administrative regulations. But in attempting to reform the boyars, he completely alienated them. Besides, he lacked the energy and determination to conceive a bold and thoroughgoing change. The war with the Turks, or rather with the Crimean Tartars, which was still being fought with mixed success, did not permit an ailing ruler to undertake so great a task. Like his predecessors, Feodor married one of his subjects, a native of the Polish frontier region, and, having lost her within a year, in 1682 took as his second wife Marta Matveyevna,[9] daughter of his secretary, Apraxin. A few months later he became mortally ill and died, leaving no heir. Just as the czars used to marry without regard to rank, they could also—at least in those days— choose a successor regardless of primogeniture. It appears that the rank of the sovereign's wife and of his heir was to be solely the reward of merit, in which respect the practice of the Russian empire was far superior to that of the most civilized states.[10]

Before he died, Feodor, seeing that his brother Ivan's afflictions made him incapable of reigning, named as heir to the Russian throne his second brother, Peter, who was only ten years old but already giving rise to great expectations (April, 1682).

If the custom of raising commoners to the rank of czarina was favorable to women, another custom of the period was extremely harsh: czars' daughters rarely married, most of them spending their lives in a convent.

Princess Sophia, the third daughter of Czar Alexei's first marriage, whose intellect was as superior as it was dangerous, having realized that her brother Feodor had not long to live, did not choose to live in a convent. Finding herself between her two remaining brothers, neither of whom was in a position to rule, one due to his ill health, the other because of his youth, she conceived the design of ruling the empire herself. During the closing days of Czar Feodor's life, she tried to revive the role once played by Pulcheria with her brother the emperor Theodosius.[11]

Chapter 4
Ivan and Peter. Horrible Insurrection of the Streltsi Militia.

Hardly had Feodor breathed his last[1] when the nomination of a ten-year-old prince to the throne, the exclusion of his elder brother,[2] and the intrigues of their sister, Princess Sophia, stirred up one of the Streltsi corps's bloodiest mutinies. Neither the Janissaries nor the Praetorian Guard had ever been so barbarous. To begin with, two days after Czar Feodor's funeral they hurried under arms to the Kremlin, which is, as we know, the palace of the czars in Moscow. They began by complaining about nine of their colonels who had not paid them promptly enough. The government was obliged to cashier the colonels and give the Streltsi the money they were demanding. The soldiers were not mollified; they wanted the nine officers surrendered to them, and condemned them by majority vote to the punishment called the *batogi,* which is administered as follows.

The victim is stripped naked and made to lie on his belly; two torturers beat him on the back with rods until the judge says "Enough." The colonels, having been treated thus by their own men, were then obliged to thank them, in accordance with the custom of Oriental criminals who, after undergoing punishment, kiss their judges' hands. They added a sum of money to their thanks, which was not customary.

While the Streltsi were beginning to make themselves feared, Princess Sophia, who was covertly inciting them and leading them from crime to crime, convened at her residence an assembly consisting of the princesses of the blood, generals, boyars, the Patriarch, bishops, and even some of the leading merchants. She put it to them that Prince Ivan, by right of primogeniture and through his own merit, ought to rule the empire, whose reins she herself secretly hoped to hold. On leaving the assembly, she promised the Streltsi an increase in pay, as well as presents. Her agents incited the soldiery above all against the Naryshkin family, and especially against the two Naryshkins who were the brothers of the young czarina dowager, Peter I's mother. They convinced the Streltsi that one of these brothers, named Ivan, had taken the czar's robe, sat on the throne, and tried to strangle Prince Ivan; they added that a hapless Dutch physician called Daniel Vangad[3] had poisoned Czar Feodor. Lastly, Sophia handed them a list of forty noblemen—whom she termed their enemies and enemies of the state— to be slaughtered. Nothing more resembles the proscriptions of Sulla

and the Roman Triumvirs,[4] renewed by Christian II in Denmark and
Sweden. From this one may see that such horrors exist in every land in
times of trouble and lawlessness.

First of all, they threw Lords Dolgoruky and Matveyev[5] out of the
window. The Streltsi caught them on their spear points, stripped them,
and dragged them out onto the square.[6] Then they burst into the palace,
where they found one of Czar Peter's uncles, Afanasy Naryshkin, the
young czarina's brother. They butchered him in the same way, forced
the doors of a nearby church where three proscripts had taken sanc-
tuary, dragged them away from the altar, stripped them, and stabbed
them to death.

So blind was their fury that, catching sight of a young nobleman of
the Soltikov family, who was popular with them and *not* on the pros-
cription list, some of them mistook him for Ivan Naryshkin, whom
they *were* seeking, and killed him without hesitation. Highly characteristic of the manners of those days is the fact that, once they discovered
their error, they carried young Soltikov's body to his father for burial,
and the unhappy father, far from daring to complain, rewarded them
for having brought him the bloody corpse of his son. His wife, his
daughters, and his daughter-in-law reproached him, in tears, for his
cowardice. "Let us await the right moment for revenge," said the old
man. Some of the Streltsi overheard this remark, rushed angrily back
into the room, dragged the father out by his hair, and cut his throat on
his own threshold.

Other Streltsi were hunting everywhere for the Dutch physician Vangad. They came across his son and asked his father's whereabouts. The
trembling young man replied that he did not know, whereupon they slit
his throat. They found another German doctor.[7] "You are a doctor,"
they said. "If you didn't poison our master Feodor, you've poisoned
others; you deserve to die." And they killed him too.

They finally found the Dutchman they were looking for, disguised as
a beggar. They haled him to the palace, where the princesses, who were
fond of the good man and trusted him, begged the Streltsi to spare his
life, assuring them that he was a very good doctor and had looked after
their brother Feodor very well. The Streltsi answered that he deserved
death not only as a doctor, but also as a sorcerer, and that they had
found a large mummified toad and a snakeskin at his house. They added
that young Ivan Naryshkin, whom they had been seeking in vain for
two days, must absolutely be surrendered to them, and that he was
certainly hiding in the palace, which they would burn down if they were
not given their victim. Ivan Naryshkin's sister and the other terrified
princesses went to his secret hiding place; the Patriarch heard his confession and gave him the last rites, after which he took down an al-
legedly miraculous icon of the Virgin and led the young man to the

Streltsi while showing them the icon. The weeping princesses gathered around Naryshkin, fell to their knees before the soldiers, and implored them in the name of the Virgin to spare their kinsman's life; but the Streltsi tore him from their hands and dragged him downstairs together with Vangad. Then they formed themselves into a kind of court and put Naryshkin and the doctor to the question. One of them, who could write, drew up an indictment. They condemned the two unfortunates to be hacked to pieces, which in China and Tartary is the punishment for parricides and is called the Death of Ten Thousand Cuts. When they had dealt in this way with Naryshkin and Vangad, they stuck their heads, hands, and feet on the iron spikes of a balustrade.

While they were assuaging their fury in the very sight of the princesses, others were massacring anyone who was hateful to them or suspect to Sophia.

These horrible executions came to an end when the two Princes Ivan and Peter were proclaimed sovereigns (June, 1682), with their sister Sophia acting as co-regent. Then she gave her approval to all the crimes committed by the Streltsi, rewarded them, and confiscated the property of the proscripts to give it to their murderers. She even gave them permission to erect a monument on which they engraved the names of those they had slaughtered as traitors to the Fatherland. Lastly, she gave them letters patent in which she thanked them for their loyalty and zeal.

Chapter 5
Princess Sophia's Administration. A Curious Religious Dispute. Conspiracy.

These were the steps by which Princess Sophia[1] in effect ascended the throne of Russia without being proclaimed czarina, and these were the earliest examples set before Peter I. Sophia received all the honors of a sovereign: her portrait on the coinage, her signature authorizing every expedition, the first place in the council, and, above all, the supreme power. She was highly intelligent, even composed poetry in her own language, and both wrote and spoke well. A pleasing countenance enhanced her manifold gifts, which were tarnished only by her ambition.

She married off her brother Ivan in accordance with the tradition of which we have already seen so many examples. A girl of the Soltikov family, a relative of that same Soltikov murdered by the Streltsi, was chosen from the depths of Siberia, where her father was commandant of a fortress, to be presented to the czar in Moscow. Her beauty prevailed over the intrigues of all her rivals, and Ivan married her in 1684. One seems, at each marriage of a czar, to be reading the story of Ahasuerus[2] or that of the second Theodosius.

In the midst of the nuptial festivities, the Streltsi provoked a new uprising, and—who would believe it?—the cause was religion, the cause was dogma. Had they been mere soldiers, they would not have become controversialists, but they were also Muscovites. From darkest India to the ends of Europe, whoever finds himself or puts himself in a position to speak to the populace with authority may found a sect. This is something which has been observed in every age, particularly since the passion for dogma has become the weapon of the bold and the yoke of the feebleminded.

In the days when there was a dispute over whether the sign of the cross should be made with three fingers or with two, the Russians had already endured several seditious outbreaks. In Moscow, a certain archpriest named Avvakum had made a dogmatic pronouncement concerning the Holy Spirit—who, according to the Gospel, is supposed to enlighten the faithful—the equality of the first Christians, and the following words of Jesus: "There shall be neither a first nor a last among you."[3] Several citizens and Streltsi embraced Avvakum's doctrines, the faction grew stronger, and a certain Raspop became its leader. Finally, the sectarians entered the cathedral where the Patriarch and his clergy were officiating, drove them all out, Patriarch and priests alike, amid a shower of stones, and devoutly took their places in order to receive the Holy Spirit (July 16, 1682, new style). They called the Patriarch a ravenous wolf among lambs, a title which the members of every denomination have freely bestowed upon one another. Princess Sophia and the youthful czars were warned in haste of these disorders. The other Streltsi, who supported the cause of righteousness, were told that the czars and the Church were in danger. The patriarchal faction of the Streltsi and citizens came to blows with the Avvakumists, but the carnage was suspended as soon as there was talk of convening a Council. A Council immediately assembled in a hall of the palace. There was no difficulty in summoning it, since every available priest was sent for. The Patriarch and a bishop disputed with Raspop and at the second syllogism hurled stones at one another's faces.[4] The Council finished by beheading Raspop and some of his faithful disciples, at the sole command of the three sovereigns, Sophia, Ivan, and Peter.[5]

In those troubled times there was a certain Lord Khovansky[6] who, having played a part in the rise of Princess Sophia, wished to be rewarded for his services by participating in her government. One may readily believe that he found Sophia ungrateful, and so he sided with the devout faction and the persecuted Raspopites. Moreover, he stirred up some of the Streltsi and the common people in the name of God. His conspiracy was more serious than Raspop's religious fervor, since an ambitious hypocrite will always go further than a simple fanatic. Khovansky was aiming at nothing less than the empire, and, so as to have nothing to fear in the future, he resolved to murder both czars, Princess Sophia, the other princesses, and everyone connected with the imperial family. The czars and princesses were obliged to retire to the Troitsa Monastery twelve leagues outside Moscow.[7] This was at one and the same time convent, palace, and fortress, like Monte Cassino, Corbie, Fulda, Kempten,[8] and many others among Christians of the Latin rite. The Troitsa Monastery belongs to the Basilian monks; it is surrounded by a broad moat and brick ramparts bristling with cannon. The monks owned all the land for four leagues around. The imperial family's safety there was due rather to the strength of the place than to its sanctity. From within the Troitsa, Sophia negotiated with the rebel, tricked him into coming halfway to meet her, and had his head cut off, besides executing one of his sons and thirty-seven Streltsi accompanying him (1682).

At this news, the Corps of Streltsi made ready to march in strength to the Troitsa Monastery, threatening to destroy everything and everybody. The imperial family barricaded itself, the boyars armed their followers, every nobleman hurried to the place, and a bloody civil war was on the point of breaking out. The Patriarch appeased the Streltsi to a certain extent, and the troops approaching from every direction intimidated them. Their fury changed to fright and their fright to the most abject submission, a perfectly usual occurrence with the rabble. Three thousand seven hundred of them, followed by their wives and children, put ropes around their necks and marched in this state to the Troitsa Monastery, which three days earlier they had wanted to reduce to ashes. These wretches appeared in front of the monastery in pairs, each pair carrying an axe and a block. They prostrated themselves and awaited their punishment. They were pardoned. They returned to Moscow blessing their masters and ready, all unbeknownst to themselves, to repeat all their criminal outrages at the earliest opportunity.

After these convulsions, the state resumed its tranquil exterior. Sophia still maintained her supremacy, abandoning Ivan to his incapacity and keeping Peter under her thumb. To increase her power, she shared it with Prince Vasily Golitsyn, whom she created commander in chief, prime minister, and lord privy seal. Golitsyn was in every respect superior to everyone else at that turbulent court. He was urbane, openhanded, full of grandiose designs, and more learned than any other Russian, because he had received a better education. He even had a thorough knowledge of Latin, then almost totally unknown in Russia. He was a lively-minded and diligent man, whose intellect was ahead of his time, and capable of transforming Russia had he only possessed as much time and authority as will to do so. These words of praise were uttered by La Neuville, then Polish envoy to Russia, and the compliments of foreigners are the least suspect.

Golitsyn kept the Streltsi militia in check by distributing the most unruly of them among regiments in the Ukraine, Kazan, and Siberia. It was under his administration that, in 1686, Poland, long Russia's rival, gave up all its claims to the great provinces of Smolensk and the Ukraine. He was the first, in 1687, to send a diplomatic mission to France, a nation which had been for twenty years at the summit of its glory through the conquests and new institutions of Louis XIV, through his magnificence, and above all through the refinement of the arts, without which we have mere grandeur, without true glory. France had had no previous communication with Russia, of which little was known. The Academy of Paleography solemnized the arrival of the embassy by striking a medal, as though it had come from India. Despite the medal, however, Ambassador Dolgoruky's mission was a failure. Indeed, he encountered strong aversion on account of the misconduct of his domestics. It would have been better to put up with their transgressions, but the court of Louis XIV could not at that time have foreseen that both Russia and France were one day to reckon their close alliance among their major assets.

The state was now peaceful on the domestic front. It was still hemmed in on the Swedish side, while expanding toward Poland, its new ally; it was in a constant state of anxiety with regard to Crimean Tartary, and remained at loggerheads with China over the matter of the frontiers.

What the Russian empire found most intolerable, and a clear demonstration that it had not yet attained a vigorous and orderly government, was the fact that the khan of the Crimean Tartars demanded an annual tribute of sixty thousand rubles, like the one imposed on Poland by Turkey.

Crimean Tartary is that same Chersonesus Taurica once famous for its trade with the Greeks, and even more so through their stories. This fertile and barbarous region is named Crimea from the title of its first khans, who called themselves *crims* before they were conquered by the sons of Genghis Khan. It was with the intent of eliminating and avenging the shame of the tribute that Prime Minister Golitsyn went in person to the Crimea in command of a large force (1687, 1688). His army in no way resembled those which the Russian government maintains nowadays: there was no discipline, not even one well-equipped regiment, no uniforms, and no order. They constituted a militia inured to toil and want, but with a plethora of baggage unheard of even in our own camps, where luxury prevails. The prodigious number of wagons carrying munitions and stores into devastated and desert country was harmful to the Crimean expedition. They found themselves without supplies in a trackless wilderness on the banks of the Samara River, where Golitsyn accomplished something never, I fancy, achieved anywhere else. He employed thirty thousand men to build on the Samara a city capable of serving as a depot for the forthcoming campaign. Begun that same year and finished in the first three months of the next, it was, to be sure, built entirely of wood, with only two brick houses and ramparts of turf, but it had artillery and it was defensible.

This was the only noteworthy achievement of a ruinous expedition. Meanwhile, Sophia was head of state: Ivan was czar in name only, and Peter, aged seventeen, was already man enough to *be* czar in reality. The Polish envoy, La Neuville, then residing in Moscow and an eyewitness of what transpired, claims that Sophia and Golitsyn urged the new commander of the Streltsi to sacrifice the young czar to them; it would appear, at any rate, that six hundred Streltsi were supposed to lay hands on him. The confidential archives entrusted to my keeping by the court of Russia confirm that the decision had been made to kill Peter I. The blow was about to be struck, and Russia would have been forever bereft of the new mode of life she has since received. The czar was once again forced to escape to the Troitsa Monastery, the usual asylum of the court when threatened by the soldiery. There he summoned the boyars loyal to him, mobilized a militia, sent word to the captains of the Streltsi, and called to his side several Germans long since settled in Moscow and all devoted to him because he was already partial to foreigners. Sophia and Ivan, who had stayed behind in Moscow, begged the Corps of Streltsi to remain faithful to them; but the cause of Peter, whose grievance was a premeditated crime against himself and his mother, prevailed over that of a princess and a czar whose mere physical appearance turned all hearts against him. All the plotters were punished with a severity to which the country was at that time as accustomed as it was to criminal outrages. Some were beheaded, after suffering the torture of the knout or the *batogi*. The commander of the Streltsi perished in this manner. Other suspects had their tongues cut out. Prince Golitsyn, who had a kinsman loyal to Peter, was spared, but was stripped of all his immense possessions and banished to Archangel. La Neuville, who was present throughout the catastrophe, says that Golitsyn's sentence was pronounced in the following terms: "You are ordered by the most clement czar to betake yourself to Karga, a town near the Pole, and to remain there for the rest of your life. His Majesty, of his extreme benevolence, grants you three kopecks per diem."

There are no towns near the Pole. Karga is on the sixty-second degree of latitude,[9] only six and a half degrees further north than Moscow. Whoever pronounced Golitsyn's sentence must have been a sorry geographer. It is claimed that La Neuville was taken in by an inaccurate account.

Lastly, Princess Sophia was taken back to her convent in Moscow, having ruled for a long while (1689); the change was punishment enough.

From this moment on, Peter ruled alone. The only part played by his brother Ivan in public affairs was to see his name on official decrees. He led a private life and died in 1696.

Chapter 6
Reign of Peter I.
Beginning of the Great Reforms.

Peter the Great was very tall, relaxed and well-proportioned, with a noble countenance, animated eyes, and a robust constitution fit for any exercise or any labor. He was level-headed, which is the basis for all true talents, and this soundness had a dash of restlessness, which induced him to try everything and achieve everything. His upbringing was quite unworthy of his brilliance; it had been to Princess Sophia's particular advantage to keep him ignorant and to abandon him to the excesses that his youth, idleness, tradition, and rank made only too permissible. However, he had recently married (June, 1689) and had taken to wife, like all the other czars, one of his own subjects, the daughter of one Colonel Lopukhin. But as he was a young man and had for some time enjoyed no other royal prerogative save that of indulging in his amusements, the grave responsibilities of marriage did not sufficiently restrain him. The pleasures of the table shared with some foreigners attracted to Moscow by Prime Minister Golitsyn did not herald the fact that Peter would one day become a reformer. Meanwhile, in spite of bad examples and even in spite of his diversions, he applied himself to the military and political arts. It should already have been possible to discern in him the potential great man.

It was even less to be expected that a prince who was overcome with involuntary dread, reaching the point of cold sweats and convulsions, when he had to cross a stream was one day to become the finest seaman of the north. He began to curb nature by throwing himself into the water despite his loathing for this element; his aversion even turned into a dominant preference.

The ignorance in which he had been raised made him blush. Virtually unaided by teachers, he taught himself enough German and Dutch to speak and write intelligibly in both languages. For him, the Germans and Dutch were the most cultivated of peoples, since the former were already practicing in Moscow some of the crafts he wanted to nurture in his empire, and the latter excelled in seamanship, which he regarded as the most indispensable of arts.

Such were his inclinations, notwithstanding the propensities of his youth. However, he had to be constantly on his guard against factions, to check the tempestuous Streltsi, and to sustain an almost unceasing war against the Crimean Tartars. This war ended in 1689 with a short-lived truce.

In the meantime, Peter strengthened his resolve to summon the arts to his native land.

His father, Alexei, had already held the same views, but neither time nor fortune had been in his favor. He passed on his own genius to his son, only more highly developed, more vigorous, and more persistent in the face of obstacles.

At great expense, Alexei had sent for the Dutch shipwright and sea captain Bothler,[1] together with carpenters and sailors, who built a large frigate and a yacht on the Volga. These vessels sailed downstream to Astrakhan. Alexei's intent was to use them, and other ships yet to be constructed, to trade advantageously with Persia across the Caspian Sea. Just then the rebellion of Stenka Razin broke out. The rebel destroyed the two vessels, which he should have preserved in his own interest. He murdered the captain, but the rest of the crew escaped to Persia, and from there reached the territory of the Dutch East India Company. One master carpenter—a good shipbuilder—stayed behind in Russia, where his presence was long overlooked. One day Peter, while taking a stroll at Izmailov, one of his grandfather's country houses, noticed among some other curiosities a small English longboat which had been completely abandoned. He asked his German mathematics teacher, Timmermann, why this little craft was of an entirely different construction from those he had seen on the Moskva. Timmermann replied that it was designed to be both sailed and rowed. The young ruler wanted to try it out there and then, but it had to be refitted and rerigged. They found the shipbuilder Brandt, of whom we have spoken above, living in retirement in Moscow. He overhauled the longboat and sailed it on the Yauza River, which washes the outlying parts of the city.

Peter had his longboat taken to a large lake near the Troitsa Monastery.[2] He had Brandt build him two frigates and three yachts, which he himself piloted. Eventually, in 1694, he went to Archangel, where, having had a small ship built by the aforementioned Brandt, he set sail on the White Sea, which no czar before him had ever laid eyes on. He was escorted by a Dutch man-of-war commanded by Captain Jolson, and followed by every merchantman berthed at Archangel. He was already learning seamanship, which, despite the alacrity of his courtiers to imitate their sovereign, he alone mastered.

It was no less difficult to train devoted and disciplined soldiers than it was to procure a navy. His first nautical attempts on a lake, before his voyage from Archangel, seemed the mere childhood amusements of a man of genius, and his earliest efforts to train troops also appeared to be no more than a game. This occurred during Sophia's regency, and had anyone suspected that the game was in earnest, it might well have cost Peter his life.

He put his trust in a foreigner, the celebrated Lefort,[3] a member of an ancient Piedmontese noble house which, nearly two centuries before, had removed to Geneva, where it occupied the highest offices. His family wanted to make him a man of business, since that alone is responsible for the importance of Geneva, once famous for nothing but controversy.[4]

Being temperamentally inclined toward higher matters, Lefort left home at the age of fourteen and spent four months as a cadet in the citadel of Marseilles. From there he went to Holland, where he served some time as a volunteer; he was wounded at the siege of Grave-sur-la-Meuse, a quite strongly fortified town which the prince of Orange, later king of England,[5] recaptured from Louis XIV in 1674. After that, seeking advancement wherever his hopes guided him, in 1675 he embarked with a German colonel named Verstein, who had been commissioned by Peter's father, Czar Alexei, to raise some troops in the Netherlands and bring them to the port of Archangel. But when they arrived, after enduring all the perils of the sea, Czar Alexei was no longer living; the government had changed. Russia was in a turmoil, and for a long while the governor of Archangel left Verstein, Lefort, and all their company in the most abject poverty and threatened to send them into the wilds of Siberia. Everyone got away as best he might. Lefort, completely destitute, went to Moscow and presented himself to the Danish Resident, named Van Horn, who made him his secretary. He learned Russian, and shortly thereafter contrived to be presented to Czar Peter, whose elder brother Ivan was not the man for Lefort. Peter took a fancy to him, and, to begin with, gave him the command of an infantry company. Lefort had scarcely any military experience; he was no scholar and had not studied any profession thoroughly. However, he had seen much and seen well; his affinity with the czar was due to his owing everything to the latter's genius. Furthermore, he spoke Dutch and German, which Peter was learning as the languages of two nations that might well serve his designs. Peter liked everything about Lefort, who attached himself to the czar. His position as favorite originated because he was amusing, and was confirmed through his ability. He was privy to the most perilous enterprise that a czar could conceive, namely, preparing himself for the day when he could with impunity smash the mutinous and barbarous Streltsi militia. The great Sultan, or Padishah, Osman's attempt to reform the Janissaries had cost him his life. Despite his youth, Peter went to work more skillfully than Osman had done. To start with, he created a company of fifty of his youngest domestics at his country house at Preobrazhenskoe. A few boyars' sons were chosen to act as officers, but, in order to teach these boyars the chain of command, of which they knew nothing, he made them rise through all the ranks. He personally set the example, serving first as drummerboy, then private, sergeant, and lieutenant in the company. Nothing was more extraordinary nor more salutary. The Russians had always waged war as we used to ourselves during the feudal epoch, when inexperienced noblemen used to lead undisciplined and ill-armed vassals into battle: a barbarous system good enough against similar armies but powerless in the face of regular troops.

This company, Peter's own creation, soon had many effectives, and later became the regiment of Preobrazhensky Guards.[6] A second company, formed on the same model, became the regiment of Semyonovsky Guards.

There already existed one reliable regiment of five thousand men. This had been raised by General Gordon,[7] a Scotsman, and consisted almost entirely of foreigners. Lefort, whose military experience was scanty but who was competent at everything, undertook to muster a regiment of twelve thousand men, and was completely successful. Five colonels were placed under his command, and he found himself all at once general of this little army, which had in fact been levied as much against the Streltsi as against the enemies of the state.

What is worthy of note here,[8] and what thoroughly confutes the foolhardy error of those who maintain that the revocation of the Edict of Nantes[9] had cost France but few men, is the fact that one third of this army-called-regiment consisted of French refugees. Lefort drilled his brand-new force as to the manner born.

Peter wanted to see one of those sham wars, one of those encampments which were just beginning to be introduced in peacetime. A fort was constructed; one detachment of his new troops was to defend it, the other to attack it. The difference between these maneuvers and all others was that instead of a mock battle they fought a real one, in which some soldiers were killed and many were wounded.[10] Lefort, who was commanding the attackers, himself received a serious wound. These bloody games were intended to toughen the troops, but prolonged labors and even prolonged setbacks were required before success was achieved. The czar combined these martial entertainments with the care he was lavishing on his navy, and, just as he had made Lefort, who had never held a command, a general, so he made him an admiral without his ever sailing a ship. Peter, however, considered him worthy to do both. It is true that the admiral had no fleet and the general had no army other than his regiment.

Little by little, they reformed the greatest failing of the Russian military, namely, the independent spirit of the boyars who led their peasant militias. It was the authentic governance of the Franks, Huns, Goths, and Vandals, the peoples who vanquished the Roman Empire in its decadence, but who would have been annihilated had they come up against the old, disciplined Roman legions or armies like those of today.

Before long, Admiral Lefort no longer held a totally empty title. He had some Dutchmen and Venetians build galleys, and even two warships of approximately thirty guns apiece, at the mouth of the Voronezh, which flows into the Don. These vessels were capable of sailing downstream and holding the Crimean Tartars in check. Hostilities with these tribesmen were continually breaking out. In 1689, the czar had to make a decision: whether to wage war on Turkey, Sweden, or China. We must begin by showing on what terms he was with China, as well as describing the first peace treaty the Chinese ever made.

Chapter 7
Meeting and Treaty with the Chinese.[1]

One must first get a clear notion of the boundaries of the Chinese and Russian empires at that time. On departing from Siberia proper, leaving far to the south a hundred hordes of Tartars, white Kalmucks, black Kalmucks, Muslim Mongols, and so-called idolatrous Mongols, one advances toward the one hundred and thirtieth degree of longitude and the fifty-second degree of latitude, on the Amur or Amour River. To the north of this river a great mountain range extends beyond the Arctic Circle to the Ocean.[2] The Amur, which flows for some five hundred leagues through Siberia and Chinese Tartary, disappears after numerous meanderings into the Sea of Kamchatka.[3] We are assured that where the river empties into the sea, they sometimes catch a monstrous fish—far bigger than the hippopotamus of the Nile—whose jawbone is of a harder and more perfect ivory. It is claimed that this ivory was once an item of trade and that it was transported across Siberia, which explains why several fragments of it are still found buried in the soil. This is the fossil ivory of which we have already spoken. However, there is a theory that there were once elephants in Siberia, and that the Tartars who conquered the Indies brought several of these creatures into Siberia, where their bones have been preserved in the ground.

The Amur River is named the Black River by the Manchu Tartars, and the River of the Dragon by the Chinese.

It was[4] in these lands, for so long unknown, that China and Russia were quarreling over the limits of their empires. Russia had a few forts near the Amur River, three hundred leagues from the Great Wall. There were numerous outbreaks of hostilities between the Chinese and Russians over these forts. Finally, both states reached a better understanding of their respective interests. The Emperor K'ang-hsi preferred peace and commerce to a futile war, and dispatched seven ambassadors to one of these forts, at Nerchinsk.[5] These ambassadors brought about ten thousand men with them, including their escort. Such was oriental ostentation, but what is truly remarkable is the fact that there was not a single example in the annals of the Chinese empire of a mission's having been sent to another power. Also unprecedented since the foundation of their empire was the very fact that the Chinese signed a peace treaty. Twice subjugated by the Tartars, who attacked and subdued them, they themselves never made war on any other people, aside from a few hordes which were either quickly routed or else left to their own devices without any treaty. Accordingly, this nation, so renowned for its ethics, was unacquainted with what we term the law of nations, i.e., those problematic rules of war and peace, those rights of diplomats, the phraseology of treaties and the commitments resulting therefrom, disputes over precedence and the point of honor.

Besides, in what language might the Chinese be expected to negotiate with the Russians in the heart of the wilderness? Two Jesuits, a Portuguese named Pereira and a Frenchman called Gerbillon, who had left Peking with the Chinese ambassadors, smoothed away all these novel problems, and were the true mediators. They negotiated in Latin with a German in the Russian service who knew that language. The head of the Russian embassy was Golovin, governor of Siberia, who put on an even more lavish display of magnificence than the Chinese, thereby giving a noble impression of his empire to those who had believed themselves to be the only great power on earth. The two Jesuits set the limits of the two jurisdictions at the Kerbechi River, near the spot where the negotiations were taking place. The Chinese kept the south, the Russians the north. It cost the latter only one small fortress, which happened to have been built beyond the boundary line. After some minor quibbles, the Russians and Chinese swore an eternal peace[6] in the name of the same God, as follows: "Should anyone ever harbor secret thoughts to rekindle the fires of war, we pray the Lord, ruler of all things, who reads men's hearts, to punish these traitors by sudden death."

This wording, common to Chinese and Christians alike, tells us two important facts: the first being that the Chinese government is neither atheistic nor idolatrous, a charge so frequently leveled at it by contradictory imputation; while the second is that every people which cultivates reason—despite all the aberrations of that ill-informed faculty—in fact acknowledges the same God. Two copies of the treaty were drawn up in Latin. First the Russian ambassadors signed the copy that they kept, and the Chinese likewise signed their own copy first, following European practice in negotiations between crowned heads. Another custom was also observed, that of the Asiatic nations and of the primitive ages of the known world. The treaty was engraved on two great marble slabs that were erected to serve as boundary stones for the two empires. Three years later, the czar sent the Dane Hildebrand Ide on a mission to China, and the commercial relations then established prospered until a rupture between Russia and China in 1722, after which interruption they resumed more vigorously than before.

Chapter 8
Expedition to the Sea of Azov. Azov Captured.
The Czar Sends Young Men to Study Abroad.

Peace with the Turks was not so easy to obtain. Indeed, the time seemed to have come to build on their ruins. Venice, which had been crushed by them, was beginning to rise again. That same Morosini who had surrendered Candia to the Turks was now capturing the Peloponnese from them.[1] His victory earned him the honorific title "Peloponnesiac," a dignity reminiscent of the Roman Republic.[2] The German Emperor Leopold enjoyed some successes against the Turkish empire in Hungary, and the Poles were at any rate beating off the incursions of the Crimean Tartars.

Peter took advantage of these circumstances to harden his troops and to take control of the Black Sea, if possible. General Gordon marched along the Don toward Azov with a regiment five thousand strong, accompanied by General Lefort with his twelve thousand men, a Streltsi corps commanded by Sheremeteyev[3] and the Prussian Shein, a troop of Cossacks, and a great artillery train. All was in readiness for the expedition.

In the early summer of 1695 the immense army moved forward under the command of Marshal Sheremeteyev toward Azov, at the mouth of the Don at the far end of the Sea of Azov, today called the Sea of Zabache. The czar was with the army, but as a simple volunteer, wishing to spend some little time learning before he himself took command. During the advance, they stormed and captured two towers that the Turks had built on opposite sides of the river.

The enterprise was not easy, Azov, quite strongly fortified, being defended by a large garrison. Some long galleys of Venetian construction, similar to Turkish *saics,* and two small Dutch warships sailed out of the Voronezh, but were not ready soon enough and were unable to enter the Sea of Azov. First attempts invariably run into obstacles. The Russians had not yet conducted a regular siege, and their attempts were not at first successful.

A certain Jacob, a native of Danzig,[4] was in charge of the artillery under General Shein, for practically all the senior gunners, engineers, and pilots were foreigners. This Jacob was sentenced by the Prussian General Shein to be beaten with the *batogi.* In those days authority was apparently strengthened by such severities. The Russians, despite their inclination toward mutiny, submitted to them, and after punishment served as before. The Danziger thought otherwise, and wanted revenge. He spiked the guns, hurried into Azov, embraced the Muslim religion, and defended the place successfully. This example demonstrates that the humanity practiced in Russia in our day is preferable to the old cruelty, and is a better way of retaining in their duty men who, thanks to an auspicious upbringing, have acquired a sense of honor. Extreme harshness was at that time necessary when dealing with the lower classes, but when society changed, the empress Elizabeth completed with clemency the task her father had initiated with laws. Her indulgence has been carried to a point unparalleled in the history of any nation. She promised that during her reign no one would suffer the death penalty, and she kept her promise. She is the first sovereign to have respected human life in this way. Malefactors have been sentenced to labor in the mines and on public works; their punishment has been useful to the state, a practice as wise as it is humane. Everywhere else we know only how to kill criminals with ceremony, without ever preventing them from committing crimes. The fear of death doubtless makes less of an impression on evildoers, most of whom are idlers, than the fear of a penalty and an irksome drudgery which begin afresh every day.

To return to the siege of Azov, which was now being defended by the very man who had directed the attacks on it, the Russians vainly attempted to take the city by storm, and after suffering heavy losses were obliged to raise the siege.

Steadfastness in every endeavor molded Peter's character. He led an even bigger army to Azov in the spring of 1696. His brother Czar Ivan had just died. Although Ivan, who was czar in name only, had not personally obstructed his authority, it had always been slightly inhibited by reason of the proprieties. After his death, Ivan's household expenses were diverted to the upkeep of the army. This was a relief for a state which did not at that time enjoy such ample revenues as it does today. Peter wrote to the Emperor Leopold, the States General,[5] and the elector of Brandenburg to obtain engineers, artillerymen, and seamen. He recruited some Kalmucks, whose cavalry is very useful against that of the Crimean Tartars.

The most gratifying of the czar's triumphs was that of his little navy, which was at last completed and well organized. It defeated the Turkish *saics* sent out from Constantinople and captured some of them. The siege was conducted in an orderly fashion, by means of trenches, though not quite in accordance with our methods; the trenches were three times as deep as ours and the parapets formed high ramparts. The besieged finally surrendered the city on July 28, new style, without receiving any of the honors of war, taking with them neither weapons nor stores. They were forced to hand over the deserter Jacob to the besiegers.

The czar's prime objective in fortifying Azov, protecting it with forts, and dredging a harbor capable of berthing the largest vessels was to make himself master of the Straits of Caffa, that Cimmerian Bosporus[6] that opens the way into the Black Sea, all places once renowned for the warlike exploits of Mithridates. Peter left thirty-two armed *saics* in front of Azov[7] and got everything in readiness to deploy against the Turks a fleet of nine sixty-gun men-of-war and forty-one ships carrying from thirty to fifty guns. He insisted that the greatest nobles and the wealthiest merchants contribute to this weaponry and, believing that the possessions of the church should serve the common cause, compelled the Patriarch, bishops, and archimandrites to donate their own money to this latest blow he was striking for the honor of his country and the good of Christendom. He ordered the Cossacks to build some of the light craft they commonly use, which can easily hug the Crimean coastline. Turkey must have been alarmed at such preparations for war, the first ever attempted on the Sea of Azov. The plan was to drive the Tartars and Turks out of the Crimea forever, and then to establish with Persia, by way of Georgia, a large-scale commerce without let or hindrance. This was the identical trade once practiced by the Greeks at Colchis[8] and in that Chersonesus Taurica which the czar seemed destined to subdue.

As conqueror of the Turks and Tartars, he wished to accustom his people to glory as well as to toil. He had his army enter Moscow beneath triumphal arches, amid firework displays and anything else likely to embellish the festivities. The soldiers who had fought on the Venetian *saics* against the Turks formed a separate troop and marched at the head of the column. Marshal Sheremeteyev, Generals Gordon and Shein, Admiral Lefort, and the other commanders preceded the sovereign in the spectacle since, as he put it, he did not as yet hold any official rank in the army. By this example, he wanted to make the whole aristocracy realize that military rank must be earned before it can be enjoyed.

The triumph seemed to derive in some sort from the ancient Romans. It resembled theirs particularly inasmuch as victors awarded a triumph in Rome exposed the vanquished to the eyes of the populace, and occasionally had them put to death. Those enslaved by the expedition followed the army, and the aforementioned Jacob, who had betrayed it, rode in a cart in which a gallows had been erected. Later he was hanged from it, after being broken on the wheel.

The first Russian medal was then struck. Its Russian inscription is noteworthy: "Peter I, Emperor of Muscovy, ever august." On the reverse is Azov, with these words: "Victor by fire and water."

Despite his success, Peter was grieved that the ships and galleys of the

Azov fleet had been built by foreigners. He was still just as eager to have a port on the Baltic as on the Black Sea.

In the month of March, 1697, he sent off to Italy sixty young Russians from Lefort's regiment, most of them to Venice and a few to Leghorn, to learn seamanship and the construction of galleys. He sent forty more to Holland to be trained in the building and handling of large ships; another group was dispatched to Germany for military training and to acquire experience in German discipline. Lastly, he made up his mind to spend a few years outside his own domains, with the intention of learning how better to govern them. He could not overcome his strong desire to obtain with his own eyes—and indeed with his own hands—instruction in seamanship and the other skills that he wanted to implant in Russia. He intended to travel incognito in Denmark, Brandenburg, Holland, Venice, and Rome. Only France and Spain did not enter into his plans: Spain, where the techniques he was seeking were at the time too neglected; and France, because there they held sway with perhaps too much ostentation, and because Louis XIV's hauteur, which had scandalized so many potentates, was ill suited to the simplicity with which he purposed to travel. Besides, with the exception of France and Rome he was on good terms with most of the powers he was about to visit. He still recalled with some irritation the scant regard Louis XIV had shown the Russian embassy in 1687, which had gained more notoriety than success. Finally, he was already supporting Augustus, elector of Saxony, whom the Prince de Conti was challenging for the crown of Poland.[10]

Chapter 9
Peter the Great's Travels.

With his mind made up to view so many states and their courts as a private citizen, he constituted himself a member of the entourage of three ambassadors, just as he had marched behind his own generals during his triumphal entry into Moscow.

The three ambassadors[1] were General Lefort; Boyar Alexei Golovin, commissioner general for war and governor of Siberia, the same man who had signed the treaty of eternal peace with the plenipotentiaries of China at the Chinese border; and Voznitsyn, *diak* or secretary of state, who had long experience of foreign courts. Four first secretaries, twelve noblemen, two pages for each ambassador, and a company of fifty guards with their officers, all from the Preobrazhensky Regiment, composed the embassy's principal retinue. In all there were two hundred persons, and the czar, whose only domestics were a valet, a footman, and a dwarf, was lost in the crowd. A twenty-five-year-old king leaving his kingdom in order to be a better ruler was something without parallel in the history of the world. His victory over the Turks and Tartars, the glamor of his triumphal entry into Moscow, the numerous foreign troops devoted to him, the death of his brother Ivan, the sequestration of Princess Sophia, and even more the general respect he enjoyed would guarantee the tranquility of his domains during his absence. He entrusted the regency to Boyar Streshnev and to Knes Romodanovsky, who were to consult with other boyars concerning matters of importance.

The troops trained by General Gordon stayed behind in Moscow to maintain order in the capital. The Streltsi, who were quite capable of disturbing it, were dispersed along the Crimean frontier, to consolidate the conquest of Azov and to keep Tartar raids in check. Having thus provided for every eventuality, he gave free rein to his passion for travel and self-instruction.

Since these journeys were the occasion or the pretext for the bloody war which for so long thwarted the czar in all his grand designs but ultimately furthered them, a war that dethroned King Augustus of Poland, gave the crown to Stanislas and took it away again, made King Charles XII of Sweden the greatest of conquerors for nine years and the most luckless of monarchs for nine more, we must, before going into these events in detail, describe the state of affairs of contemporary Europe.

Sultan Mustapha II reigned in Turkey. His feeble regime was making little headway against either the German Emperor Leopold, who was enjoying military successes in Hungary, the czar, who had just taken Azov from him and was threatening the Black Sea, or even Venice, which had at last seized the whole of the Peloponnese.

King John Sobieski of Poland, forever renowned for his victory at Khotin and the relief of Vienna, had died on June 17, 1696, and his crown was being contested by Augustus, elector of Saxony, who carried it off, and by Armand, prince de Conti, who merely enjoyed the honor of being elected.

Sweden had just lost (April, 1697), with few regrets, Charles XI, that country's first truly absolute monarch and father of a king even more absolute, but in whose person despotism in Sweden died out. He left his fifteen-year-old son Charles XII on the throne. For the czar, this was an apparently auspicious combination of circumstances, as he would now be able to enlarge his territories into the Gulf of Finland and Livonia. Peter was not content to make the Turks uneasy on the Black Sea; settlements on the Sea of Azov and near the Caspian could not satisfy his dreams of a navy, of trade, and of power. Glory itself, so passionately desired by every reformer, was not to be found in Persia or Turkey, but in our own part of Europe, where great talents of every kind are immortalized. Besides, Peter had no wish to introduce either Turkish or Persian manners into his empire, but ours instead.

Germany, at war simultaneously with Turkey and France, and allied with Spain, England, and Holland against Louis XIV, was ready to make peace, and the plenipotentiaries were already assembled at Ryswick Castle near The Hague.

It was at this juncture that Peter and his embassy set off in the month of April, 1697, by way of Novgorod the Great. From there they traveled across the provinces of Estonia and Livonia, which had once been hotly fought for by the Russians, the Swedes, and the Poles, and ultimately acquired by Sweden through force of arms.

Livonia's fertility and the location of its capital Riga might well have proved tempting to the czar. At any rate he was eager to inspect its fortifications. Count Dahlberg, governor of Riga, took umbrage at this; he refused to gratify Peter's wish and seemed to show scant respect for the embassy. Such conduct did not help to dampen the czar's doubtless heartfelt desire to become the master of these provinces one day.

From Livonia they entered Brandenburg Prussia, part of which had been inhabited by the ancient Vandals. Polish Prussia was included in European Sarmatia. Brandenburg was a poor country, whose elector— who later assumed the title of king[2]—nevertheless put on a new and ruinously expensive show of magnificence. He made it a point of honor to receive the embassy in his city of Königsberg with kingly ostentation.

The most lavish gifts were exchanged. There was a striking contrast between the French mode of dress affected by the court of Berlin and the long Asiatic robes of the Russians, their caps embellished with pearls and precious stones and their scimitars hanging at their belts. The czar was dressed in the German fashion. A Georgian prince who was with him, wearing Persian costume, displayed yet a different kind of magnificence. This was the same man who was captured at the battle of Narva and who died in Sweden.

Peter despised all this show. One could have wished that he had similarly despised the pleasures of the table which the Germany of the day gloried in.[3] It was during one of these repasts, all too fashionable in those days and as dangerous to the health as they were to morals, that he drew his sword against his favorite, Lefort. But he expressed as much regret over this momentary outburst as did Alexander over the murder of Clytus. He begged Lefort's pardon, saying that he wanted to reform his nation but was as yet unable to reform himself. In his manuscript, General Lefort has more praise for the czar's depth of character than blame for his immoderate anger.

The embassy passed through Pomerania and Berlin, part of it making its way through Magdeburg, the other through Hamburg, a city that was already growing powerful because of its extensive commerce, but not then as opulent or hospitable as it has become since. They turned off toward Minden, passed through Westphalia, and finally arrived in Amsterdam by way of Cleves.

The czar reached Amsterdam two weeks before his embassy. At first he stayed at the Dutch East India Company house, but shortly thereafter took modest lodgings in the Admiralty shipyards. He put on a pilot's coat, and thus arrayed went to the village of Saardam,[4] where in those days they built many more ships than they do today. This village is as extensive, as populous, and as wealthy as many prosperous cities— and cleaner, too. The czar marveled at the throng of ceaselessly busy men, the orderliness and precision of their work, the prodigious speed with which a vessel could be constructed and fully rigged, and the incredible quantity of storehouses and machinery which made the task easier and safer. Peter began by buying a boat, for which he made a built-up mast[5] with his own hands. After that, he worked in every area of shipbuilding, leading the same life as the artisans of Saardam, dressing like them, eating the same food, laboring in the forges, the rope walks, and the stupendous number of mills which surround the village and where they saw fir and oak, extract oil, manufacture paper, and draw ductile metals. He had himself enrolled among the shipwrights under the name of Peter Mikhailov. He was generally known as Master Peter (Peterbaas), and the workmen, who were at first flabbergasted at having a sovereign for a comrade, were soon on familiar terms with him.

While he was manipulating the dividers and the axe in Saardam, he received confirmation of the Polish schism and the double nomination of the elector Augustus and the prince de Conti. The shipwright of Saardam immediately promised King Augustus thirty thousand men. From his workshop, he issued orders to his army of the Ukraine, which had been mustered to fight the Turks.

His troops, commanded by General Shein and Prince Dolgoruky, had just beaten the Tartars, and even a body of Janissaries sent by Sultan Mustapha, near Azov (July, 1696). As for Peter, he went on diligently acquiring skills. From Saardam he went to Amsterdam to work with the celebrated anatomist Ruysch. He performed surgical operations, which, in an emergency, could be of use to his officers or himself. He studied the natural sciences in the home of Burgomaster Witsen, a citizen forever worthy of respect by virtue of his patriotism and of the use to which he put his immense wealth, which, like a citizen of the world, he spent lavishly, sending learned men at enormous cost to every corner of the globe to seek out its greatest rarities and chartering vessels at his own expense for voyages of discovery.

Peterbaas suspended his labors only to pay an informal visit to King William of England, Stadtholder of the United Provinces, in Utrecht and The Hague. General Lefort alone was present as a third party with the two monarchs. Afterwards, Peter attended the ceremonial entrance of his ambassadors, and their audience. In his name, they presented the delegates of the States General with six hundred of the most beautiful sables; and the States, above and beyond the usual gift of a gold medallion and chain, gave the ambassadors three magnificent coaches. Peter and William received the first official visits of all the ambassadors plenipotentiary at the Congress of Ryswick, with the exception of the French, whom they had not informed of their arrival, not only because the czar was taking King Augustus's part against the prince de Conti, but also because King William, whose friendship he was cultivating, did not desire peace with France.

On his return to Amsterdam, Peter resumed his earlier pursuits, with his own hands completing a sixty-gun ship whose keel he had laid, and which he dispatched to Archangel, the only deep-water port he possessed at the time. Not only did he hire French refugees, Swiss, and Germans, but he sent craftsmen of every kind to Moscow—only, however, those whose work he had personally inspected. There are very few arts and crafts which he did not study thoroughly and painstakingly. He took a special delight in redrafting maps, for the geographers of those days used to assign random locations to all the cities and rivers of his little-known domains. We still possess the map on which he traced the linking of the Caspian and Black Seas, which he had already planned and entrusted to a German engineer named Brakel. The joining of these two seas was easier than that of the Atlantic Ocean and the Mediterranean carried out in France, but at the time the mere notion of uniting the Sea of Azov and the Caspian was awe-inspiring. New establishments in Russia struck him as being all the more appropriate as his successes gave him fresh expectations.

His troops gained the day against the Tartars quite close to Azov (August 11, 1697) and some months later captured the city of Or or Or-Kapi, which we call Perekop. This triumph earned him the respect of those who reproached the sovereign for having left his realm in order to practice various trades in Amsterdam. They saw that the affairs of the monarch were not suffering from the labors of the traveling philosopher and craftsman.

In Amsterdam he continued his customary pursuits as shipwright, engineer, geographer, and naturalist until the middle of January, 1698, when he left for England, still in the guise of a member of his own embassy.

King William sent the royal yacht and two warships to meet him. His mode of life was the same as the one he had prescribed for himself in Amsterdam and Saardam. He took lodgings near the great Deptford shipyards and applied himself almost exclusively to his studies. The Dutch shipbuilders had taught him only their methods and practice; in England, he became better acquainted with the theory. English ships were built according to mathematical principles. He became adept at this science, and was soon capable of giving lessons in it. He worked, following the English method, on the construction of a vessel that turned out to be one of the most seaworthy ships afloat. Clockmaking, already brought to a fine art in London, attracted his interest, and he learned its entire theory to perfection. Captain Perry the engineer, who followed him from London to Russia, tells us that from the casting of cannon to the spinning of rope there was no trade that he did not observe and to which he did not set his hand whenever he was in the workshops.

The English, who wished to cultivate his friendship, thought it desirable that he should engage workmen as he had done in Holland, but in addition to artisans, he obtained what he would not have found so readily in Amsterdam, namely, mathematicians. Ferguson,[6] a Scot and a fine geometrician, entered his service. He is the man who introduced arithmetic into the offices of the Russian treasury, where previously they had employed the Tartar method of counting with balls threaded on brass wire. This took the place of writing but was cumbrous and faulty, because after the computation it is impossible to verify whether one has made a mistake. Thanks to the Arabs, we became acquainted with the Indian numerals now in use as recently as the ninth century; the Russian empire did not acquire them until a thousand years after that. Such is the destiny of all the arts; their voyage around the world had been a slow one. Two young men from the school of mathematics accompanied Ferguson, and this was the beginning of the naval academy that Peter founded at a later date. He observed and calculated eclipses with Ferguson. Perry the engineer, though highly dissatisfied at having been insufficiently recompensed, admits that Peter was well grounded in astronomy. He was conversant with the movements of the celestial bodies, and even with the laws of gravity that govern them. Completely unknown before the great Newton, and yet now so conclusively demonstrated, this force, in obedience to which all the planets weigh upon each other and remain in their orbits, was already understood by a sovereign of Russia while elsewhere men's heads were stuffed with nonsensical vortices,[7] and in the homeland of Galileo ignoramuses were commanding other ignoramuses to believe that the earth was motionless.[8]

For his part, Perry went off to work connecting rivers and building bridges and lock gates. The czar's plan was to link the ocean, the Caspian Sea, and the Black Sea by canals.

We must not omit the fact that some English merchants, under the aegis of Admiral Lord Carmarthen, gave Peter fifteen thousand pounds sterling to obtain for themselves the right to sell tobacco in Russia. By a piece of ill-conceived severity, the Patriarch had proscribed this item of trade; the Russian Church forbade the use of tobacco, regarding it as sinful. Peter, who was more enlightened and who among all the other changes he was planning contemplated the reform of the church, introduced the tobacco trade into his domains.

Before Peter left England, King William offered a spectacle most worthy of such a guest, that of a naval battle. At the time, no one suspected that one day the czar would wage real sea fights against the Swedes, and that he would win victories on the Baltic. Lastly, William made him a present of the craft in which he himself usually sailed to Holland. It was named the *Royal Transport*, and was as well-built as it was sumptuous.[9] Peter returned to Holland in this vessel at the end of May, 1698, bringing with him three man-of-war captains,[10] twenty-five master mariners—also called captains—forty lieutenants, thirty pilots, thirty surgeons, two hundred and fifty gunners, and more than three hundred artisans. This colony of craftsmen of all kinds went from Holland to Archangel aboard the *Royal Transport*. Individuals were then sent wherever their services were required. Those who were hired in Amsterdam took the road for Narva, which then belonged to Sweden.

While Peter was transporting the skills of England and Holland into his own country, the officers he had dispatched to Rome and Italy[11] were engaging some artists. General Sheremeteyev, head of his embassy in Italy, went from Rome to Naples, Venice, and Malta; the czar traveled to Vienna with the other ambassadors. After his inspection of the English navy and the Dutch workshops, the military discipline of Germany still remained to be seen. Diplomacy played as important a role in his travels as did self-instruction. The Emperor was the czar's indispensable ally against the Turks. Peter saw Leopold incognito, and the two emperors conversed standing, so as to spare themselves the bother of protocol.

There was nothing memorable about his stay in Vienna except for the ancient festivity of the host and hostess which Leopold revived in his honor, but which had not previously been observed during his reign. This entertainment, which is called the *Wirtschaft*,[12] is celebrated in the following manner. The Emperor is the innkeeper and the Empress the innkeeper's wife, while the king of the Romans,[13] the archdukes and archduchesses are generally their servants, who welcome to the hostelry every nation dressed in the most ancient form of its national costume. Those invited to the feast draw lots for tickets, on each of which is written the name of the nation and the social rank to be portrayed. One person receives a ticket for a Chinese mandarin, another for a Tartar mirza,[14] a Persian satrap, or a Roman senator. A princess draws the ticket of a gardener's wife or a milkmaid; a prince becomes a peasant or a soldier. Dances befitting all these types are devised. The host, the hostess, and their family wait at table. Such is this venerable institution.[15] On this occasion, Joseph, king of the Romans, and the countess von Traun represented ancient Egyptians, while the archduke Charles and the countess von Wallenstein were Flemings of Charles V's time. The archduchess Marie Elizabeth and Count von Traun were disguised as Tartars; the archduchess Josephine with Count von Vorkla was dressed Persian style; the archduchess Marianne and Prince Maximilian of Hanover appeared as peasants from North Holland. Peter was attired as a Frisian peasant and was addressed as such, while people constantly spoke to him about the great czar of Russia. These are very minor details, but anything that recalls the old ways to us may well, in some respects, deserve to be mentioned.

Peter was on the point of leaving Vienna to put the finishing touches to his education in Venice when he received news of a rebellion which was causing unrest at home.

Chapter 10
A Conspiracy Punished. Streltsi Militia Disbanded. Changes in Customs and Manners, Changes in the State and in the Church.

He had taken care of everything before he left Russia, even the means of suppressing a rebellion. The actual cause of the revolt was the important and beneficial things he was accomplishing for his country.

Some elderly boyars to whom the old ways were dear and some priests to whom the new ones appeared sacrilegious were at the root of the troubles. Princess Sophia's former adherents bestirred themselves. One of her sisters, confined with her in the same convent, is said to have contributed greatly to inflaming people's minds. Everywhere it was pointed out how serious was the threat that foreigners would come to instruct the nation.[1] Finally—and who would believe it?—the czar's authorization to sell tobacco in his empire despite the clergy's protests was one of the major causes of the sedition. Superstition, that baneful and universal scourge so dear to the populace, passed from the Russian people to the Streltsi stationed on the Lithuanian frontier. They banded together and marched on Moscow with the intention of placing Sophia on the throne and preventing the return of a czar who had flouted custom by presuming to educate himself abroad. The army corps commanded by Shein and Gordon, which was better disciplined than the Streltsi, beat them fifteen leagues outside Moscow, but the superiority of a foreign general over the old militia in which numerous Muscovite burghers were enrolled made the nation even angrier.

In order to stifle these rumblings, the czar secretly left Vienna, crossed Poland, and paid an incognito visit to King Augustus, in agreement with whom he was already taking steps to enlarge his territories on the Baltic. He finally reached Moscow (September, 1698), where his arrival took everyone by surprise. He rewarded the troops who had defeated the Streltsi. The prisons were full of these wretches. If their crime was great, so was its punishment. Their leaders, several officers, and a few priests were condemned to death.[2] Some were broken on the wheel and two women were buried alive. Two thousand Streltsi were killed, either hanged outside the city wall or executed in other ways.[3] For two days, their bodies were exposed along the highways, and especially around the convent where Princesses Sophia and Evdokiya were domiciled. Stone columns were erected with their crime and punishment engraved thereon. A very large number of the Streltsi who had wives and children in Moscow were dispersed with their families to Siberia, the kingdom of Astrakhan, and the Azov region. In this way at least their punishment was useful to the state, since they served to clear and to populate territories lacking both inhabitants and agriculture.

Perhaps if the czar had not needed to make so terrible an example, he would have sentenced some of the executed Streltsi to labor on public works, instead of letting them be lost both to himself and to the state. Human life must be valued highly, especially where populating the land is of the greatest concern to a lawgiver, but Peter deemed it advisable to stun and subdue the national spirit once and for all by the sheer spectacle and number of executions. The entire Streltsi corps, which not one of his predecessors would have dared even to reduce in size, was smashed forever, and its very name abolished. This tremendous change took place without the slightest resistance because he was prepared. The Turkish sultan Osman, as I have already observed, was deposed and murdered during the same period simply for allowing the Janissaries to suspect that he wished to decrease their number. Peter, having made better arrangements, was more fortunate. Of all the mighty Streltsi militia, nothing remained save a few feeble regiments that were no longer a threat. In 1705, however, still retaining their old spirit, they mutinied in Astrakhan, but were quickly suppressed.

The harshness Peter displayed in this affair of state was equaled by the humanity he showed when, shortly afterwards, he lost his favorite Lefort, who died at the early age of forty-six (March 12, 1699, new style). He gave him the honors of a state funeral of the kind generally accorded to great sovereigns. The czar personally took part in the procession, carrying a pike and marching behind the captains, dressed in the uniform of a lieutenant, the rank he had assumed in General Lefort's regiment. Thus at one and the same time he gave the aristocracy a lesson in respect for merit and for military rank.

After Lefort's death, it was discovered that the projected changes in the state did not originate with him, but with the czar. His conversations with Lefort had indeed confirmed his ideas, but he had conceived them all himself and carried them out unaided.

As soon as he had destroyed the Streltsi, he founded regular regiments on the German model, with short military tunics instead of the clumsy robes they had worn before. Their drill also became more standardized.

The Preobrazhensky Guards were already in existence. Their name was derived from that first company of fifty men whom the czar, while still a boy, had drilled in his country retreat at Preobrazhenskoe during the rule of his sister Sophia. The other guards regiment was already established as well.[4]

Just as he himself had risen through the lowest military ranks, he wanted the sons of his boyars and knes to start off as private soldiers before becoming officers. He assigned others to the Voronezh and Azov squadrons, where they had to serve an apprenticeship as ordinary seamen. No one dared to refuse a master who had already set the example. The English and Dutch were working to put this fleet in order and were building lock gates and shipyards equipped with drydocks, and resuming the great task—abandoned by the German Brakel—of joining the Don and the Volga. From that time on, reforms were undertaken in his council of state, the treasury, the church, and society itself.

The treasury was administered more or less as in Turkey. Each boyar paid a stipulated sum for his lands, which he levied from his serfs. As tax collectors, the czar appointed members of the middle class and local functionaries not powerful enough to usurp the right to pay into the public treasury only as much as they thought fit. The new financial management caused Peter more trouble than anything else. He had to experiment with several methods before settling on one.

Reforming the church, which is universally believed to be both difficult and dangerous, was not either for Peter. The Patriarchs—like the Streltsi—had on occasion fought against the royal prerogative, Nikon with effrontery, Joachim (one of Nikon's successors) with pliancy. The bishops had arrogated to themselves the power of life and death, as well as that of condemnation to penal servitude and capital punishment,[5] powers that are hostile to both the spirit of religion and the civil authority. This longstanding usurpation was taken away from them. When, at the turn of the century, the Patriarch Adrian died, Peter declared that there would be no more Patriarchs. The dignity was totally abolished, and the immense wealth assigned to the patriarchate was channeled into the public treasury, which badly needed it. If the czar did not make himself head of the Russian church, as the kings of Great Britain are of the Anglican church, he was in effect its absolute master, because the synods did not dare disobey a despotic sovereign or dispute with a monarch who was more enlightened than themselves.

One has only to glance at the preamble to his edict of 1721 concerning ecclesiastical regulations to see that he was acting both as legislator and as absolute monarch: "We would think ourselves guilty of ingratitude toward the Almighty if, having reformed the military and civil estates, we neglected the spiritual, etc. Wherefore, following the example of the most ancient kings, whose piety is a byword, we have taken upon ourselves the charge of giving the clergy good regulations." It is true that he instituted a synod to carry out his ecclesiastical laws, but the synod's members had to begin their tenure of office by taking an oath whose wording Peter had himself composed and signed. It was an oath of obedience; here are its terms: "I swear to be a faithful and obedient servant and subject to my true and natural sovereign and to the august successors whom it shall please him to appoint by virtue of his incontrovertible authority. I acknowledge him to be the supreme arbiter of this spiritual body; I swear by the God who sees all that I understand and construe this oath in the full force and meaning presented by its language to those who read or hear it." This oath is even stronger than the Oath of Supremacy in England. To be sure, the Russian monarch was not one of the fathers of the synod, but it was he who dictated their decrees. He did not touch the censer, but he directed the hands that bore it.

Pending this great work, he believed that in his domains, which were underpopulated, the celibacy of the monks was contrary both to nature and to the common good. The time-honored tradition of the Russian church is that secular priests marry at least once. Indeed, they are obliged to marry, and in the old days, when they had lost their wives they ceased to be priests. But a host of young men and women taking vows to remain idle in a cloister where they live at the expense of others seemed dangerous to him. He gave orders that one could only enter a monastery at fifty, i.e., at an age when scarcely anyone is tempted to do so, and forbade all persons holding public offices to be accepted into a monastery at any age whatsoever.

Since Peter's death this rule has been abolished, at a time when it was deemed advisable to be more indulgent to the monasteries, but the dignity of Patriarch has never been revived, the enormous revenues of the patriarchate being used to pay the troops.

To begin with, these changes aroused some murmurings. A priest wrote that Peter was the Antichrist because he did not want a Patriarch, and the art of printing, encouraged by the czar, served to vilify him. However, another priest replied that the monarch could not be the Antichrist, because the number 666 did not occur in his name, and he did not have the mark of the beast on him. The complaints were suppressed in short order. In actual fact, Peter gave far more to his church than he took from it, for by degrees he made the clergy more orderly and more learned. In Moscow, he founded three colleges for the teaching of languages, and those who intended to enter the priesthood were obliged to study there.

One of the most needed reforms was the abolition, or at least the moderation, of four major fasts, to which the Orthodox Church had long subjugated the faithful. These fasts were as pernicious for those laboring on public works—and especially for the soldiery—as was the ancient Jewish superstition that forbade fighting on the Sabbath. The czar accordingly dispensed at least his troops and his laborers from these fasts, during which, moreover, if eating was prohibited, it was quite in order to get drunk. He likewise absolved them from days of abstinence. Naval and regimental chaplains were obliged to set the example, and did so willingly.

The calendar was an important matter. In times past, the year was regulated by religious leaders in every country on earth, not only because of feast days, but because astronomy was originally studied by almost no one but priests. In Russia the year began on September 1, but Peter ordered that henceforth the year would start on January 1, as in our part of Europe. The changeover was scheduled for the year 1700, at the opening of the new century, which he celebrated by a jubilee and great solemnities. The common people marveled at the czar's power to change the course of the sun. A few obstinate persons, convinced that God had created the world in September, kept to the old ways, but the change was effected in government offices, in chanceries, and before long throughout the empire. Peter did not adopt the Gregorian calendar—rejected by English mathematicians—which every land will sooner or later have to accept.[6]

Since the fifth century, the period during which writing was introduced, Russians had written first on scrolls of bark or parchment, and then on paper. The czar was obliged to issue a decree commanding everyone to write in *our* style.[7]

His reforms extended to everything. Marriages were contracted before his time as they were in Turkey and Persia, where the groom does not see the bride until after the contract is signed and it is too late to back out. This is a good custom for peoples who practice polygamy and lock up their womenfolk, but a poor one for countries where one takes but a single wife and divorce is rare.

The czar desired to accustom his subjects to the manners and customs of the lands he had visited, and from which he had taken all the teachers then instructing his own nation.

It was to everyone's advantage that the Russians be dressed no differently than those who were teaching them the useful arts, since hatred for foreigners is all too human and all too easily fueled by differences in attire. The ceremonial costume, which at that time partook of the Polish, the Tartar, and the ancient Hungarian modes, was, as we have observed, very dignified, but the garb of the middle and lower classes was similar to those coats pleated at the waist that are still given to certain paupers in some of our charity hospitals. The robe was once generally worn in every nation. It required less skill and was less bothersome to make. Beards were allowed to grow for the same reason. At court, the czar had no trouble introducing western costume and the practice of shaving, but the ordinary people were harder to persuade, and he had to impose a tax on long robes and beards. Patterns of close-fitting coats were hung up at the city gates. Anyone who refused to pay had his robe shortened and his beard cut off. All this was carried out gaily, and this very gaiety disarmed any defiance.[8]

The attention of every legislator has always been turned to making men fit for society, but to achieve this end it is not enough that they be gathered together in towns: it is essential that people display civility. Such urbanity everywhere assuages the vexations of life. The czar introduced social gatherings, the Italian *ridotti,* a term incorrectly rendered by the journalists as *redoubt.*[9] To these assemblies he invited ladies with their daughters dressed in the fashion of southern Europe; he even issued rules for these little social fetes. And so everything, right down to his subjects' good manners, was accomplished by Peter and by time.

In order that these innovations might be better appreciated, he abolished the word *golut,* or slave, used by Russians wishing to speak to the czar or to submit petitions; he commanded that they use the word *raab,* meaning subject. The alteration in no way detracted from their obedience, and was designed to gain their attachment. Each month saw a new institution or change. He turned his attention to such details as setting painted posts along the highway from Moscow to Voronezh to serve as milestones from verst to verst, i.e., at intervals of seven hundred and fifty paces. At every twentieth verst, he built a sort of caravanserai.

Even while taking endless pains over ordinary people, merchants, and travelers, he wanted to inject some formality into his court, hating ostentatious display in his own person but deeming it necessary for others. In imitation of those orders of chivalry that proliferate at every European court, he founded the Order of St. Andrew.[10] Golovin, Lefort's successor as Grand Admiral, was the first recipient of this order. The honor of being admitted was considered a great reward. It was a reminder that it is up to oneself to earn the people's respect. This mark of honor costs a sovereign nothing, and flatters a subject's self-esteem without making him powerful.

All these useful innovations were welcomed with applause by the soundest segment of the population, while the complaints of those who favored the old ways were drowned by the acclamations of the enlightened.

While Peter was beginning his work of creation in Russia itself, an advantageous treaty with the Turkish empire gave him the freedom of action he needed to extend his frontiers in a different direction. Mustapha II, defeated by Prince Eugene at the Battle of Zenta in 1697, having lost the Morea to the Venetians and being unable to defend Azov, was compelled to make peace with his adversaries. A treaty was concluded at Karlowitz (January 26, 1699) between Peterwardein and Zalánkemén, places renowned for Mustapha's defeats. Temesvár was the boundary between the Imperial possessions and the Ottoman domains. Kamenets was returned to the Poles; the Venetians kept for some time the Morea and certain cities they had captured in Dalmatia, while Peter I remained in control of Azov and several forts built in its vicinity. It was scarcely feasible for the czar to enlarge his territories at the expense of the Turks, whose forces, hitherto divided but now combined, would have fallen upon him. His naval plans were too grandiose for the Sea of Azov, while his settlements on the Caspian did not require a battle fleet. He accordingly turned his eyes toward the Baltic, without, however, abandoning the squadrons of the Don and the Volga.

Chapter 11
War with Sweden. The Battle of Narva.

A mighty spectacle then unfolded near the Swedish frontier (1700). One of the principal causes of all the disturbances occurring from Ingria to Dresden and devastating so many states for eighteen years was the abuse of the supreme power by King Charles XI of Sweden, father of Charles XII. This fact cannot be too often repeated, as it is relevant to every throne and every nation. The greater part of Livonia, together with the whole of Estonia, had been abandoned by Poland to King Charles XI, who succeeded Charles X during the negotiations which led to the Treaty of Oliva. The territory was ceded, as is customary, subject to the maintenance of all its privileges, for which Charles XI showed scant regard. Johan Reinhold Patkul, a Livonian nobleman, came to Stockholm in 1692 at the head of a six-man delegation from his province in order to convey to the Swedish crown Livonia's firm yet respectful protests.[1] Charles XI's only response was to imprison the six delegates and sentence Patkul to lose his honor and his life. He lost neither, but escaped, remaining for some time in the canton of Vaud in Switzerland. Later, on learning that Augustus, elector of Saxony, had promised on his accession to the throne of Poland to recover the provinces that had been wrested from that kingdom, he hurried to Dresden to point out how easy it would be to recapture Livonia and to exact vengeance from a seventeen-year-old king for the conquests of his forebears.

Just at that time, Czar Peter was thinking of seizing Ingria and Carelia, provinces which had once belonged to the Russians. The Swedes had taken possession of them by right of conquest in the days of the false Dmitrys, and had retained them by treaty. A new war and new treaties might well give them back to Russia. Patkul went from Dresden to Moscow, and, inciting two monarchs to his personal vengeance, cemented their alliance and urged on their preparations for seizing everything east and south of Finland.

At precisely the same time, Frederick IV, the new king of Denmark, formed a league with the czar and the king of Poland against young Charles, whose defeat seemed inevitable. Patkul, in his capacity as major general, had the satisfaction of besieging the Swedes inside Riga, the capital of Livonia.

(September, 1700) The czar sent some sixty thousand men marching toward Ingria. It is true that in this huge army there were scarcely twelve thousand seasoned soldiers, and these he had trained himself (for example, his two guards regiments and a few others). The remainder consisted of ill-armed militia, with some Cossacks and Circassian Tartars, but he was hauling one hundred and forty-five pieces of ordnance in his train. He laid siege to Narva, a small town in Ingria with a serviceable harbor, and it seemed highly probable that the place would shortly be taken.

All Europe knows how Charles XII, not yet eighteen, attacked all his enemies one after the other, invaded Denmark, put an end to the Danish war in less than six weeks, sent a relief force to Riga, where he raised the siege, and marched against the Russians before Narva in the icy month of November.

The czar, banking on the capture of the city, had gone to Novgorod (November 18), taking with him his favorite, Menshikov—who later became a field marshal and a prince—then a lieutenant in the bombardier company of the Preobrazhensky Regiment. He was a man whose remarkable career deserves to be discussed at greater length elsewhere. Peter left his army and his instructions for the siege with the prince von Croy, a native of Flanders who had entered his service shortly before.[2] Prince Dolgoruky was commissioner for the army. Jealousy between these two commanders and the czar's absence were in part responsible for the astonishing defeat at Narva. In October, Charles XII, having disembarked with his troops at Pernau in Livonia, moved northward to Reval and overcame a Russian advance guard nearby. He continued his march and beat yet another corps. The fugitives returned to the camp in front of Narva, infecting it with their own panic. In the meantime, it was already November, and Narva, though incompetently besieged, was on the point of surrendering. The young king of Sweden had less than nine thousand men with him at the time, and could bring to bear only ten pieces of artillery against the one hundred and forty-five cannon protecting the Russian entrenchments. Every contemporary account, every historian without exception, assesses the strength of the Russian army besieging Narva at eighty thousand fighting men. The documents I have been sent say sixty thousand, while others give forty. Be that as it may, Charles certainly had less than nine thousand men, and the battle is one of those which prove that—since the Battle of Arbela[3]—great victories have often been won by the smaller number.

Charles did not hesitate to attack the vastly bigger army with his little force, and availing himself of a strong wind blowing thick snow straight at the Russians, he charged their entrenchments under the covering fire of several cannon which had been deployed to good advantage (November 30). The Russians had no time to recognize one another in the midst of the swirling snow driving into their faces, pounded by cannon they could not see and with no idea how small was the army they were fighting.

The duke von Croy tried to issue commands, and Prince Dolgoruky refused to obey them. The Russian officers rebelled against their German colleagues, murdering the duke's secretary, Colonel Lyon, as well as several others. Everyone deserted his post; tumult, confusion, and panic spread throughout the ranks. The Swedish troops had nothing to do but kill men who were running away. Some hurled themselves into the Narva River, where a host of soldiers were drowned; others threw down their weapons and fell to their knees before the Swedes. The duke von Croy, General Hallart, and the German officers, who were more afraid of the mutinous Russians than of the Swedes, surrendered to Count Stenbock. The king of Sweden, now in control of all the artillery, saw thirty thousand beaten men at his feet, laying down their arms and marching past him bareheaded. Knes Dolgoruky and all the other Muscovite commanders surrendered to him like the German generals, and only later did they learn that they had been vanquished by eight thousand men. Among the prisoners was the king of Georgia's son, who was sent to Stockholm. His name was the Czarevich—or son of the czar—Mittelleski,[4] which is an additional proof that the title of czar or tsar owes nothing at all to the Roman Caesars.

Charles XII lost barely twelve hundred soldiers in this battle. The czar's journal, sent to me from Saint Petersburg, says that only six thousand Russians were lost, including those who perished during the siege and battle of Narva and those who were drowned while running away. Lack of discipline and panic were therefore the prime movers in that engagement. There were four times as many prisoners of war as there were victors, and, if Nordberg is to be believed,[5] Count Piper, later taken prisoner by the Russians, reproached them for the fact that at this battle the prisoners were eight times more numerous than the Swedish army. If such were indeed the case, the Swedes would have captured seventy-two thousand men, which goes to show how rarely we are apprised of all the details. What is both undeniable and extraordinary is the permission granted by the king of Sweden for half the Russian soldiers to depart unarmed and for the other half to cross the river with their weapons.[6] The strangely overconfident Charles thus returned to the czar men who, once they had been taught discipline, became formidable troops.

Charles had all the advantages which may be derived from winning a battle: immense storehouses, barges laden with provisions, evacuated or captured outposts, and the entire country at the mercy of the Swedes—such were the fruits of victory. With Narva relieved, no Russian survivors to be seen, and the entire region undefended all the way to Pleskov, the czar apparently lacked any means of carrying on the war, and the king of Sweden, who had in less than one year defeated the monarchs of Denmark, Poland, and Russia, was regarded as the foremost man in Europe, at an age when others do not yet aspire to any reputation. But Peter, who was of an unshakably resolute nature, was not discouraged in any of his plans.

A Russian bishop composed a prayer[7] to Saint Nicholas on the subject of this defeat, and it was recited throughout Russia. This composition, which reveals both the spirit of the age and the profound ignorance from which Peter rescued his country, calls "the raging and frightful Swedes" sorcerers, and complains at having been forsaken by Saint Nicholas. Russian bishops of our day would not write such stuff, and, without meaning any disrespect to Saint Nicholas, they soon realized that Peter was the one to appeal to.

Chapter 12
Measures Taken after the Battle of Narva; the Disaster Completely Salvaged. Peter's Victory near Narva Itself. His Labors in the Empire. The Person Who Later Became Empress Taken Prisoner during the Sack of a City. Peter's Successes; His Triumph in Moscow.[1]

The czar, having left his army at Narva near the end of November, 1700, to confer with the king of Poland, learned en route of the Swedish victory. His determination was as unwavering as Charles XII's valor was unyieldingly intrepid. He postponed his talks with Augustus so as to apply a speedy remedy to this chaotic situation. His scattered troops went to Novgorod the Great and from there to Pleskov on Lake Peipus.

It was already a considerable achievement to maintain the defensive after such a sharp setback. "I am well aware," he would say, "that the Swedes will long be superior to us, but in the long run they themselves will teach us how to beat them."

When he had taken care of the most urgent needs, Peter ordered a general mobilization and hurried to Moscow to arrange for the casting of cannon, since he had lost all of his guns at Narva. There was a shortage of bronze, so he took the bells from churches and monasteries. This action was untainted by superstition, or, if it comes to that, by impiety. With these bells the Russians accordingly manufactured one hundred heavy cannon, one hundred and forty-three field pieces—three- and six-pounders—mortars, and howitzers. He sent them to Pleskov. In other lands, the leader gives the orders and they are carried out, but in those days the czar had to do everything himself. While he was expediting these preparations, he was negotiating with the king of Denmark, who undertook to provide him with three infantry and three cavalry regiments, a pledge that the king subsequently dared not honor.

Hardly was the treaty signed when Peter hurried off again to the theater of war. He met King Augustus at Birze, on the frontier between Courland and Lithuania (February 27, 1701). It was necessary to strengthen Augustus's resolution to sustain the war against Charles XII, and also to commit the Polish Diet to the war. It is fairly common knowledge that a king of Poland is only the head of a republic. The czar enjoyed the advantage of always being obeyed, but a king of Poland, a king of England, and—nowadays—a king of Sweden must constantly negotiate with their own subjects. Patkul and the king's Polish supporters attended these conferences. Peter promised subsidies and twenty thousand men. Livonia was to be returned to Poland in the event that the Diet was willing to stand behind its king and help him recover the province. However, the czar's proposals had less effect on the Diet than their own fear. The Poles were afraid of being harassed simultaneously by the Saxons and the Russians, and they were even more afraid of Charles XII. And so the majority agreed that they would neither serve their king nor fight.

The king of Poland's followers grew angry with the opposition party, and eventually, because Augustus had tried to restore an important province to Poland, civil war broke out in the kingdom itself.

As an ally, then, Peter found Augustus to be ineffectual, and his Saxon troops an inadequate source of aid. The universal dread of Charles XII compelled Peter to rely solely on his own forces.

Having hastened from Moscow to Courland for his talks with Augustus, on March 1 he rushed back from Courland to Moscow to expedite the fulfillment of his promises, and in fact dispatched Prince Repnin with four thousand men to Riga, on the banks of the Dvina, where the Saxons had taken up defensive positions.

The prevailing terror increased when Charles, crossing the Dvina (July) in spite of the Saxons deployed to advantage on the opposite bank, won a total victory; when, without losing a moment, he subdued Courland and was seen advancing into Lithuania, while the Polish faction hostile to Augustus was given encouragement by the victor.

Nevertheless, Peter carried out all his plans. General Patkul, the moving spirit behind the Birze conference, who was now in Peter's service, furnished him with German officers, trained his troops, and filled the place left empty by General Lefort. He perfected what his predecessor had begun. The czar supplied post-horses for every German, Livonian, or Polish officer—or even private soldier—coming to join his armies, and looked into the details of their weaponry, clothing, and rations.

On the confines of Livonia and Estonia, to the west of the province of Novgorod, lies the vast Lake Peipus, into which flows, from southern Livonia, the Velikaya River. From its northern end runs the Narva River,[2] which washes the walls of the city of Narva near the spot where the Swedes had won their famous victory. This lake is thirty common leagues in length, while in width it varies from twelve to fifteen leagues. It was necessary to maintain a fleet on it to prevent Swedish ships from attacking the province of Novgorod. To be within striking distance of their coast, but more particularly to train his seamen, Peter spent all of the year 1701 building one hundred half-galleys, carrying about fifty men apiece, on this lake. Other fighting ships were commissioned on Lake Ladoga. He personally directed all the work and taught his new sailors how to handle their craft. Those who had seen service on the sea of Azov in 1697 were now serving near the Baltic. He would frequently leave these labors to go to Moscow and his other provinces to consolidate all the innovations he had undertaken and to put new ones into effect.

every in wartime public works

Monarchs have won renown by employing the leisure of peacetime in the construction of public works, but Peter, who in spite of the debacle of Narva was busily engaged in linking the Baltic, Caspian, and Black Seas by canals, was more worthy of real glory than he would have been by winning battles. It was in 1702 that he began to dig the deep canal between the Don the the Volga. Others were to connect—by way of intervening lakes—the Don and the Dvina, whose waters empty into the Baltic at Riga, but this second project was still far in the future, since Peter was a very long way from possessing Riga.

Charles was ravaging Poland, while Peter was bringing shepherds and their flocks from Poland and Saxony to Moscow to supply the wool for weaving good cloth. He founded textile and paper mills, and at his command metalworkers, foundrymen, and armorers were sent for. The mines of Siberia were worked. He labored to enrich and defend his domains.

Charles pursued the course of his victories, leaving what he considered to be enough troops in the general area of the czar's territories to safeguard all of Sweden's possessions. His mind was already made up to dethrone King Augustus and then to chase the czar to Moscow with his victorious armies.

That year, there were a few minor skirmishes between the Russians and Swedes in which the latter were not invariably triumphant, and even in those encounters where they did emerge victorious, the Russians were acquiring experience. Eventually, one year after the Battle of Narva, the czar already had troops so highly trained that they defeated one of Charles's best generals.

Peter was at Pleskov; during his stay there he dispatched numerous army corps in all directions to attack the Swedes, and it was no foreigner, but a Russian, who beat them. Near Dorpat on the Livonian border (January 11, 1702), General Sheremeteyev captured several positions from General Schlippenbach by a skillful maneuver, then beat Schlippenbach himself. For the first time, Swedish colors were seized: four in all, which was a lot in those days.

Shortly thereafter, Lakes Peipus and Ladoga were the scene of naval battles. The Swedes enjoyed the same advantages—discipline and long experience—as they did on land. However, the Russians in their half-galleys sometimes fought with success, and during a full-scale engagement on Lake Peipus in May, Field Marshal Sheremeteyev took a Swedish frigate.

It was thanks to Lake Peipus that the czar kept Livonia and Estonia in a continual state of alarm. His galleys would often disembark several regiments there, taking them on board again if the outcome was not favorable, while if it was, the advantage would be followed up. The Swedes, victorious everywhere else, were twice defeated (June and July) in the vicinity of Dorpat.

In every one of these actions, the Russians outnumbered the Swedes, which is why Charles XII, who waged war so triumphantly elsewhere, never concerned himself about the czar's successes. He ought to have borne in mind, however, that every day these large bodies of men were gaining experience and might very well become a threat to himself.

During the land and sea fighting around Livonia, Ingria, and Estonia, the czar learned that a Swedish fleet was bound for Archangel, to destroy it (July). He marched there himself, and people were astonished to hear that he was on the White Sea coast when they had believed him to be in Moscow. He took every defensive measure, forestalled the Swedish raid, personally drew up the plans of a citadel named the New Dvina, laid its foundation stone, returned to Moscow, and from there proceeded to the theater of war.

Charles was advancing in Poland, but the Russians were doing the same in Ingria and Livonia. Field Marshal Sheremeteyev marched against Schlippenbach's Swedes. He joined battle near the little Embac River and won, capturing sixteen flags and twenty guns. Nordberg gives December 1, 1701, as the date of the action, while Peter the Great's journal assigns it to July 19, 1702.

Sheremeteyev advanced, commandeering everything, and in August took the small city of Marienburg on the frontier of Livonia and Ingria. There are many towns with that name in the North, but this one, though no longer in existence, is nevertheless more famous than any of the others, by reason of the adventure of the empress Catherine.

The little town having surrendered unconditionally, the Swedes, whether inadvertently or intentionally, set fire to its warehouses. The angry Russians destroyed the place and led its entire population into captivity. There was in Marienburg a young Livonian girl who had been brought up by the local Lutheran pastor, one Gluck. She was one of the prisoners, but became the sovereign of those who had captured her, ruling Russia under the name of the empress Catherine.

It was not the first time that a commoner had become czarina. Nothing was more commonplace in Russia, and in every Asiatic kingdom, than marriages between sovereigns and their own subjects; but that a foreign girl, captured in the ruins of a pillaged city, should become the absolute ruler of the empire to which she had been led as a captive is a spectacle which fortune and merit have revealed but once in the annals of the world.

The consequences of this victory in Ingria were not belied. The fleet of Russian half-galleys on Lake Ladoga compelled the Swedes to withdraw to Viborg at the far end of the great lake.[3] From there they could watch, at the opposite end, the siege of the fortress of Noteburg undertaken by General Sheremeteyev on the czar's instructions. This was a far more important venture than was realized at the time, since it gave potential access to the Baltic, which was one of Peter's unchanging objectives.

Noteburg was a very strongly fortified place built on an island in Lake Ladoga,[4] which, dominating the lake as it did, made its possessor master of the Neva, which flows into the sea. It came under attack night and day from September 18 to October 12. At last the Russians stormed it through three breaches in its walls. The Swedish garrison was reduced to one hundred men still able to fight, which, astonishingly enough, they did, obtaining honorable terms of capitulation in the very breach. Even then the commander, Colonel Schlippenbach,[5] refused to surrender (October 16) unless he was allowed to send for two officers from the nearest Swedish outpost to examine the breaches and report to the king his master that the remaining eighty-three fighting men and one hundred and fifty-six sick or wounded had surrendered to an entire army only when it had become impossible to hold the place any longer. This characteristic touch in itself reveals what kind of enemies the czar was up against, and how essential his exertions and insistence on military discipline had been.

He distributed gold medals to his officers and rewarded all the enlisted men, but he also punished some individuals who had run away during an assault. Their comrades spat in their faces and then shot them, in order to add disgrace to their execution.

Noteburg was rebuilt and its name changed to Schlüsselburg, i.e., "Key City," because it is the key to Ingria and Finland. Its first governor was that same Menshikov who had now become an excellent officer and who, having distinguished himself during the siege, deserved the honor. His example encouraged all who possessed merit without high birth.

After the campaign of 1702, the czar wanted Sheremeteyev and all the officers who had won renown to enter Moscow in triumph. All the prisoners taken during the campaign marched behind their conquerors (December 17). Before them were borne the Swedish flags and standards, together with the ensign of the frigate captured on Lake Peipus. Peter himself took a hand in the preparations for the festivities, as he had done in the ventures that they were intended to commemorate.

This pageantry was designed to inspire emulation, without which it would have been vain. Charles scorned it, and ever since the Battle of Narva had despised his enemies, their efforts and their triumphs alike.

Chapter 13
Reforms in Moscow. Fresh Triumphs. Foundation of Saint Petersburg. Peter Takes Narva, Etc.

The czar employed his brief stay in Moscow early in the winter of 1703 to put into effect all his new regulations and to improve the civilian as well as military condition. His very amusements were devoted to making his subjects appreciate the new mode of life he was introducing. With this in mind, he invited the boyars and their ladies to the wedding of one of his buffoons, demanding that everyone should come dressed in the old style. A meal was served as it would have been in the sixteenth century.[1] An ancient superstition forbade the lighting of fires on wedding days even in the bitterest cold, a custom which was strictly observed on the day of the marriage feast. In former times, the Russians drank no wine, but instead hydromel and brandy.[2] On that day, Peter permitted no other kind of drink. All protests were vain, for he laughingly answered: "Your ancestors behaved like this; the old ways are always the best." This pleasantry played a major role in reforming those who invariably preferred the past to the present, or at least in discrediting their complaints, and there still exist nations that could profit by such examples.

A more practical institution was a printing press with Cyrillic and Roman type, all of whose machinery came from Holland, with which they at once began printing Russian translations of books on ethics and the useful arts. Ferguson founded schools of geometry, astronomy, and navigation.

An equally necessary foundation was an immense poorhouse, not of the kind that encourages idleness and perpetuates poverty, but one like those the czar had seen in Amsterdam, where old people and children are put to work, and all the inmates lead useful lives.

He established several industries, and as soon as he had set in motion all the new crafts that he had inaugurated in Moscow, he hurried to Voronezh and laid the keels of two eighty-gun ships with long, watertight caissons beneath the floor timbers to raise the vessels and let them pass safely over the sandbars and sandbanks encountered near Azov. This ingenious device is almost exactly like the one used in Holland to cross the Pampus.

Having made ready for his Turkish campaign, Peter rushed back to confront the Swedes (March 30, 1703), going to inspect the vessels he was building in the shipyards of Olonets, between Lakes Ladoga and Onega, a town where he had installed munitions factories. The whole place had a martial atmosphere, while in Moscow he was causing the peaceful arts to bloom. A mineral spring discovered later in Olonets increased its fame. From Olonets he went to fortify Schlüsselburg.

I have already mentioned that he wanted to rise through all the military grades; he was a lieutenant of bombardiers under Prince Menshikov before the favorite became governor of Schlüsselburg. He now assumed the rank of captain and served under Field Marshal Sheremeteyev.

There was, near Lake Ladoga, an important fortress called Niantz or Nya, close by the Neva. It was necessary to gain control of this to secure his conquests and promote his designs. He had to besiege it by land and prevent any relief from arriving by water. The czar assumed personal responsibility for escorting boats laden with soldiers and warding off Swedish convoys. Sheremeteyev directed the siegeworks, and the citadel surrendered on May 12. Two Swedish ships arrived too late to relieve the citadel; the czar attacked them with his small craft and captured them. His diary contains an entry to the effect that, in recompense for this service, "the captain of bombardiers was created a knight of the Order of Saint Andrew by Admiral Golovin, senior knight of the order."

After taking the fort of Nya, he at last determined to build his city of Saint Petersburg at the mouth of the Neva, on the Gulf of Finland.

King Augustus's affairs were in ruins. The succession of Swedish victories in Poland had emboldened the opposition party, and his very friends had forced him to send back to the czar some twenty thousand Russian reinforcements. They maintained that this sacrifice would deprive the malcontents of any pretext for going over to the king of Sweden, but one's foes are disarmed by force alone, whereas they are encouraged by weakness. These twenty thousand men, trained by Patkul, did yeoman service in Livonia and Ingria while Augustus was losing his own lands. Thus reinforced, and above all thanks to his possession of Nya, the czar was now in a position to found his new capital.

And so it was in that wild and marshy spot, which can be reached from solid ground by only one road, that he laid[3] the first foundations of Saint Petersburg at sixty degrees of latitude and forty-four degrees thirty minutes of longitude. The first stones used in the foundation were debris from some of the bastions of Niantz. A start was made by erecting a small fort on one of the islands that nowadays is at the heart of the city. The Swedes did not concern themselves with this settlement in a swamp inaccessible to ships of the line, but shortly afterwards they observed fortifications being pushed forward, a city coming into being, and eventually—in 1704—the little isle of Kronslot, which covers the town, becoming an impregnable fortress under whose cannon the largest fleets might take shelter.

These undertakings, which would seem to call for a period of peace, were executed in wartime. Workmen in every trade came from Moscow, Astrakhan, Kazan, and the Ukraine to labor on the new city. Neither the natural obstacles of the site, which had to be both reinforced and elevated, nor its distance from any source of aid, nor the unforeseen problems that kept cropping up at every step and in every part of the work, nor, finally, the epidemics that carried off a phenomenal number of workmen could dishearten the founder, who had his city within five months. It was a mere collection of hutments surrounded by ramparts, with only two houses of brick, and for the moment it was enough; persistence and time took care of the rest. Saint Petersburg was only five months old when a Dutch merchantman arrived in search of trade (November). Its master was rewarded with presents, and the Dutch lost no time learning the way to Saint Petersburg.

While governing his colony, Peter was forever ensuring its security by the conquest of nearby enemy outposts. A Swedish colonel named Croniort had taken up positions on the Sestra River and thus posed a threat to the newborn city. Peter attacked him with his two guards regiments, defeated him, and made him withdraw to the other side of the river (July 9). Having ensured his city's safety, he went to Olonets to order the construction of several small vessels, and returned to Saint Petersburg on board a frigate he had built, together with six transports, while awaiting the completion of the other ships (September).

All this while, he was offering a helping hand to the king of Poland, sending him (November) twelve thousand infantrymen and a subsidy of three hundred thousand rubles, which amounts to more than one and a half million French francs. We have already pointed out that his total revenues only came to some five million rubles. The upkeep of his navy, his armies, and all his new institutions might have been expected to drain his treasury. He had, almost simultaneously, fortified Novgorod, Pleskov, Kiev, Smolensk, Azov, and Archangel, and was engaged in founding a capital city. Yet he still had the wherewithal to aid his ally with both men and money. The Dutchman Kornelis de Bruyn, then traveling in Russia, with whom Peter conversed as he did with all foreigners, reports that the czar told him that he still had a balance of three hundred thousand rubles in his coffers after taking care of all the expenses of the war.

In order to put his newborn city of Saint Petersburg beyond the reach of danger, he went in person to take soundings in the area, picked the spot for the foundation of Fort Kronslot, made a wooden model of it, and left Menshikov in charge of carrying out the work based on the model. From there, he went to spend the winter in Moscow (November), so as to consolidate by degrees all the changes he was effecting in its laws, customs, and usages. He introduced a new system of organizing his finances, and urged on the work undertaken on the Voronezh, at Azov, and in a port that he was establishing on the Sea of Azov beneath the fortress of Taganrog.

In its alarm, the Sublime Porte sent him (January, 1704) an ambassador to protest all these preparations. Peter replied that he was master of his own domains, just as the Grand Seignior was of his, and that he was in no way committing a breach of the peace by making Russia worthy of respect on the Black Sea.

On his return to Saint Petersburg (March 30), finding his new citadel of Kronslot—which had been founded in the sea—now completed, he furnished it with artillery. To strengthen his positions in Ingria and to wipe the slate clean of his shameful defeat at Narva, he had sooner or later to take that city. During his preparations for the siege, a small flotilla of Swedish brigantines appeared on Lake Peipus to thwart his plans. The Russian galleys went out to meet it, attacked it, and captured every ship in it, along with its ninety-eight guns. Then (April) Narva was besieged by land and sea, and, more remarkable still, the city of Dorpat in Estonia was under siege at the same time.

Who would believe that there was a university at Dorpat? Gustavus Adolphus had founded it, but the place was no more famous for that. Dorpat is known solely for the period of the two sieges. Peter went constantly from one town to the other to press on the attacks and direct all the operations. The Swedish General Schlippenbach was near Dorpat with some two thousand five hundred men.

The besieged were awaiting the moment when Schlippenbach could get some reinforcements into the town. Peter devised a strategem that is insufficiently exploited. He equipped two infantry regiments and one of cavalry with Swedish uniforms, standards, and colors. The bogus Swedes attacked the trenches. The Russians pretended to run away, and the garrison, deceived by appearances, made a sortie, at which time the sham assailants and those under attack joined forces and fell upon the garrison, half of which was killed while the other half reentered the city (June 27). Schlippenbach in fact soon came up to support them, but was utterly defeated. At last Dorpat was forced to capitulate (July 23), at the very moment when Peter was about to order an all-out assault.

A fairly serious reverse that the czar suffered at the same time on the road to his new city of Saint Petersburg neither prevented him from continuing to build the city nor from pressing on with the siege of Narva. He had, as we have seen, sent troops and money to King Augustus, who was in the process of being unthroned. Both forms of aid proved equally futile. The Russians, together with the Lithuanians of Augustus's party, were thoroughly beaten in Courland (July 31) by the Swedish General Lewenhaupt. If the victors had then concentrated their attacks on Livonia, Estonia, and Ingria, they could have ruined the czar's labors and made him lose all the fruits of his great enterprises. Every day Peter was undermining the outer walls of Sweden, while Charles, instead of countering him adequately, was seeking a less profitable but more brilliant reputation.

As early as July 12, 1704, a simple Swedish colonel commanding a detachment made the Polish nobility elect a new king in the Field of Elections, called Colo, near Warsaw. The Cardinal-Primate of the realm and several bishops bowed to the will of a Lutheran monarch, despite all the pope's threats of excommunication. Everything yielded to force. No one is ignorant of the manner of Stanislas Leszczynski's election, or of how Charles XII caused him to be acknowledged king in most of Poland.

Peter did not abandon the dethroned sovereign, but redoubled his aid the more Augustus's fortunes declined; and while his adversary was making kings, he was beating the Swedish generals in Estonia and Ingria one by one, hurrying to the siege of Narva, and ordering assaults. There were three famous bastions at Narva, famous at least in name: they were called Victory, Honor, and Glory. The czar, sword in hand, carried all of them by storm. The besiegers entered the town, sacked it, and indulged in all the forms of cruelty that were only too frequent when Swedes and Russians were fighting each other.

Peter then set an example that must have won the hearts of his new subjects (August 20). He raced all over the town to put a stop to the looting and murdering, snatched women from the hands of his soldiers, and, after killing two hotheads who disobeyed his orders, entered the city hall where the citizens were flocking to take refuge. There, laying his bloody sword on the table, he said: "This sword is stained, not with the blood of the townsfolk, but with the blood of my own soldiers, which I have shed to save your lives."[4]

Chapter 14
All Ingria Remains in the Hands of Peter the Great, While Charles XII Triumphs Elsewhere. The Rise of Menshikov. Saint Petersburg in Safety. Peter's Plans Always Carried Out Despite Charles's Victories.

Peter, now master of all Ingria, appointed Menshikov as its governor and gave him the title of prince and the rank of major general. In other lands pride and prejudice might well be displeased that a pastry cook's apprentice should become a general, a governor, and a prince, but Peter had already accustomed his subjects not to be surprised at seeing talent richly rewarded while mere nobility received nothing. Menshikov, who had been lifted out of his original profession at an early age by a stroke of luck that placed him in the czar's household, had learned several languages, become proficient in both civil and military affairs, and, having first discovered how to make himself agreeable to his master, contrived to become indispensable.

He expedited the construction of Saint Petersburg, where several brick and stone houses, an arsenal, and magazines were already being built. They were completing the fortifications; the palaces came later.

Scarcely was Peter secure in Narva when he again offered assistance to the unthroned king of Poland, to whom he promised more troops in addition to the twelve thousand men already sent, and in fact dispatched (August 19, 1704) General Repnin with six thousand cavalry and an equal number of infantry to the Lithuanian border. Not for an instant did he lose sight of his Saint Petersburg colony; the city was building and his navy was growing, with ships of the line and frigates emerging from the shipyards at Olonets. He went to supervise their completion and took them back to Saint Petersburg (October).

All Peter's returns to Moscow were marked by triumphant entries, and so it was that year (December 30). He left Moscow only to attend to the launching of his first eighty-gun ship, whose dimensions he had specified the previous year on the Voronezh.

As soon as campaigning could begin in Poland (May 1705), he hurried off to the army he had sent to the Lithuanian frontier to relieve Augustus, but while he was helping his ally, a Swedish fleet was sailing to destroy the scarcely completed Saint Petersburg and Kronslot. It comprised twenty-two vessels of between fifty-four and sixty-four guns, six frigates, two bomb ketches,[1] and two fireships. The troops aboard the transports went ashore on the small island of Kotlin. A Russian colonel named Tolbukhin, who had made his regiment lie flat on the ground while the Swedes were disembarking, suddenly ordered them to their feet, and their fire was so brisk and so well directed that the Swedes were bowled over and forced to return to their ships, abandon their dead, and leave behind three hundred prisoners (June 17).

However, their fleet remained in the vicinity, threatening Saint Petersburg. They made a second landing and were once again repulsed. Troops led by the Swedish general Maidel advanced by land from Viborg toward Schlüsselburg. This was the most serious attempt yet made by Charles XII against the territories conquered or created by Peter. The Swedes were everywhere repelled (June 25), and Saint Petersburg remained at peace.

For his part, Peter was moving toward Courland, desirous of penetrating as far as Riga. His plan was to take Livonia while Charles XII finished subjugating Poland to the new king he had given her. The czar was still at Vilno in Lithuania, and Marshal Sheremeteyev was approaching Mitau, the capital of Courland, where, however, he encountered General Lewenhaupt, already famous for more than one victory. A pitched battle was fought at a place called Gemauerthof or Gemauert.[2]

In these affairs, where experience and discipline prevail, the Swedes, though outnumbered, always had the upper hand. The Russians suffered a total defeat, and all their artillery was captured (July 28). After losing three battles in this manner, at Gemauerthof, Jacobstadt, and Narva, Peter invariably made good his losses, and even turned them to account.

After the Battle of Gemauerthof, he marched in strength to Courland, appeared before Mitau, took the town, and besieged its citadel, which he entered after its capitulation (September 14).

In those days, Russian troops had the reputation of signaling their victories by looting, a tradition all too ancient in every land. At the capture of Narva, Peter had so changed this practice that when the Russian soldiers detailed to guard the vaults of Mitau Castle, where the Grand Dukes of Courland were buried, saw that the bodies had been taken out of their tombs and despoiled of their ornaments, they refused to take possession and demanded that a Swedish colonel first be summoned to acknowledge the state of the premises. And indeed a Swedish officer did come and handed them a signed statement admitting that the Swedes were responsible for the disarray.

The rumor that had run through the entire empire to the effect that the czar had been utterly undone at the Battle of Gemauerthof caused him even more harm than the battle itself. Some veterans of the old Streltsi on garrison duty in Astrakhan were emboldened, on hearing this false report, to mutiny. They killed the governor of the city, and the czar was obliged to send Marshal Sheremeteyev with troops to quell the mutiny and punish the mutineers.

Everything conspired against him. The good fortune and valor of Charles XII, the woes of Augustus, the forced neutrality of Denmark, the uprisings of the former Streltsi, the rumblings of a people who were then capable of discerning only the inconvenience of Peter's reforms and none of their benefits, the dissatisfaction of the great, now subject to military discipline, the empty treasury—none of this disheartened Peter for an instant. He crushed the rebellion, and, having guaranteed the security of Ingria and made sure of the citadel of Mitau in spite of the victorious Lewenhaupt, who lacked sufficient troops to oppose him, he was then at liberty to cross Samogitia[3] and Lithuania.

He shared with Charles XII the glory of being predominant in Poland. He advanced to Tykocin,[4] where he saw King Augustus for the second time. He offered him consolation for his misfortunes, promised to avenge him, and presented him with some flags that Menshikov had taken from his rival's troops. They then traveled to Grodno, capital of Lithuania, and stayed there until December 14. On his departure (December 30, 1705), Peter left Augustus some money and an army and, as was his wont, went off to spend part of the winter in Moscow, to foster the growth of the arts and his new legislation after conducting a very arduous campaign.

Chapter 15

While Peter Upholds His Conquests and Organizes His Domains, His Enemy Charles XII Wins Battles, and Rules in Poland and Saxony. Augustus, Despite a Russian Victory, Submits to Charles XII. He Gives Up the Crown, Surrenders Patkul, the Czar's Ambassador; Patkul, Sentenced to the Wheel, Is Murdered.

No sooner was Peter in Moscow than he learned that the ever-victorious Charles was advancing on Grodno to fight his army. King Augustus had been compelled to run away from Grodno and was retreating in haste to Saxony with four regiments of Russian dragoons, thus weakening his protector's army as well as disheartening him by his retreat. The czar found all the roads to Grodno held by the Swedes and his army dispersed.

While he himself, with the greatest difficulty, was redeploying in Lithuania, the celebrated Schulenburg, Augustus's last hope, who later acquired so much fame by his defense of Corfu against the Turks, was advancing toward Greater Poland with about twelve thousand Saxons and six thousand of the Russian troops entrusted to the hapless prince by the czar. Schulenburg was rightly hopeful of restoring Augustus's fortunes. He saw Charles XII occupied in the Lithuanian region, and there were only about ten thousand Swedes under General Rehnskjöld capable of stopping him. He accordingly moved forward confidently as far as the Silesian border, which is the gateway from Saxony to Upper Poland. Near the little town of Fraustadt on the Polish border, he encountered Marshal Rehnskjöld coming to do battle.

However strenuously I try not to repeat what I have already written in my *History of Charles XII,* I must at this point reiterate that there was in the Saxon army a French regiment which, having been taken prisoner en masse at the famous Battle of Hochstedt,[1] had been forced to serve with the Saxons. My sources tell me that it was responsible for protecting Schulenburg's artillery; they add that the Frenchmen, impressed by Charles XII's prestige and discontented with the Saxon service, laid down their weapons as soon as they saw the enemy and asked permission to enlist in the Swedish army, where they in fact remained throughout the war. This was the beginning of and the signal for a total rout. Not three Russian battalions escaped, and even then every soldier who did escape was wounded; all the rest were killed without mercy (February 6, 1706). Chaplain Nordberg claims that the Swedish battle cry in this engagement was *in God's name,* whereas the Russians' was *massacre them all.* But it was the Swedes who massacred everyone in the name of God. In one of his manifestos,[2] the czar even affirms that many Russian, Cossack, and Kalmuck prisoners were killed three days after the battle. The irregulars on both sides had accustomed the generals to these atrocities. None greater was committed during the Dark Ages. King Stanislas has done me the honor of informing me that during one of these skirmishes that were so frequent in Poland, a Russian officer who had been a friend of his threw himself on Stanislas's mercy after the defeat of the corps that he commanded, whereupon General Stenbock shot the man dead in his arms with a pistol.

Here were four battles lost by the Russians to the Swedes, without counting Charles XII's other victories in Poland. The czar's troops in Grodno ran the still more calamitous risk of total encirclement. Fortunately, Peter was able to redeploy and even reinforce them. He had simultaneously to provide for the safety of this army and that of his territorial gains in Ingria. He dispatched his army to the east, under the command of Prince Menshikov, then southward to Kiev.

While it was on the march (August), he himself went to Schlüsselburg, Narva, and his colony at Saint Petersburg, where he made all secure. From the shores of the Baltic he hurried to the banks of the Dnieper, returning to Kiev by way of Poland, and always striving to nullify Charles XII's victories, which he had been unable to prevent, while making early preparations for a fresh conquest, namely, Viborg, capital of Carelia on the Gulf of Finland. He went off to besiege it (October), but this time it resisted his attack, relief arrived at an opportune moment, and he raised the siege. His adversary Charles XII, though winning battles, made no real conquests. He was then pursuing King Augustus in Saxony, constantly more intent on humiliating that monarch and overwhelming him with the weight of his power and reputation than anxious to recapture Ingria from the vanquished enemy who had taken it away from him.

Charles terrorized Upper Poland, Silesia, and Saxony. King Augustus's entire family, his mother, his wife, his son, as well as the principal families of the land, withdrew into the heart of the Empire. Augustus sued for peace; he would rather surrender unconditionally to his conqueror than place himself in the hands of his protector. He was negotiating a treaty that would deprive him of the crown of Poland and cover him with confusion. The treaty was secret and had to be concealed from the czar's generals, in whose company he was, so to speak, a refugee in Poland, while Charles XII was imposing his will in Leipzig and governing Augustus's Electorate. Already (September 14) the fatal treaty was signed by his plenipotentiaries. By its terms he relinquished the Polish crown, promised never to assume the title of king of that country, acknowledged Stanislas, repudiated his alliance with his benefactor the czar, and—supreme humiliation—undertook to hand over to Charles XII the czar's ambassador Johan Reinhold Patkul, general of the Russian army, who was fighting to defend Augustus. Some time previously, he had arrested Patkul on trumped-up charges and in defiance of international law, and in defiance of that same law delivered him to his enemy. It would have been better to die sword in hand than to conclude such a treaty. Not only was he losing his crown and his good name, but he was also jeopardizing his own freedom, since at the time he was in the hands of Prince Menshikov in Poznan, the few Saxons with him then being paid with Russian silver.

Prince Menshikov was confronted in that area by a Swedish army reinforced by Polish adherents of the new King Stanislas and commanded by General Meyerfeld. Unaware that Augustus was negotiating with his enemies, Menshikov proposed to attack them. Battle was joined near Kalicz (October 19), in King Stanislas's home palatinate.[3] It was the first pitched battle against the Swedes to be won by the Russians, and Prince Menshikov had the honor of winning it. The enemy losses were four thousand dead and two thousand five hundred and ninety-eight prisoners.

It is difficult to comprehend how Augustus could ratify an agreement that cost him the entire fruit of this victory. However, Charles was all-powerful in Saxony, where his name inspired such terror, continued Russian successes were so unlooked-for, the Polish faction in opposition to King Augustus was so strong, and, lastly, Augustus himself was so poorly advised that he signed the fateful pact. Not satisfied with that, he wrote his envoy Pfingsten a letter more wretched than the treaty itself, in which he craved forgiveness for his victory, "protesting that battle was joined without his consent; that the Russians and Poles of his own party had forced his hand; that with this in mind he had carried out maneuvers in order to abandon Menshikov; that Meyerfeld could have beaten the Russians if he had seized the opportunity; that he would either return all the Swedish prisoners or break with the Russians, and that finally he would give the king of Sweden every appropriate satisfaction for having dared to beat his troops."

All this is unique, incredible, and yet the strictest truth. When one thinks that with this weakness Augustus was one of Europe's bravest princes, it is easy to see that it is moral courage that ruins or preserves states and that exalts or debases them.

Two acts put the finishing touches to the misfortunes of the king of Poland and elector of Saxony, and to Charles XII's abuse of his success. The first was a congratulatory letter that Charles forced Augustus to write to the new King Stanislas. The second was horrible: this same Augustus was compelled to surrender to Charles the czar's ambassador and general, Patkul. Europe knows well enough that this minister was later broken on the wheel at Casimir, in the month of September, 1707. Chaplain Nordberg admits that all the orders for the execution were written in Charles's own hand.

There is not one jurist in Europe, there is not even one slave who does not feel the sheer horror of this barbarous injustice. The unfortunate man's first crime was to have respectfully pointed out the rights of his homeland,[4] as leader of six Livonian noblemen representing the entire state. He was condemned for having fulfilled the first of duties, that of serving his country in accordance with the laws. This iniquitous sentence had given him the full natural right of all men to choose their own fatherland. Having become ambassador of one of the world's greatest monarchs, his person was sacred. The right of the stronger violated in him the rights of nature and of nations. Once, the glitter of fame covered up such acts of cruelty; nowadays it is tarnished by them.

Chapter 16
An Attempt Is Made to Create a
Third King of Poland.
Charles XII Departs from Saxony with a
Thriving Army and Makes a Triumphal
Progress across Poland. Perpetration
of Atrocities. The Czar's Behavior. Victories of
Charles, Marching at Last on Russia.

Charles XII was enjoying his triumphs at Altranstadt near Leipzig. The Protestant princes of the Empire came flocking to pay homage and ask for his protection. Nearly all the great powers sent him ambassadors. The Emperor Joseph I deferred to his every wish. And so Peter, realizing that Augustus had renounced both Russian protection and his throne, and that part of Poland recognized Stanislas, listened to the proposals made at Zholkva to elect a third king (January, 1707).[1]

In a Diet held at Lublin, several counts palatine were nominated. Prince Rakoczy entered the lists, the same Prince Rakoczy who had in his youth been long imprisoned by the Emperor Leopold, and who after regaining his freedom was later his rival for the throne of Hungary. The negotiations were very far advanced, and there were very nearly three kings of Poland all at once. Prince Rakoczy having failed, Peter tried to give the throne to Sieniawski, the Grand General of the Republic, a powerful man of good standing and leader of a third party, which was unwilling to recognize either the deposed Augustus or Stanislas, who had been elected by an opposing faction.

In the midst of these troubles, peace was mentioned, as it invariably is. Buzenval, the French emissary to Saxony, acted as go-between to reconcile the czar and the king of Sweden. It was then the opinion of the court of France that Charles, being no longer obliged to fight either the Russians or the Poles, might unleash his armies against the Emperor Joseph, with whom he was displeased and to whom he had been dictating harsh terms during his stay in Saxony. Charles, however, replied that he would discuss peace with the czar in Moscow. It was on that occasion that Peter said: "My brother Charles wants to play Alexander, but he won't find his Darius in me."

Meanwhile, the Russians were still in Poland, and even in Warsaw itself, while the Poles barely recognized the king Charles XII had given them, and Charles was enriching his army with the spoils of Saxony.

Finally, he left (August 22) his headquarters at Altranstadt at the head of forty-five thousand men, an army which it seemed unlikely that his adversary could ever withstand, since Charles had utterly routed him at Narva with eight thousand men.

It was while passing beneath the walls of Dresden (August 27) that he paid King Augustus that curious visit which must arouse the admiration of posterity, according to Nordberg; it may at least cause some surprise. Putting himself in the hands of a prince whom he had deprived of a kingdom was taking a great risk.[2] He crossed Silesia again and reentered Poland.

That country was utterly devastated by warfare, ruined by party politics, a prey to every sort of calamity. Charles advanced through Mazovia, choosing the least negotiable highway. The inhabitants, who had taken refuge in the marshes, tried to make him at least pay for his passage. Six thousand peasants appointed an old man of their company as their spokesman. This outlandish figure, clad all in white and armed with two carbines, harangued Charles, and as what he was saying was none too clearly understood, it was decided to kill him in the king's sight, right in the middle of his speech. The desperate peasants withdrew and took up arms. All that could be found were seized. They were compelled to hang one another, and the last man was forced to put the noose around his own neck and be his own executioner. All their houses were burned to ashes. Chaplain Nordberg is our authority for these acts, which he personally witnessed. One can neither impugn his evidence nor refrain from shuddering.

Charles arrived within a few leagues of Grodno in Lithuania (February 6, 1708) and was informed that the czar in person was in the town with some troops. Without consulting anyone, Charles took a mere eight hundred guardsmen and hurried to Grodno. A German officer named Muhlenfeld,[3] commanding a body of troops at one of the city gates, did not doubt, on seeing Charles XII, that his entire army was behind him, and yielded the gate instead of fighting for it. The alarm spread through the town, and everyone believed the Swedish army had entered. The few Russians who tried to resist were cut to pieces by the Swedish guard. All his officers assured the czar that a victorious army was taking possession of every outpost in the city. Peter retired beyond the ramparts, and Charles posted a guard of thirty men at the very gate through which the czar had just left.

Amid all the confusion, some Jesuits whose house had been commandeered as a lodging for the king of Sweden because it was the finest in Grodno came by night to the czar and this time gave him the true facts.

Peter instantly reentered the town and broke through the Swedish guard. There was fighting in the streets and squares, but the king's army was already arriving. The czar was at last obliged to give way and to yield the place to the might of the conqueror who made Poland tremble.

Charles had reinforced his troops in Livonia and Finland, and that sector caused Peter the gravest anxiety for his new territories, as did the Lithuanian quarter for his ancestral domains and for Moscow itself. He accordingly had to consolidate his positions in each of these far-flung regions. Charles could not make rapid headway by traveling eastward through Lithuania, during inclement weather, in swampy terrain infested with contagious diseases that poverty and famine had spread from Warsaw to Minsk. Peter stationed his troops in positions on fords, garrisoned important outposts, and did everything in his power to impede his enemy's advance at every step. He then raced toward Saint Petersburg to put everything in order there (April).

While Charles was lording it over the Poles, he took nothing from them, but Peter, making good use of his new navy by descending on Finland, by capturing and destroying Borgå (May 21), and by taking much booty from the enemy, made profitable gains.

Charles, long detained in Lithuania by incessant rain, finally advanced toward the little river Beresina, a few leagues from the Dnieper. Nothing could withstand his energy; he threw a bridge across the river in full view of the Russians; he beat the detachment guarding the river crossing and reached Holowczyn, on the river Wabis,[4] where the czar had posted a sizable body of men who were supposed to check Charles's headlong rush. The little Wabis river is only a stream during the dry season, but at that time it was a deep, rushing torrent, swollen by the rains. On the far bank was a marsh, behind which the Russians had thrown up an entrenchment a quarter of a league in length, defended by a broad moat and covered by a parapet furnished with artillery. Nine cavalry regiments and eleven of infantry were deployed to advantage along these lines. A river crossing appeared impossible.

The Swedes, in accordance with military practice, prepared pontoon bridges and positioned batteries to cover their advance, but Charles did not wait until the pontoons were ready; his eagerness to fight could never tolerate the slightest delay. Marshal von Schwerin, who long served under him, has on several occasions corroborated to me the fact that on the day of action he would ask his generals, engrossed in the details of his arrangements: "Will you soon be done with these trifles?" and he would then be the first to advance at the head of his drabants.[5] This was especially true on that memorable day.

He dashed into the river, followed by his regiment of guards. The mass of bodies dammed the swift current, but they were shoulder-deep in water and could not use their weapons. Had only the parapet artillery been efficiently manned and the infantry battalions opened fire at the proper moment, not a solitary Swede would have escaped.

After fording the river (July 25), the king crossed the marsh too on foot. As soon as the army had passed these obstacles in full view of the Russians, it formed up in battle order. The entrenchments were attacked seven times, the Russians yielding only at the seventh attack. All that was captured from them was twelve field pieces and twenty-four mortars, as the Swedish historians themselves concede.

It was therefore obvious that the czar had succeeded in training seasoned troops, and the victory of Holowczyn, while covering Charles with glory, ought certainly to have made him aware of all the dangers he was courting by penetrating into such distant lands. It was impossible for the army to march, except as separate, individual units advancing from wood to wood and from swamp to swamp, fighting every step of the way, but the Swedes, accustomed to overthrowing everything in their path, feared neither danger nor fatigue.

Chapter 17
Charles XII Crosses the Dnieper, Goes Far into the Ukraine, and Fails to Make Proper Arrangements. One of His Armies Is Defeated by Peter the Great; His Supplies Are Lost. He Marches on into the Wilds. Adventures in the Ukraine.

At last Charles reached the banks of the Dnieper, at a small town called Mogilev.[1] It was at this fateful spot that he was to announce whether he would march eastward to Moscow or southward to the Ukraine. His army, his enemies, and his friends alike were expecting him to march on the capital. Whichever route he chose, Peter had been following him ever since Smolensk with a powerful army. No one supposed that Charles would take the Ukrainian route. His strange decision was inspired by Mazeppa, hetman of the Cossacks, who was an old man of seventy. Having no children, he should to all appearances have been thinking only of ending his days in peace. Gratitude should also have ensured his attachment to the czar, to whom he owed his position, but, whether he had genuine grounds for complaint against that monarch, whether he had been dazzled by Charles XII's name, or whether he was simply seeking independence, he had betrayed his benefactor and secretly defected to the king of Sweden, deluding himself that he could make his entire nation join his rebellion.

Charles never doubted that he would triumph over the whole Russian empire when his victorious troops were supported by so warlike a people. From Mazeppa he was to receive the additional stores, munitions, and artillery he might need. To this powerful aid was to be joined an army of sixteen to eighteen thousand fighting men, led from Livonia by General Lewenhaupt and bringing in its train a prodigious quantity of ammunition and victuals. Charles was not concerned that the czar might be within striking distance of this army and able to deprive him of such vital support. He did not inquire whether Mazeppa was in a position to keep all his promises, whether the Cossack's standing was high enough to change an entire nation that takes counsel only of itself, and whether, in short, his army would still have sufficient resources in an emergency. Should Mazeppa prove faithless or powerless, Charles was relying on his own valor and good fortune. And so the Swedish army advanced beyond the Dnieper toward the Desna, and it was between these two rivers that Mazeppa was expected. The way was arduous, and Russian skirmishers in the area made the march dangerous.

Menshikov, commanding several regiments of cavalry and dragoons [*sic*], attacked (September 11, 1708) the king's vanguard, threw it into disorder, killed many Swedes, lost even more of his own men, but did not lose heart. Charles, who hurried to the battlefield, only repelled the Russians with difficulty. For a while, he risked his own life fighting several dragoons who surrounded him. Meanwhile, Mazeppa still had not come, provisions were beginning to run low, and the Swedish soldiers, watching the king share all their perils, their hardships, and their short rations, did not become discouraged, but despite their admiration for Charles they criticized him and grumbled.

The king's order to Lewenhaupt to get his army on the move and bring supplies with all possible speed had been given twelve days too late, which under the circumstances was a long time. Lewenhaupt finally set out; Peter let him cross the Dnieper, and when the army was bogged down between the river and its small tributaries, he crossed the river behind Lewenhaupt and attacked him with his massed regiments, which were following him in almost perfect formation. Battle was joined between the Dnieper and the Sozh.[2]

Prince Menshikov returned with the same cavalry detachment that had tried conclusions with Charles XII; General Bauer was following him, and, for his part, Peter was leading the cream of his army. The Swedes thought they were up against forty thousand fighting men, a fact which was long believed on the strength of their account. My latest sources inform me that Peter had only twenty thousand men that day, not many more than the enemy. The czar's energy, patience, and determination, as well as that of his troops, who were inspired by his presence, decided the outcome, not of that day, but of the three succeeding ones, during which there was fighting on several occasions.

To begin with, they attacked the Swedish rearguard near the village of Lesnaya, which has given its name to the battle. The first encounter was bloody but indecisive. Lewenhaupt withdrew to a wood and preserved his baggage train intact (October 7). On the following day, the Swedes had to be driven from the wood; this engagement was more murderous and more successful. It was there that the czar, seeing his troops in disarray, shouted that deserters were to be shot and that he himself was to be fired upon if he retreated. The Swedes were repulsed, but by no means routed.

Eventually, a relief force of four thousand dragoons arrived. For the third time, the Russians charged the Swedes, who retreated toward a little town named Propoisk, where they were once more attacked. They marched toward the Desna and were pursued. They were never completely broken, but they lost more than eight thousand men, seventeen guns, and forty-four standards. The czar captured fifty-six officers and nearly nine hundred men. The whole of the great supply train being taken to Charles fell into the hands of the victor.

This was the first time that the czar in person defeated, in a pitched battle, those who had distinguished themselves by so many victories over his troops. He was thanking God for his triumph when he learned that General Apraxin had just gained (September 17) the upper hand in Ingria, a few leagues away from Narva, an advantage which was indeed of lesser consequence than the victory of Lesnaya, yet this concurrence of happy events invigorated his hopes and the courage of his army.

Charles XII learned all this disastrous news when he was about to ford the Desna, in the Ukraine. Mazeppa had at long last come to him. He was supposed to bring twenty thousand men and huge quantities of supplies, but arrived with only two regiments, and appeared more like a fugitive requesting aid than a prince coming to bestow it. The Cossack had in fact begun his march with some fifteen or sixteen thousand of his people, having originally told them that they were going to fight the king of Sweden, that they would have the glory of halting that hero's advance, and that the czar would be eternally in their debt for so great a service.

A few miles from the Desna, he finally disclosed his plans, but these good people were horrified and absolutely refused to betray a monarch with whom they had no quarrel for the sake of a Swede entering their country sword in hand, who, after his departure, would no longer be able to defend them but would leave them at the mercy of the enraged Russians and of the Poles, once their overlords and still their foes. They returned to their homes and informed the czar of their chief's defection. Only about two regiments, whose officers were in Mazeppa's pay, remained with him.

He was still master of several strongholds in the Ukraine, notably of Baturin, where he resided and which is regarded as the Cossack capital. It is located near forests on the Desna River, but far away from the battlefield where Peter had beaten Lewenhaupt. There were still a few Russian regiments in the area. Prince Menshikov was detached from the czar's army and reached Baturin by going the long way around. Charles could not guard all the approaches; indeed, he was not even familiar with them. He had neglected to seize the important outpost of Starodub, which leads directly to Baturin through seven or eight leagues of forest traversed by the Desna. His foe always had the advantage of him in knowing the country. Menshikov and Prince Golitsyn passed through Starodub easily and appeared before Baturin (November 4). The town, taken with practically no resistance, was pillaged and reduced to ashes. Stores intended for the king of Sweden were removed, as was Mazeppa's treasure. The Cossacks elected a new hetman, named Skoropadsky, who was acceptable to the czar. Peter wanted an impressive demonstration to make the people conscious of the enormity of treason. The archbishop of Kiev and two other prelates publicly excommunicated Mazeppa, who was hanged in effigy (November 22), and several of his accomplices died broken on the wheel.

In the meantime, Charles XII, at the head of some twenty-five to twenty-seven thousand Swedes, now joined by the survivors of Lewenhaupt's army and reinforced by the two or three thousand men brought to him by Mazeppa, was still beguiled by the hope of persuading the entire Ukraine to declare for him. He crossed the Desna far from Baturin and close to the Dnieper, in the teeth of the czar's troops surrounding him on every side, some following his rearguard and the rest spread out beyond the river to oppose his crossing.

He marched on through deserts where he found nothing but the burned-out ruins of villages. The cold made itself felt in early December with such excessive severity that during one of his marches nearly two thousand men dropped dead before his eyes. The czar's troops suffered less, because they were better provisioned; Charles's men, whose very clothes were in short supply, were more exposed to the bitter weather.

In this deplorable state of affairs, Count Piper, the Swedish chancellor, whose advice to his master was invariably sound, begged him to call a halt and to spend at least the worst of the winter in a small Ukrainian village called Romny, which could be fortified and where with Mazeppa's aid he could collect some supplies. Charles replied that he was not the man to shut himself up inside a town. Piper then implored him to withdraw across the Desna and the Dnieper to Poland, where he could give his troops the winter quarters they needed, avail himself of the Polish light cavalry, which was absolutely indispensable to him, lend support to the king he had appointed, and contain Augustus's party, which was beginning to rise again. Charles answered that this would be tantamount to running away from the czar, that the weather would become more favorable, and that he had to subjugate the Ukraine and march on Moscow.[3]

The Russian and Swedish armies were inactive for some weeks, so fierce was the cold in the month of January, 1709, but as soon as a soldier could use his weapons, Charles attacked all the minor outposts that lay in his line of march. He had to send out foraging parties in all directions to rob the peasants for twenty leagues around of their sustenance. Peter, who was in no hurry, kept an eye on his movements and let him wear himself out.

It is impossible for the reader to follow the route taken by the Swedes in these regions. Several rivers crossed by them are not to be found on the maps. We must not suppose that geographers know these lands as we know Italy, France, and Germany. Of all the disciplines, geography still has the greatest need of improvement, and ambition has hitherto taken more pains to devastate the earth than to describe it.

Let us be satisfied to know, in brief, that Charles traveled right through the Ukraine in February, everywhere burning villages and coming upon those burned by the Russians themselves. He advanced in a southeasterly direction to the arid deserts on the edge of the mountains that separate the Nogai Tartars from the Don Cossacks. To the east of these mountains are found the altars of Alexander. He was thus beyond the Ukraine, on the Tartar road to Russia, and when he had come this far he had to retrace his steps in order to survive. The natives hid in their dens with their livestock; sometimes they would fight for their food with the soldiers who came to steal it from them. Captured peasants were put to death; such, they say, are the rights of war. I must at this point transcribe some lines by Chaplain Nordberg.[4]

"To show," he says, "how much the king loved justice, we shall insert a note in his own hand to Colonel Hielmen: 'Colonel, I am well pleased that the peasants who carried off a Swede have been caught. When they have been convicted of their crime, they will be punished in accordance with the exigencies of the case by being put to death.' [Signed] Charles, and below, Budis."[5]

Such are the sentiments of justice and humanity found in a royal confessor; but if the peasants of the Ukraine had been able to hang the conscripted peasants of Ostrogothia who thought they had the right to come from so far away to steal the food belonging to their wives and children, would not the Ukrainian confessors and chaplains have been able to sanctify *their* justice?

Mazeppa had been engaged in lengthy negotiations with the Zaporozhsky Cossacks, some of whom inhabit the banks of the Dnieper while others live on its islands.[6] It is the latter group which constitutes that tribe without wives or families, existing on plunder, accumulating provisions on their islands during the winter and selling them in the spring in the small city of Poltava. The other Zaporozhskys live in townships on the right and left banks of the river. They all combine to choose their own hetman, who is subordinate to the hetman of the Ukraine. The hetman of the Zaporozhskys sought out Mazeppa, and the two barbarians had a parley, each with a horse's tail[7] and a club borne before him.

In order to give some notion of what the Zaporozhsky hetman and his people were like, I do not deem it unworthy of this history to report how the treaty was concluded. Mazeppa gave the hetman and his senior officers a great feast served on silver plate. When these chieftains were drunk on brandy, they swore on the Gospels, at the table, that they would supply Charles XII with men and victuals, after which they carried off the silver and the furniture. The majordomo of the household rushed after them and remonstrated that such conduct was not in keeping with the Gospels on which they had sworn. Mazeppa's servants tried to take back the silver; the Zaporozhskys gathered together and came in a body to complain to Mazeppa of this unprecedented insult offered to such decent people, and demanded that the majordomo be turned over to them for punishment in accordance with their laws. He was surrendered to them, and the Zaporozhskys, in accordance with their laws, shoved the poor man back and forth from one to another as one kicks a ball, after which they plunged a dagger into his heart.

Such were the new allies that Charles XII was obliged to make welcome. He formed two thousand of them into a regiment; the rest marched in individual bands against the czar's Cossacks and Kalmucks, who were scattered throughout this area.

The little town of Poltava, where the Zaporozhskys came to trade, was stocked with provisions and was well suited to serve Charles as a stronghold. It is situated on the Vorskla river, fairly close to the mountain range that dominates it to the north. To the east lies a vast wilderness; the west is more fertile and more densely populated. The Vorskla flows into the Dnieper fifteen full leagues downstream.[8] From Poltava, one may go north to the Moscow highway through the gorges used by the Tartars. This route is an arduous one, and the precautions taken by the czar had made it almost impracticable, but to Charles nothing seemed impossible, and he still counted on taking the road to Moscow after capturing Poltava. And so early in May he laid siege to the town.

Chapter 18
Battle of Poltava.

Peter was waiting for Charles at Poltava. He had deployed his armies within easy reach of one another, so that they could combine to attack the besiegers. He had visited all the territories surrounding the Ukraine: the Duchy of Severia, though which flows the Desna—now famous because of Peter's victory—whose waters are already deep in this region; the Bolkhov country, source of the Oka River; and the deserts and mountains leading to the Sea of Azov. Finally, he went to Azov itself. He had its harbor dredged, ships built, and the citadel of Taganrog strengthened, thus making good use, for the benefit of his empire, of the time elapsing between the Battles of Desna and Poltava.

As soon as he learned that the town was besieged, he mustered his forces. His cavalry, dragoons [sic], infantry, Cossacks, and Kalmucks advanced from a score of different places. His army lacked for nothing, neither heavy nor light artillery, nor munitions of all types, nor provisions, nor medical supplies. This was yet another advantage he had given himself over his opponent.

On June 15, 1709, he reached Poltava with an army of some sixty thousand fighting men. The Vorskla River was betweeen Charles and himself, the besiegers to the northwest, the Russians to the southeast. Peter marched upstream to a point above the town, built bridges, sent his army across the river (July 3), and threw up a long earthwork—which was started and completed in a single night—facing the enemy army. Charles was now in a position to judge whether or not the man he despised, and expected to dethrone in Moscow, understood the art of war. His dispositions made, Peter stationed his cavalry between two woods, covering it with several redoubts provided with artillery. Having thus taken every precaution, he reconnoitered the besiegers' camp so as to plan his attack (July 6).

This battle was to determine the fate of Russia, Poland, and Sweden, and of the two monarchs on whom the eyes of Europe were fixed. In most of the nations attentive to these important issues, nothing was known of the whereabouts of the two sovereigns or of their circumstances, but, seeing the victorious Charles XII leave Saxony at the head of a most redoubtable army and observing that he was everywhere in pursuit of his foe, no one doubted that he would overwhelm him or that, having laid down the law in Denmark, Poland, and Germany, he would dictate peace terms in the Kremlin at Moscow and make a czar after making a king of Poland. I have seen letters from several ambassadors confirming their respective courts in this widely held belief.

The risk run by the two rivals was not equal. If Charles lost a life so often jeopardized, it would be, after all, only one hero the less. The Ukrainian provinces, the Lithuanian and Russian frontiers would no longer be devastated; Poland would resume her tranquility together with her lawful king, who was already reconciled with his benefactor the czar; and, lastly, Sweden, drained of men and money, would be able to find grounds for consolation. But if the czar perished, tremendous labors beneficial to the entire human race would be buried with him, and the vastest empire in the world would fall back into the chaos from which it had barely emerged.

Some Swedish and Russian units had more than once crossed swords beneath the city walls. During one of these encounters (June 27), Charles had been wounded by a musket ball and the bones of his foot shattered. He underwent painful surgery, which he endured with his usual courage, and was forced to spend several days in bed. While in this state, he learned that Peter was about to attack. His notions of glory would not permit him to wait in his entrenchments, and he came out, carried on a litter. Peter the Great's journal admits that the Swedes attacked the artillery redoubts protecting his cavalry so fiercely and stubbornly that, despite his resistance and despite a ceaseless fusillade, they captured two of them. Someone has written that the Swedish infantry in possession of the two redoubts believed that the battle was won, and yelled in triumph. Chaplain Nordberg, who was far from the battlefield with the baggage, which was the proper place for him, maintains that this is a calumny, but whether or not the Swedes cried victory, they did not win it. The fire from the other redoubts did not slacken, and everywhere the tenacity of the Russian defense was equal to the ardor of the attack. The Russians committed no tactical blunders. The czar drew up his army in battle order outside his earthworks methodically and with dispatch.

The battle became general. In his own army, Peter was performing the duties of major general; General Bauer was commanding the right wing, Menshikov the left, and Sheremeteyev the center. The action lasted for two hours. Charles, pistol in hand, went from rank to rank on his litter, carried by his drabants. A cannonball killed one of his stretcher-bearers and smashed the litter. Charles then had himself carried on pikes, for it is hardly likely, no matter what Nordberg may say, that during so brisk an engagement a fresh litter could have been found in readiness. Peter took several bullets through his clothing and his hat, both monarchs being continually in the thick of the fire throughout the encounter. Finally, after two hours of fighting, the Swedes were bested all along the line, confusion broke out among them, and Charles XII was forced to run from the man he had so despised. During his flight, the same hero who had been unable to mount a horse during the battle was put on one, necessity having somewhat restored his strength. He galloped off, suffering intense agony made still more excruciating through the pain of having been hopelessly beaten. The Russians counted nine thousand two hundred and twenty-four Swedish dead on the field; during the action they took from two to three thousand prisoners, mostly cavalrymen.

Charles XII fled headlong with about fourteen thousand soldiers, but very little field artillery, provisions, powder, or shot. He marched south toward the Dnieper, between the Vorskla and the Sol[1] Rivers, in Zaporozhsky country. In this region, beyond the Dnieper, are vast desert tracts leading to the Turkish border. Nordberg affirms that the victors did not dare pursue Charles; however, he does admit that Prince Menshikov appeared on the heights with ten thousand cavalrymen and a sizable artillery train when the king was crossing the Dnieper.

Fourteen thousand Swedes surrendered to these ten thousand Russians (July 12). Lewenhaupt, their commander, signed the fatal capitulation by which he turned over to the czar the Zaporozhskys who, having fought for his king, found themselves with the fugitive army. The most important prisoners taken during the battle and the capitulation were Prime Minister Count Piper, with two secretaries of state and two ministerial secretaries, Field Marshal Rehnskjöld, Generals Lewenhaupt, Schlippenbach, Rosen, Stackelberg, Creutz, and Hamilton, three senior aides-de-camp, the army's auditor general, fifty-nine staff officers, five colonels (including a prince of Württemberg), and sixteen thousand nine hundred and forty-two private soldiers and junior officers. To summarize, counting the king's household domestics and other noncombatants, eighteen thousand seven hundred and forty-six men fell into the hands of the victor. This figure, when added to the nine thousand two hundred and twenty-four killed in the battle, and the approximately two thousand men who crossed the Dnieper with the king, proves that Charles actually had twenty-seven thousand men under his command on that memorable day.[2]

Charles had set out from Saxony with forty-five thousand soldiers, and Lewenhaupt had brought more than sixteen thousand from Livonia. Of all that splendid army nothing remained, and out of a large artillery train lost and sunk in the marshes during his advance he had preserved a mere eighteen iron guns, two howitzers, and twelve mortars. And it was with these puny weapons that he had undertaken the siege of Poltava and attacked an army well provided with formidable artillery. He is consequently accused of having displayed more valor than good sense after his departure from Germany. On the Russian side, only fifty-two officers and twelve hundred and ninety-three men were killed, which proves that their deployment was better than Charles's and that their fire-power was incomparably superior.

A former envoy to the court of the czar states in his memoirs that when Peter learned of Charles XII's intention of withdrawing to Turkey, he wrote imploring him not to take so desperate a step, but to place himself in Peter's hands rather than in those of the natural enemy of every Christian prince. He gave Charles his word of honor not to take him prisoner, but to put an end to their dispute by a reasonable agreement. The letter was taken by courier to the river Bug, which separates the wilds of the Ukraine from the territories of the Grand Seignior. The messenger arrived when Charles was already in Turkey, and took the letter back to his master. The ambassador adds that he owes this information[3] to the very man charged with carrying the message. The anecdote is not implausible, but it occurs neither in Peter the Great's journal nor in any of the documents entrusted to me. The paramount importance of this battle lies in the fact that, of all the battles which have ever stained the earth with blood, it is the only one that, instead of creating destruction, has served the happiness of the human race, since it gave the czar a free hand to civilize a great portion of the world.

From the beginning of this century to the year in which I am writing,[4] more than two hundred pitched battles have been fought in Europe. The sole consequences of the most brilliant and bloody victories have been the conquest of some small provinces, which have afterwards been ceded by treaty and then recaptured in other battles. Armies one hundred thousand strong have often fought, but their most violent exertions have enjoyed only a feeble and ephemeral success. The greatest efforts have produced the smallest results. There is not one instance in our modern nations of any war that has compensated, by a little good, for the evil it has done. But the result of the Battle of Poltava has been the felicity of the greatest empire on earth.

Chapter 19
Aftermath of the Victory of Poltava. Charles XII a Fugitive among the Turks. Augustus, Unthroned by Charles, Returns to His Domains. Peter the Great's Conquests.

Meanwhile, all the most important prisoners were being presented to the victor. The czar gave them back their swords and invited them to dinner. It is well enough known that while drinking their health he said: "I drink to the health of my masters in the art of war." However, most of his masters—at any rate, all the junior officers and enlisted men—were soon sent to Siberia. There was no protocol for exchanging prisoners between the Russians and Swedes. The czar had proposed one before the siege of Poltava; Charles refused it, and his Swedes were in every respect the victims of his indomitable pride.

This perennially inopportune pride brought about the misadventures and calamities which befell Charles in Turkey, calamities more befitting one of Ariosto's heroes than a judicious monarch, for as soon as he was in the vicinity of Bender he was advised to write to the Grand Vizier, as was customary, but he believed it too much beneath his dignity. A similar obstinacy set him at loggerheads one after the other with all the ministers of the Porte. He could never adapt to different times or places.[1]

At the earliest reports of the Battle of Poltava, there was a drastic change in thinking and in the conduct of affairs in Poland, Saxony, Sweden, and Silesia. While Charles had been imposing his will on others, he had demanded of the Austrian Emperor Joseph I that the Catholics be dispossessed of five hundred churches in favor of Silesians of the Augsburg persuasion. The Catholics took back nearly all of the Lutheran churches as soon as they were apprised of Charles's misfortune. The Saxons' one idea was to take vengeance for the extortions of a conqueror who, they said, had cost them twenty-three million crowns. Their elector, the king of Poland, immediately (August 8) protested against his forced abdication and, having gotten back into the czar's good graces, lost no time reascending the throne of Poland. Sweden, in a state of consternation, believed for a long time that her king was dead,

142

and the Senate, in its uncertainty, could not make up its mind about anything.

Peter made up *his* mind forthwith to reap the advantage of his victory, sending Marshal Sheremeteyev with an army to Livonia, on whose frontiers that general had distinguished himself on so many occasions. Prince Menshikov was dispatched posthaste with a large cavalry force to support the few Russian troops left behind in Poland, to put heart into all the nobles of Augustus's faction, to expel the rival monarch, who was now considered a mere rebel, and to disperse some remaining Swedish troops commanded by General Krassau.

Peter himself set out shortly. Passing through Kiev and the Palatinate of Chelm and Upper Volhynia, he reached Lublin and held consultations with the General of Lithuania.[2] He next reviewed the Army of the Crown, which took the oath of loyalty to King Augustus (September 18). Then he went to Warsaw, and at Thorn enjoyed the finest of all triumphs, namely, accepting the thanks of a king to whom he was restoring his domains (October 7). It was there that he concluded a treaty against Sweden with the kings of Denmark, Poland, and Prussia. Already it was a question of regaining all the territories conquered by Gustavus Adolphus. Peter revived the time-honored czarist pretensions to Livonia, Ingria, Carelia, and part of Finland; Denmark claimed Scania, and the king of Prussia, Pomerania.

Charles's ill-starred valor was thus shaking all the edifices erected by the fortunate valor of Gustavus Adolphus. The Polish aristocracy came in a body either to ratify its oaths to its king or to beg his forgiveness for having deserted him. Nearly all of them recognized Peter as their protector.

To the armed might of the czar, the treaties, and the unexpected and drastic change in his affairs, Stanislas could oppose nothing but patience. He published a document known as the *Universal,* in which he announced his readiness to relinquish the crown if the Republic so demanded.

When Peter had discussed everything with the king of Poland and ratified the treaty with Denmark, he hurried off to conclude his negotiations with the king of Prussia. It was not as yet customary for sovereigns to carry out in person the duties of their ambassadors; it was Peter who introduced this new and little-imitated procedure. The elector of Brandenburg, first king of Prussia, went to confer with the czar at Marienwerder, a little city in western Pomerania built by the Teutonic Knights and incorporated within the new kingdom of Prussia. The kingdom was small and impoverished, yet its new king displayed the most ostentatious pomp whenever he traveled. He had already received Peter with this brilliant display during the czar's first visit, when he left his empire to educate himself abroad. He welcomed the vanquisher of Charles XII with greater magnificence still. At first, Peter merely concluded a defensive treaty with the king of Prussia (October 20), which, however, later consummated the ruin of Swedish affairs.

Not a moment was wasted. Having speedily carried out negotiations that everywhere else are so protracted, Peter rejoined his army at Riga, capital of Livonia, where he began by shelling the place (November 21), personally lighting the fuses of the first three bombshells. He then established a blockade, and, satisfied that Riga could not slip through his fingers, went off to oversee the building of his city of Saint Petersburg, the construction of houses, and his fleet. He laid down with his own hands the keel of a fifty-four-gun ship (December 3), and then set off for Moscow. He amused himself by working on the preparations for the triumph that he flaunted in the capital. He gave the orders for all the festivities, worked on them himself, and made all the arrangements.

The year 1710 opened with that ritual then so necessary to his subjects, in whom it inspired sentiments of grandeur, and so agreeable to those who had once feared that they would see the Swedes, over whom they were now exulting, enter their walls as conquerors. Beneath seven magnificent arches they watched the parade of the defeated foe's artillery, their flags and standards, their king's litter, the captive soldiers, officers, generals, and ministers, all marching by to the sound of bells, trumpets, a hundred cannon, and the acclamations of a countless throng, who made themselves heard whenever the guns fell silent. The victors brought up the rear of the procession on horseback, with the generals to the fore and Peter dressed as a major general. At each triumphal arch there were delegates from the various classes of society, and at the last arch a select band of boyars' children dressed in Roman costume, who presented the victorious monarch with laurel wreaths (January 1).

This public fete was followed by a no less gratifying ceremony. In 1708, there had been an incident that was all the more unpleasant as Peter's fortunes were then at a low ebb. Matveyev, his ambassador at the court of Queen Anne in London, having taken his leave, was forcibly arrested by two officers of the law at the behest of some English tradesmen and taken before a justice of the peace to guarantee the sums he owed them. The English merchants claimed that commercial law should take precedence over diplomatic privilege. The czar's ambassadors and all the other diplomats, who took his part, said that their persons must always be inviolable. The czar wrote to Queen Anne, loudly demanding justice, but she was unable to oblige him because the law of England allowed tradesmen to prosecute their debtors and did not exempt diplomats from this proceeding. The murder of Patkul, the czar's ambassador, executed the year before by order of Charles XII, emboldened the English not to respect a quality that had been so cruelly profaned. The other ambassadors then in London were obliged to answer for the czar's, and, in brief, the only thing the queen could do in his behalf was to urge Parliament to enact a law by whose terms it would henceforth no longer be permissible to arrest an ambassador for debt. But after the Battle of Poltava, a more genuine act of atonement was called for. The queen apologized publicly through the agency of a solemn diplomatic mission. Mr. Whitworth, who had been chosen for this ceremony (February 16), began his address with the following words: "Most high and mighty emperor." He informed Peter that those who had dared to arrest his ambassador had been imprisoned and dishonored.[3] Nothing of the kind had in fact occurred, but it sufficed merely to say that it had, and the title of emperor, which the queen had not given Peter before the Battle of Poltava, was a clear enough indication of the respect he now enjoyed in Europe. In Holland, Peter was already commonly addressed by this title, and not only by those who had watched him work beside them in the Saardam shipyards and who took a more personal interest in his glory. All the leading citizens of the state tried to outdo one another in calling him emperor, and they used to celebrate his victory by festivities held in the presence of the Swedish ambassador.

He enhanced the respect he had earned by his victory by not wasting an instant in taking advantage of it. To begin with, he laid siege to Elbing, a Hanseatic town of royal Prussia, in Poland, where the Swedes still maintained a garrison. The Russians stormed and entered the city, and the garrison surrendered (March 11). The place had been one of Charles XII's major arsenals, containing one hundred and eighty-three bronze cannon and one hundred and fifty-seven mortars. Peter immediately hurried from Moscow to Saint Petersburg. No sooner there (April 2), he took ship at his new fortress of Kronslot, sailed along the coast of Carelia, and, in the teeth of a violent gale, anchored his fleet off Viborg, capital of Finnish Carelia, while his armies approached across frozen marshland. The town was invested, and at the same time the blockade of the Livonian capital was tightened. Shortly after its walls were breached, Viborg surrendered, and a garrison consisting of some four thousand men capitulated, without obtaining the honors of war. The garrison were taken prisoner in spite of the capitulation (June 23). Peter felt aggrieved about several infractions committed by the Swedes. He promised to restore these troops to freedom when the Swedes had responded to his complaints. They had to ask for instructions concerning the affair from their ever-inflexible king, and the soldiers, whom Charles could have liberated, remained in captivity. It was thus that the prince of Orange, King William III of England, had in 1695 arrested Marshal de Boufflers, despite the capitulation of Namur. Several examples of such violations are recorded; it could have been hoped that there had been none.

After Viborg had fallen, the siege of Riga soon became a regular siege, conducted energetically. The Russians had to break the ice in the Dvina River, which washes the northern walls of the city. An epidemic that had been ravaging the area for some time spread to the besieging army and carried off nine thousand men. Nevertheless, the pace of the siege was not slackened. It was a lengthy one, and the garrison obtained the honors of war, but the terms of surrender (July 15) stipulated that every Livonian officer and enlisted man would remain in the Russian service, as citizens of a country which had been severed from Russia and usurped by Charles XII's ancestors. The privileges of which the Livonians had been divested by his father[4] were restored, and all the officers entered the service of the czar, which was the noblest vengeance he could exact for the murder of his ambassador, the Livonian Patkul, condemned for having defended the self-same privileges. The garrison comprised about five thousand men. Shortly thereafter the citadel of Peenemünde was taken, and more than eight hundred artillery pieces were found in the city as well as in the fort.

In order to be in complete control of Carelia, Peter still needed the fortified town of Kexholm on Lake Ladoga, which, being on an island, was considered impregnable. A short while later it was bombarded, and soon surrendered (September 19). The Isle of Oesel north of Livonia was subdued with the same rapidity (September 23).

The cities of Pernau and Reval lie on the Gulf of Finland in northern Estonia, which is a province of Livonia. Once they were taken, the conquest of Livonia would be complete. Pernau capitulated after a siege lasting a few days (August 25), and Reval submitted without a single shot being fired (September 10), but the besieged population found a way of escaping from the victor at the very moment of surrender. Some Swedish ships dropped anchor in the roadstead during the night, and the garrison went on board together with most of the townspeople. On entering the city, the besiegers were astonished to find it deserted. When Charles XII won the victory of Narva, he little thought that one day his troops would need to resort to such stratagems.

As for Poland, Stanislas, seeing his party destroyed, had taken refuge in Pomerania, which still belonged to Charles XII. Augustus was king, and it was hard to tell whether Charles had won more fame by unthroning him than Peter had by reestablishing him.

The king of Sweden's domains were even worse off than himself; the contagious disease that had raged through Livonia passed into Sweden, carrying off thirty thousand people in the city of Stockholm alone. It also devastated the provinces, which were already excessively underpopulated, since for ten consecutive years most of the men had left the countryside to perish in their master's footsteps.

Charles's misfortunes pursued him into Pomerania, to which eleven thousand Swedish troops had withdrawn from Poland. The czar, the kings of Denmark and Prussia, the elector of Hanover, and the duke of Holstein formed a common alliance to neutralize this army and force its commander General Krassau to remain neutral. The regency in Stockholm, what with the plague devastating the city and no news from the king, was only too happy to sign the pact of neutrality, which seemed likely to spare at least one of its provinces the horrors of war. The Emperor of Austria approved of this singular treaty, one of whose provisions was that the Swedish army in Pomerania could not leave to defend its monarch anywhere else. It was even resolved, in the Empire, to raise an army to enforce this unprecedented covenant. The fact of the matter is that the Emperor, then at war with France, hoped to have the Swedish army enter his own service. All this negotiating was conducted while Peter was taking possession of Livonia, Estonia, and Carelia.

Charles XII, who all this while had been sending messages from Bender to the Ottoman Porte, leaving no stone unturned to commit the Divan to declare war on the czar, received this news as one of the most fatal blows dealt him in his adversity. He maintained that the Senate in Stockholm had tied his army's hands. It was on this occasion that he wrote to the Senate saying he would send one of his boots to govern it.[5]

Meanwhile, the Danes were preparing an assault on Sweden. Every nation in Europe was then at war: Spain, Portugal, Italy, France, Germany, Holland, and England were still fighting over the succession of King Charles II of Spain, while the entire North was up in arms against Charles XII. The only element lacking for every village in Europe to be exposed to havoc was a quarrel with the Ottoman Porte. Such a quarrel broke out when Peter was at the height of his fame, and precisely because he *was* at the height of his fame.

PART II

Chapter 1
The Pruth Campaign.

Sultan Achmet III did declare war on Peter I, but not for the king of Sweden's sake. It was, as we may readily believe, purely in his own interests. The khan of the Crimean Tartars looked fearfully on a neighbor who had grown so mighty. The Porte had taken umbrage at his ships in the Sea of Azov and the Black Sea, the fortification of the city of Azov, the already famous harbor of Taganrog—in brief, at Peter's numerous triumphs, and at ambition itself, which always feeds on success.

It is neither probable nor true that the Ottoman Porte made war on the czar in the Sea of Azov because a Swedish vessel in the Baltic had seized a barque aboard which was found a letter from a never-identified diplomat. Nordberg has written that this letter contained a plan for the conquest of the Turkish empire, that it was taken to Charles XII in Turkey, that Charles forwarded it to the Divan, and that on the strength of this letter war was declared. This fable reveals clearly enough its fictitious character. The Tartar khan was even more uneasy than the Divan at Constantinople because of his proximity to Azov, and he was the man whose urgings persuaded the Turks to take the field.[1]

Livonia was not yet altogether within the czar's grasp, when, no later than August, Achmet III determined to show his colors. He could barely have heard of the fall of Riga. The proposal to make cash restitution for the king of Sweden's material losses at Poltava would be the most preposterous idea conceivable, if that of demolishing Saint Petersburg were not more so. There was a good deal of the quixotic about Charles's conduct at Bender, but the Divan's would have been more quixotic still had it really made such demands.

The Tartar khan, who was the prime instigator of this war, visited Charles at his retreat (November, 1710). Their interests were identical, since Azov is the frontier of Little Tartary.[2] Charles and the Crimean khan were the principal losers by the czar's aggrandizement, but the khan was not head of the sultan's armies. He was like the feudatory princes of Austria who served the Empire with their own troops under the command of the Emperor's general.

The first step taken by the Divan was to arrest Tolstoy, the czar's ambassador, together with thirty of his domestics, in the streets of Constantinople, and to lock him up in the Castle of the Seven Towers (November 29). This barbarous custom, of which savages would be ashamed, is explained by the fact that the Turks always have foreign ambassadors in permanent residence at Constantinople, whereas they themselves never send ordinary ambassadors abroad. They consider the ambassadors of the Christian monarchs to be commercial attachés. Moreover, despising the Christians no less than the Jews, they do not deign to observe the law of nations in their case except when they are compelled to do so. At all events, they have persisted in their fierce pride right up to the present day.

The celebrated vizier Achmet Koprülü, who took Candia under Mahomet IV, committed an outrage against the son of a French ambassador and, having pushed brutality to the point of striking him, threw him in prison. Louis XIV, for all his pride, showed his resentment in no other way than by sending a different minister to the Porte. The Christian princes, very particular among themselves on the point of honor, having even embodied it in the common law, seem to have overlooked it so far as the Turks are concerned.

Never was a sovereign more affronted in the person of his ambassadors than the czar of Russia. Within the course of a very few years, he had seen his ambassador to London jailed for debt, his plenipotentiary in Poland and Saxony broken on the wheel by order of the king of Sweden, and his minister to the Ottoman Porte seized and imprisoned like a common criminal in Constantinople.

The queen of England, as we have already seen, gave Peter satisfaction for the outrage in London. The horrible affront he received in the person of Patkul was expunged in Swedish blood at the Battle of Poltava, but fortune let the violation of international law by the Turks go unpunished.

The czar was obliged to leave the western front (January 17) to fight on the Turkish border. To begin with, he sent forward to Moldavia[3] ten regiments that had been stationed in Poland. He commanded Marshal Sheremeteyev to depart for Livonia with his army corps, and, leaving Prince Menshikov at the head of affairs in Saint Petersburg, he himself went to Moscow to issue all the orders for the forthcoming campaign.

A regency council was established (January 18), the guards regiments set out, and Peter instructed his young nobles to come and learn the soldier's trade under him, appointing some to the rank of cadet and commissioning others as junior officers. Admiral Apraxin went to Azov as commander in chief of the land and naval forces. Having taken all these steps, Peter gave orders in Moscow that a new czarina be recognized. It was that same person who had been taken prisoner at Marienburg in 1702. In the year 1696, Peter had repudiated his wife Evdokiya Lopukhina,[4] by whom he had two children. Divorce is allowable by the laws of the church, and had it been forbidden, he would have passed a law permitting it.

The youthful captive from Marienburg who had been given the name Catherine[5] rose above her sex and her misfortunes. She made herself so agreeable that the czar wanted her near him. She accompanied him on his journeys and his arduous enterprises, sharing his hardships and alleviating his afflictions by her gaiety and her complaisance. She was quite unacquainted with that paraphernalia of luxury and indolence of which other women have made real necessities. What made the favor she enjoyed the more singular was the fact that she was neither envied nor thwarted, and that no one suffered because of her. She frequently calmed the czar's wrath, and made him an even greater man by making him a more merciful one. At last she became so indispensable to him that in 1707 he secretly married her. He already had two daughters by her, and the following year she presented him with a princess, who later married the duke of Holstein. Peter and Catherine's clandestine marriage was proclaimed on the same day[6] that the czar set off with her to put his fortune to the test against the Ottoman empire (March 17, 1711). His preparations all promised a favorable outcome. The hetman of the Cossacks was to contain the Tartars, who had already been despoiling the Ukraine since February; one Russian army was moving up toward the Dniester, while another corps, under Prince Golitsyn, was marching through Poland. Everything started off well, for near Kiev Golitsyn encountered a large band of Tartars, plus some Cossacks, some Polish supporters of Stanislas, and even a few Swedes. Golitsyn utterly routed them, killing five thousand men. These Tartars had already enslaved ten thousand people in the steppes. From time immemorial it has been a Tartar custom to carry more cords than scimitars, to bind the poor wretches whom they take unawares. The captives were all released and their captors put to the sword. The whole army, had it been assembled in one place, must have totaled sixty thousand men. It was supposed to be further augmented by the king of Poland's troops. That monarch, who owed the czar everything, came to see him on June 3 at Jaroslaw, on the banks of the San River, promising strong reinforcements. War against the Turks was declared in the name of both kings, but the Polish Diet did not ratify Augustus's promises, and refused to break off relations with Turkey. The czar was fated to have in King Augustus an ally who was never able to help him. He had the same hopes as regards Moldavia and Wallachia, and was likewise deceived.

Moldavia and Wallachia ought to have thrown off the Turkish yoke. These are the lands of the ancient Dacians, who, in company with the Gepidae, long troubled the Roman Empire. Trajan subjugated them, and the first Constantine converted them to Christianity. Dacia became a province of the Byzantine empire, but before long the same peoples contributed to the collapse of the Western Empire by serving under Odoacer and Theodoric.[7]

The Dacian territories remained possessions of the Byzantine empire, and when the Turks took Constantinople, they were ruled and oppressed by individual princes. Ultimately, they were totally subjugated by the padishah, or Turkish emperor, who awards their investiture. The hospodar or voivode chosen by the Porte to govern these provinces is always an Orthodox Christian. By this choice, the Turks have displayed their tolerance, while our ignorant ranters berate them for their persecutions. The prince nominated by the Porte is its tributary, or rather its tax-farmer. The Porte confers the dignity on whoever pays the most for it and gives most presents to the vizier, just as it awards the Greek patriarchate of Constantinople. Occasionally some dragoman, i.e., an interpreter to the Divan, obtains the position. Moldavia and Wallachia are rarely united under the same voivode; the Porte divides the two provinces to make more sure of them. Demetrius Cantemir had obtained Moldavia. The Voivode Cantemir claimed descent from Tamerlane because Tamerlane's name was Timur and because Timur was a Tartar khan. From the name of Timurkan the *Kan*temir family name was supposedly taken.

Bassaraba Brancovan[8] had been invested with Wallachia. Bassaraba had no genealogist to trace his ancestry from a Tartar conqueror. Cantemir thought the time had come to break away from Turkish domination and to make himself independent thanks to the czar's patronage. His behavior toward Peter was identical with Mazeppa's toward Charles. At first he even prevailed upon Bassaraba, hospodar of Wallachia, to join the conspiracy, all of whose fruits he hoped to gather for himself, planning to make himself master of both provinces. The bishop of Jerusalem,[9] who was then in Wallachia, was the moving spirit of the plot. Cantemir promised the czar troops and provisions, just as Mazeppa had promised the king of Sweden, and was no better at keeping his word.

General Sheremeteyev advanced to Jassy, capital of Moldavia, to supervise and support the execution of these grandiose schemes. Cantemir met him there and was received with princely honors, but the only princely act he performed was to publish a manifesto against the Turkish empire. The hospodar of Wallachia, who soon perceived Cantemir's ambitious designs, abandoned him and returned to his duty. The bishop of Jerusalem, rightly fearing for his head, ran away and hid. The peoples of Wallachia and Moldavia remained loyal to the Ottoman Porte, while those who were expected to supply the Russian army with victuals took them instead to the Turkish army.

The vizier Baltaji Mehemet had already crossed the Danube at the head of one hundred thousand men and was marching toward Jassy along the banks of the Pruth—once called the Hierasa—which empties into the Danube and more or less corresponds to the boundary between

Moldavia and Bessarabia. He sent Count Poniatowsky, a Polish nobleman devoted to the king of Sweden, to beg that monarch to call upon
him and inspect his army. Charles could not bring himself to do this; he
demanded that the Grand Vizier first call upon *him* at his place of refuge
near Bender. His pride got the better of his interests. When
Poniatowsky returned to the Turkish camp and made excuses for
Charles XII's refusal: "I fully expected," said the vizier to the Tartar
khan, "that the haughty infidel would treat us like this." Such reciprocal
arrogance, which invariably alienates high-ranking personages, did not
help the king of Sweden's affairs. What is more, he was shortly to
realize that the Turks were acting only in their own interests, not in his.

While the Turkish army was crossing the Danube, the czar, advancing by way of the Polish frontier, crossed the Dnieper to disengage
Marshal Sheremeteyev, who, on the banks of the Pruth south of Jassy,
was in imminent danger of encirclement by a hundred thousand Turks
and an army of Tartars. Before his passage of the Dnieper, Peter had
been afraid to expose Catherine to perils which were daily becoming
more terrible, but Catherine considered this attentiveness as an affront
to her affection and courage, and was so insistent that the czar could not
do without her. The army was overjoyed to see her riding at the head of
the line. She rarely used a carriage. On the far side of the Dnieper, they
had to march through desert country, cross the river Bug and then the
Tiras, now known as the Dniester, after which they came upon yet
another wilderness before reaching Jassy on the Pruth. Catherine put
heart into the army, filled it with gaiety, sent aid to sick officers, and
even looked after the rank and file.

At last the Russians arrived at Jassy, where they were supposed to set
up supply depots (July 4). Hospodar Bassaraba of Wallachia, who was
once again acting in the interests of the Porte, while pretending to act in
those of the czar, suggested that he make peace, although the Grand
Vizier had not empowered him to do so. The Russians scented a trap
and simply requested provisions, which the hospodar neither could nor
would furnish. It was difficult to fetch them from Poland. The supplies
promised by Cantemir, which he hoped in vain to get from Wallachia,
failed to arrive, and the situation was becoming most disturbing. An
ominous scourge was added to all these setbacks: clouds of locusts
covered the countryside, devouring and contaminating the crops. There
were frequent water shortages as the Russians marched on beneath a
burning sun and across parched deserts, and it was necessary to take
water to the army in casks.

By a singular coincidence, Peter's advance brought him within reach
of Charles XII, for Bender is only twenty-five leagues from the spot
where the Russian army was encamped near Jassy. Bands of Cossacks
penetrated as far as Charles's retreat, but the Crimean Tartars skirmish-

ing in the area safeguarded the king of Sweden from being taken by surprise. In his camp, Charles was waiting impatiently and fearlessly for the outcome of the war.

Peter made haste to cross to the right bank of the Pruth, as soon as he had established some supply depots. It was crucial to prevent the Turks deployed along the left bank from fording the river and getting at him. His maneuver was intended to make him master of Moldavia and Wallachia. He sent General Janus ahead with the vanguard to thwart a Turkish crossing, but the general arrived just as they were coming across their pontoon bridges. He fell back, and his infantry was pursued until the czar came up in person to disengage it.

And so before long the Grand Vizier's army approached the czar's along the riverbank. The two armies were very different: that of the Turks, reinforced by the Tartars, was said to number nearly two hundred and fifty thousand men, while the Russians at that time had only thirty-seven thousand or so. A fairly sizable army corps under General Ronne was on the other side of the Moldavian mountains on the Siretul River,[10] but the Turks had severed Peter's communications with him. The czar was beginning to run low on supplies, and his troops, though encamped not far from the river, could obtain scarcely any water, being exposed to a large concentration of artillery stationed on the left bank by the Grand Vizier together with a detachment which maintained a ceaseless fire on the Russians. Judging from this highly detailed and very faithful account, it would seem that the Vizier Baltaji Mehemet, far from being the imbecile portrayed by the Swedes, handled himself with a good deal of intelligence. Fording the Pruth within full sight of the enemy, forcing him to retreat and pursuing him, suddenly severing all communications between the czar's army and a large force of his cavalry, encircling this army without leaving it any means of retreat, cutting off its food and water, keeping it at the mercy of batteries of cannon on the opposite shore—none of this was the work of a man lacking energy and foresight.

Peter was now in a worse position than Charles XII at Poltava. Hemmed in like him by a superior force, suffering more than he had from the lack of supplies, and, also like him, having put his faith in the word of a prince who lacked the power to keep it, he decided to retreat, and tried to choose an advantageous campsite by returning to Jassy.

He struck camp during the night of July 20, but was barely on the march before the Turks fell on his rearguard at daybreak. The regiment of Preobrazhensky Guards held off this headlong assault for a long while. The Russians formed up and constructed breastworks with wagons and the baggage. The same day (July 21), the entire Turkish army attacked them once again. The proof that the Russians were capable of defending themselves, whatever may have been said to the contrary, is the fact that they *did* defend themselves for a considerable time, that they killed large numbers of the enemy, and that their line was not broken.

With the Ottoman army were two of the king of Sweden's officers, Count Poniatowsky and Count Sparre, as well as some Cossack supporters of Charles XII. My sources inform me that these generals advised the Grand Vizier not to fight, but rather to cut off the enemies' food and water and force them to surrender or die. Other accounts claim that, on the contrary, they incited the Grand Vizier to put to the sword an exhausted and declining army which was already starving to death. The former notion appears more prudent, the latter more in conformity with the character of generals trained by Charles XII.

What actually happened was that the Grand Vizier fell upon the rearguard at dawn and threw it into disarray. All the Turks found confronting them to begin with was a single line of four hundred men. The Russians formed up rapidly,[11] and a German general named Hallart had the glory of making such speedy and such effective dispositions that the Russians resisted the Ottoman army for three hours without losing any ground.

The discipline to which the czar had subjected his troops now repaid his efforts handsomely. At Narva, sixty thousand men had been defeated by eight thousand because they were undisciplined, whereas at the Pruth a rearguard of approximately eight thousand Russians withstood the attack of one hundred and fifty thousand Turks, killed seven thousand of them, and repulsed them.

After this bitter engagement, both armies dug in during the night, but the Russian army was still surrounded and without food or water. It was near the banks of the Pruth but could not approach the river, for as soon as a few soldiers ventured to go and fetch some water, a Turkish detachment stationed on the opposite bank rained iron and lead upon them from a large number of guns loaded with canister shot. For its part, the Turkish army that had attacked the Russians maintained a withering barrage.

The odds were that eventually the Russians would be irretrievably lost, thanks to their position, their numerical inferiority, and the shortage of supplies. Skirmishing went on without a pause; the czar's cavalry, almost all of which lacked mounts, was no longer able to give assistance unless it fought on foot. The situation appeared desperate. One has merely to glance at an accurate map depicting the czar's camp and the Ottoman army to see that there never had been a more vulnerable position, that retreat was out of the question, and that the choice was between winning total victory, perishing to the last man, or enslavement by the Turks.

Every contemporary account and every contemporary memoir

unanimously agree that the czar, uncertain whether or not to run the risk of another battle and to expose his wife, his army, his empire, and the fruits of so many endeavors to seemingly inevitable destruction, retired to his tent overcome with grief and shaken by the convulsions that sometimes racked him and that were redoubled by his distress. All alone, a prey to many cruel anxieties and unwilling even to be seen in this sorry state, he forbade anyone to enter his tent. It was then that he realized how fortunate he was to have permitted his wife to accompany him. Catherine entered his tent despite his orders to the contrary.

A woman who had braved death throughout all this fighting, exposed like everybody else to the Turkish bombardment, had earned the right to speak. She persuaded her husband to try the way of negotiation.

It is the immemorial practice throughout the Orient, when requesting an audience of sovereigns or their representatives, not to approach them without bearing gifts. Catherine gathered together the few jewels she had brought with her on this military expedition, from which all ostentation and luxury were banned, and added two black fox pelisses; the ready cash that she collected was intended for the Kehaya.[12] She herself picked out an intelligent officer who, with two servants, was to make the presents to the Grand Vizier and afterwards make sure that the Kehaya received safely the gift set aside for him. The officer was entrusted with a letter to Baltaji Mehemet from Marshal Sheremeteyev. Peter's memoirs corroborate the existence of the letter; they give none of the details of Catherine's transactions, but everything is pretty well confirmed by Peter's personal declaration in 1723, when he had Catherine crowned empress. "She was of the greatest assistance to us," he said, "on every dangerous occasion, and especially at the Battle of the Pruth, where our army was reduced to twenty-two thousand men." If indeed the czar had at that time no more than twenty-two thousand soldiers facing the threat of death by starvation or the sword, the service rendered by Catherine was as great as the favors showered upon her by her husband. Peter the Great's manuscript journal[13] states that on the very day of the great battle of July 20 he had thirty-one thousand five hundred and fifty-four infantrymen and six thousand six hundred and ninety-two cavalrymen, nearly all of them dismounted. It would seem therefore that he had lost sixteen thousand two hundred and forty-six soldiers during the battle. Other accounts affirm that the Turkish losses were much higher than his own, and that as they attacked in a disorderly mob, none of the shots fired at them went astray. If such is the case, the Battle of the Pruth, fought on July 20 and 21, was one of the most murderous actions in several centuries.

We have either to suspect Peter the Great of being in error when, during the coronation of the empress, he expresses his gratitude to her "for having saved his army, reduced to twenty-two thousand men," or else accuse his journal of falsification, since it is stated therein that on the day of the battle his army on the Pruth, not including the detachment encamped on the Siretul, "amounted to thirty-one thousand five hundred and fifty-four infantrymen and six thousand six hundred and ninety-two cavalrymen." By this reckoning, the battle must have been more dreadful than all the historians and all the accounts pro and con have hitherto reported. There is certainly some misunderstanding here, which is quite normal in descriptions of campaigns when one goes into detail. The safest course is always to confine oneself to the principal outcome, namely victory or defeat; one rarely knows the precise cost of either.

To whatever number the Russian army had been reduced, they flattered themselves that so dauntless and stubborn a defense would impress the Grand Vizier, that they would obtain peace upon terms honorable for the Ottoman Porte, and that this treaty, while making the vizier agreeable to his master, would not be too humiliating for the Russian empire. It seems to me that Catherine's great merit was to have seen such a possibility at a time when the generals appeared to see nothing but inevitable disaster.

In his *History of Charles XII,* Nordberg cites a letter from the czar to the Grand Vizier, in which Peter expresses himself as follows: "If, contrary to my expectations, I have had the misfortune to displease His Highness, I am ready to make atonement for the grievances which he may hold against me. I beseech you, most noble general, to put a stop to this bloodshed, and I implore you to call an immediate halt to the excessive fire of your artillery. Be pleased to accept the hostage I have just sent you."

This letter bears all the hallmarks of a forgery, as do most of the documents reported haphazardly by Nordberg. It is dated July 11, new style, whereas the letter to Baltaji Mehemet was not written until the twenty-first, new style. It was not the czar who wrote, but Marshal Sheremeteyev. The expression "the czar has had the misfortune to displease His Highness" was certainly not used in the letter, such terms being appropriate only to a subject begging his master's pardon. There was no question of a hostage, none having been sent. The letter was delivered by an officer while the guns were still thundering on both sides. In his letter, Sheremeteyev merely reminded the vizier of certain peace offers made by the Porte at the opening of the campaign through the intermediary of the British and Dutch ambassadors, when the Divan was calling for the surrender of the citadel and port of Taganrog, the real occasions of the war.

Some hours elapsed before a response was received from the Grand Vizier. There were fears that the bearer had been killed by cannon fire or taken prisoner by the Turks. A second courier was dispatched with a duplicate of the letter (July 21, 1711), and a council of war was held in Catherine's presence. Ten generals signed the following recommendation:

"If the enemy refuses to accept the conditions offered him, and if he asks that we lay down our arms and surrender unconditionally, our generals and ministers are of the unanimous opinion that we must cut our way through the enemy ranks."

In consequence of this resolution, they fortified the baggage train with earthworks, and had advanced to within a hundred paces of the Turkish lines when the Grand Vizier at last called for a cessation of hostilities.

In their accounts, the entire Swedish faction has denounced this vizier as a cowardly scoundrel who accepted bribes. In the same way, many writers have accused Count Piper of taking money from the duke of Marlborough to incite the king of Sweden to continue the war against the czar, and a French minister has been charged with negotiating the Treaty of Seville for cash. Such charges should be brought on direct evidence only. Prime ministers very rarely stoop to such shameful and dastardly practices, which are sooner or later revealed by those giving the money and by their ledgers, which bear them out. A minister is always the cynosure of all eyes in Europe; his credit is based on his honor, and he is invariably rich enough to have no need to be a traitor.

The rank of viceroy of the Ottoman Empire is so splendid, in wartime the profits to be made are so immense, abundance and magnificence prevailed to such a high degree in Baltaji Mehemet's tents, while simplicity and above all scarcity were so great in the czar's army, that it was far more the Grand Vizier's place to give than to receive. A paltry mark of attention from a woman sending some pelisses and rings, as is customary in every court, or rather in every Oriental Porte, could not be regarded as bribery. Baltaji Mehemet's frank and open conduct would seem to confound the accusations that have tarnished so many writings dealing with this affair. Vice Chancellor Shafirov entered the vizier's tent with much pomp; everything was transacted in public and could not have occurred otherwise. The negotiations themselves were opened in the presence of a man devoted to the king of Sweden, a servant of Count Poniatowsky, one of Charles XII's officers, who acted as an interpreter in the early stages, and the articles of agreement were publicly drafted by the first secretary to the vizierate, one Hummer Effendi. Count Poniatowsky was himself present. The gift for the Kehaya was presented in a public ceremony. Everything took place in accordance with Oriental custom, gifts were exchanged, and nothing could less resemble an act of treason. What convinced the vizier to conclude a treaty was the fact that at that very moment the army corps commanded by General Ronne on the Siretul river in Moldavia had crossed three other rivers and was even then nearing the Danube, where Ronne had just taken the city and fortress of Braila, defended by a large garrison under the command of a pasha. The czar had another army corps advancing from the Polish frontier. It is moreover highly probable that the vizier was not cognizant of the shortages from which the Russians were suffering. An inventory of stores and munitions is not communicated to the enemy. On the contrary, one brags in his presence of enjoying plenty, precisely when one is suffering the most. There were no deserters from the Russians to the Turks or vice versa, differences in clothing, language, and religion precluding such an eventuality. The Turks were not acquainted, as we are, with desertion, and consequently the Grand Vizier did not know exactly how deplorable the condition of Peter's army was.

Baltaji, who did not care for war, yet who had waged it very well, believed that his expedition would be successful enough if he returned to the Grand Seignior's control the cities and seaports for which he was fighting, if he sent General Ronne's victorious army back to Russia from the banks of the Danube, and if he closed forever the entrance to the Sea of Azov—the Cimmerian Bosporus—and the Black Sea to the enterprising czar; finally, if he did not jeopardize undoubted gains by fighting a new battle in which, after all, despair might possibly prevail over strength. He had seen his Janissaries repulsed the day before, and there were many instances of victories won by the lesser number against the greater. Such were his reasons. Neither Charles's officers present in his army nor the Tartar khan approved of them. The Tartars' interest lay in their power to raid along the Russian and Polish borders, while Charles XII's lay in wreaking vengeance on the czar, but the general and prime minister of the Ottoman Empire was prompted neither by the private revenge of a Christian prince nor by the love of booty motivating the Tartars. No sooner was a truce agreed upon than the Russians bought from the Turks the stores they needed. The articles of this pact in no way resemble the traveler La Motraye's account, parroted by Nordberg. Among the conditions upon which he insisted, the vizier at first wanted the czar's promise to play no further role in the affairs of Poland. Poniatowsky stressed this point. However, basically it suited the Turkish empire that Poland should remain disunited and powerless, and so this article was reduced to withdrawing Russian troops from the frontier. The Tartar khan demanded a tribute of forty thousand sequins.[14] This point was debated for a long time but was not approved.

For a long time too the vizier demanded that Cantemir be surrendered to him, as Patkul had been surrendered to the king of Sweden. Cantemir was in precisely Mazeppa's position. The czar had instituted criminal proceedings against Mazeppa and had had him executed in effigy. The Turks had no such custom; they were ignorant of trials in absentia and public sentences. These widely advertised condemnations and executions in effigy are all the less common among them as their law prohibits human portraiture of any kind whatsoever. They insisted in vain on the extradition of Cantemir. Peter wrote these very words to Vice Chancellor Shafirov:

"I will rather abandon to the Turks all the territory between here and Kursk, for I will still retain the hope of recovering it, but the loss of my word is irreparable; I cannot violate it. The only thing that is truly our own is honor. To relinquish that is to cease being a monarch."

An agreement was finally reached and the treaty signed near a village named Faleshty,[15] on the banks of the Pruth. The treaty stipulated that Azov and its adjacent territory would be returned, along with the stores and artillery it contained before the czar captured it in 1696; that the port of Taganrog on the Sea of Zabache would be demolished, together with that of Samara on the river of the same name and other, smaller citadels. There was a final codicil touching the king of Sweden that revealed clearly enough the extent of the vizier's displeasure with him. It was specified that the king would not be interfered with by the czar if he returned home, and that in addition the czar and himself were at liberty to make peace if they so desired.

It is perfectly obvious from the unusual wording of this codicil that Baltaji Mehemet had not forgotten Charles XII's arrogance. Who can tell whether his haughtiness had not even disposed Mehemet toward peace? The czar's ruin would restore Charles's preeminence, and it is not in human nature to give power to those we despise. At long last Charles, who had refused to come to the vizier's army when tactful behavior was called for, came rushing up when the deed depriving him of all his hopes was about to be consummated. The vizier did not go to meet him, but contented himself with sending two pashas in his place; he himself only came to greet Charles at a little distance from his tent.

Their conversation consisted, as we know, exclusively of recriminations. Several historians have been of the opinion that the vizier's reply to the king, when the latter reproached him for failing to exploit his opportunity to take the czar prisoner, was that of an imbecile. "If I *had* captured the czar," he said, "who would have governed his empire?" It is, however, easy to comprehend that this was the answer of an angry man, and the words which he added—"Not every king can be away from his country"—reveal clearly enough how great was his desire to mortify the Guest of Bender.

Charles derived no other benefit from his journey but to tear the Grand Vizier's robe with his spur. The vizier, who could well have made him repent his action, pretended not to notice, in which he showed himself far superior to Charles. Had anything in that monarch's brilliant and tumultuous life been able to make him realize how much fortune can confound greatness, it would have been the fact that at

Poltava a pastry cook[16] had made his entire army lay down its weapons, and that at the Pruth a woodcutter had been the arbiter of the fates of both the czar and himself, for the Vizier Baltaji Mehemet had been a woodcutter in the seraglio, as his name indicates, and far from being ashamed of this, he was proud of it, so greatly do Oriental ways differ from our own.

The sultan and all Constantinople were to begin with well content with the vizier's conduct. Public celebrations were held for an entire week, and Mehemet's Kehaya, who took the treaty to the Divan, was forthwith elevated to the dignity of Bouyouk Imraour, i.e., Grand Master of the Stables. This is not the treatment accorded to those by whom one believes oneself to have been ill served.

Nordberg appears to have known little of Ottoman government, since he says that "the Grand Seignior treated his vizier with consideration, and that Baltaji Mehemet was a man to be reckoned with." The Janissaries have often been a threat to the sultans, but there is not a single example of a vizier who was not readily sacrificed at a word from his master, and Mehemet was in no position to stand alone. It is, moreover, self-contradictory on Nordberg's part to affirm on the same page that the Janissaries were angry with Mehemet but that the sultan feared his power.

The king of Sweden was reduced to the expedient of intriguing at the Ottoman court. A king who had been himself a kingmaker was seen presenting memoranda and petitions to a sultan unwilling to accept them. Charles employed every device available to a schemer, like a subject desirous of discrediting a minister in his master's eyes. This was how he comported himself with the vizier Mehemet and all his successors; on one occasion he would address the Sultana Validé[17] through a Jewess, on another he would employ a eunuch. Finally, there was the man who mingled with the Grand Seignior's guards, pretended to be a madman in order to attract his attention, then handed him a memorandum from the king. Out of all these stratagems, Charles received, in the first instance, nothing more than the mortification of having his thaïm— i.e., the daily subsistence allowance of fifteen hundred francs which he owed to the generosity of the Porte—cut off. Instead of a thaïm, the Grand Vizier sent him an order advising him to leave Turkey.

Charles was more than ever determined to stay, still imagining that he would return to Poland and the Russian empire with an Ottoman army. Everyone knows the final outcome, in 1714, of his stiff-necked audacity, and how he did battle with an army of Janissaries, Spahis, and Tartars with his secretaries, lackeys, cooks, and stableboys; how he was a captive in the land where he had enjoyed the most lavish hospitality; and how he ultimately returned to his domains disguised as a courier, after spending five years in Turkey.[18] It must be confessed that if there was method in his conduct, it was not the method of other men.

Chapter 2
Aftermath of the Pruth Incident.

It is helpful to recall at this point a fact already related in my *History of Charles XII*. During the armistice that preceded the Treaty of the Pruth, it happened that two Tartars captured two Italian officers belonging to the czar's army and approached a Janissary officer to sell them into slavery. The vizier punished this crime against good faith by executing both Tartars. How are we to reconcile this severe scrupulousness with his violation of international law in the person of Ambassador Tolstoy, whom the same Grand Vizier had had arrested in the streets of Constantinople? There is always a reason for the inconsistencies of human behavior. Baltaji Mehemet was incensed with the Tartar khan because of his reluctance to hear any talk of peace, and he desired to make him realize that *he* was the master.

Once the pact was signed, the czar withdrew by way of Jassy as far as the frontier,[1] followed by a corps of eight thousand Turks sent by the vizier, not only to observe the progress of the Russian army but also to prevent any nomadic Tartars from harassing it.

To begin with, Peter honored the treaty by having the fortresses of Samara and Kammeny Zaton dismantled. However, the surrender of Azov and the demolition of Taganrog ran into difficulties. According to the terms of the treaty, there was a distinction to be made between the artillery and munitions of Azov belonging to the Turks and those which the czar had placed there since he had conquered the stronghold. The Russian governor of Azov spun the negotiations out, and the Porte was justifiably annoyed. The sultan was impatient to receive the keys of Azov; the vizier kept promising them, and Peter's governor kept on procrastinating. Because of this, Baltaji Mehemet lost both his master's good graces and his office; the Tartar khan and his other enemies prevailed against him. He was implicated in the disgrace of several pashas, but the Grand Seignior, who recognized his fidelity, deprived him of neither his possessions nor his life. He was sent to Mitylene (November, 1711) as governor. This simple demotion, the preservation of his fortune, and above all the new command in Mitylene manifestly belie all the arguments Nordberg advances to have us believe that the vizier had been corrupted by the czar's money.

Nordberg writes that the bostangi bachi[2] who came to ask Baltaji Mehemet to return the imperial bul and to notify him of his arrest proclaimed him "traitorous and disobedient to his master, bought and

164

sold by the enemy, and guilty of not having watched over the interests of the king of Sweden." To begin with, such a declaration is not at all in keeping with Turkish practice. The sultan's commands are issued in secret and carried out in silence. Secondly, if the vizier had been proclaimed traitorous, rebellious, and corrupt, he would have been punished by death in a land where such crimes are never pardoned. Finally, if he had been punished for failing to devote sufficient attention to Charles XII's interests, it is obvious that the Swedish monarch would in effect have enjoyed an influence at the Ottoman Porte that would have made representatives of other powers tremble, in which case they would assuredly have sought his favor and anticipated his desires. On the contrary, however, Jussuf Pasha, the aga of the Janissaries who succeeded Baltaji Mehemet as vizier, held—just like his predecessor—very definite opinions concerning Charles's behavior. Far from serving him, he thought only of ridding himself of a dangerous guest, and when Charles XII's confidant and companion Poniatowsky came to pay him his respects on his new dignity, Jussuf told him: "I warn you, infidel, that at the first plot you attempt to hatch, I will have you thrown into the sea with a rock tied to your neck."

This compliment, which Count Poniatowsky himself reports in an account that he wrote at my urging, leaves no doubt at all concerning Charles XII's slender influence at the Porte. Everything Nordberg relates with respect to Turkish affairs bears the stamp of an impassioned and misinformed man. Among errors due to blind prejudice and among political falsehoods must be classified all his unfounded allegations about the so-called corruption of a Grand Vizier, i.e., of a man who had at his disposal more than sixty million per annum[3] without being accountable to anyone. I still have in my possession the letter that Count Poniatowsky wrote to King Stanislas immediately following the Peace of the Pruth. He blames Baltaji Mehemet for his antipathy to the king of Sweden, his distaste for war, and his pliancy, but is most careful not to accuse him of corruption. He was too well informed about the position of Grand Vizier to think that the czar might have been able to set a price on the treason of a viceroy of the Ottoman Empire.

Shafirov and Sheremeteyev, who were hostages in Constantinople, were not treated at all as they would have been if convicted of purchasing peace and deceiving the sultan as the vizier's accomplices. They remained at liberty in the city, escorted by two companies of Janissaries.

Ambassador Tolstoy emerged from the Seven Towers immediately after the Treaty of the Pruth, and the British and Dutch ministers acted as go-betweens with the new vizier to ensure that its articles were honored.

Azov had finally been restored to the Turks, and the fortresses specified in the treaty were being demolished. Although the Ottoman Porte rarely becomes involved in disputes between Christian monarchs, on this occasion it was gratified to find itself the arbiter between Russia, Poland, and the king of Sweden. It wanted the czar to withdraw his troops from Poland, and to deliver Turkey from so dangerous a neighbor; it longed for Charles to return home, so that the Christian kings would continue to be divided, but it never had any intention of providing Charles with an army. The Tartars still desired war, in the same way that artisans wish to practice their lucrative trades. The Janissaries wanted it, but out of pride, hatred for the Christians, and love of lawlessness rather than for any other reasons. However, the negotiations carried out by the British and Dutch ambassadors prevailed against the opposition party. The Treaty of the Pruth was ratified, but in its new form there was an additional clause to the effect that the czar would within three months withdraw all his troops from Poland, and that the Turkish emperor would send Charles XII about his business forthwith.

One may judge from this new pact whether or not the king of Sweden enjoyed as much influence at the Porte as we have been told. He was obviously sacrificed by the new vizier, Jussuf Pasha, just as he had been by Baltaji Mehemet. His historians have no other expedient to conceal this latest affront than to accuse Jussuf of having been bribed, just like his predecessor. Imputations of this sort, so often reiterated without proof, are far more likely to be the outcry of an impotent cabal than the testimony of history. Party prejudice, obliged to admit the facts, alters their circumstances and causes; and it is thus, unhappily, that every contemporary history comes down adulterated to posterity, which can scarcely distinguish truth from falsehood.

Chapter 3
Marriage of the Czarevich, and Solemn Proclamation of Peter's Marriage to Catherine, Who Recognizes Her Brother.

The ill-starred Pruth campaign did more damage to the czar than the Battle of Narva, for after Narva he had succeeded in turning his very defeat to account, making good all his losses, and taking Ingria away from Charles XII. But after the Treaty of Faleshty with the sultan, which cost him his harbors and fortresses on the Sea of Azov, he had to give up his dominion over the Black Sea. Yet he still retained fairly ample scope for his ventures. All his establishments in Russia remained to be perfected, his victories over Sweden were still to be pursued, King Augustus had to be propped up in Poland, and his allies needed to be treated with kid gloves. Hardships had damaged his health, and he had to take the waters of Carlsbad in Bohemia, but even as he was doing so, he was ordering an attack on Pomerania, Stralsund was being blockaded, and five small towns were captured.

Pomerania is the most northerly province of Germany, bounded on the east by Prussia and Poland, on the west by Brandenburg, on the south by Mecklenburg, and on the north by the Baltic Sea. It had virtually changed masters with each succeeding century. Gustavus Adolphus seized it during the famous Thirty Years' War, and eventually it was formally transferred to Sweden by the Treaty of Westphalia,[1] with the exception of the diocese of Kamminke and a few small fortresses located in Farther Pomerania. The whole province ought by rights to have belonged to the elector of Brandenburg, under the terms of dynastic settlements made with the dukes of Pomerania. The line of dukes had died out in 1637; consequently, by Imperial law, the House of Brandenburg had a manifest right to this province, but in the Treaty of Osnabrück[2] the supreme law, necessity, prevailed over family settlements, and ever since almost the whole of Pomerania had been the prize of Swedish valor.

The czar's plan was to strip the Swedish crown of every province it possessed in the Empire. In order to carry out this scheme, he had to form an alliance with the electors of Brandenburg and Hanover, and with Denmark. Peter himself wrote every clause of his contemplated treaty with these powers, and every detail of the operations required to gain control of Pomerania.

In the meantime, on October 25, 1711, in Torgau, he married his son Alexei to the princess of Wolfenbüttel, sister of the empress of Austria, Charles VI's wife, a fateful marriage which was to cost both bride and groom their lives.

The czarevich had been born of Peter's first marriage, with Evdokiya Lopukhina, whom he married, as we have seen, in 1689. She was later confined in a convent at Suzdal. Her son, Alexei Petrovich, born March 1, 1690, was now in his twenty-second year. The prince was not yet known in Europe. An ambassador whose memoirs on the court of Russia have been published[3] says, in a letter written to his master and dated August 25, 1711, that "the prince was tall and handsome, with a strong resemblance to his father, was kindhearted and very devout, had read the Holy Scriptures five times and took great delight in reading ancient Greek history; the ambassador found the prince knowledgeable and quick-witted, a mathematician well versed in warfare, navigation, and the science of hydraulics; he knew German and was learning French, but his father had never wanted him to do what they call his military training."

This is very different from the portrait the czar himself painted of his hapless son some time later. We shall see with what pain his father reproached Alexei with all the shortcomings contrary to the good qualities the ambassador admired in him.

It is for posterity to choose between a foreigner, who may be judging without due reflection or else flattering Alexei's character, and a father who believed it his duty to sacrifice his natural feelings for the good of his empire. If the minister was no better acquainted with Alexei's mind than with his physical appearance, his testimony carries little weight. He states that the prince was tall and handsome, whereas the documents I have received from Saint Petersburg say that he was neither.

His stepmother Catherine was not present at the wedding, for, although she was regarded as the czarina, she was not officially acknowledged as such, and the title of "Highness" by which she was addressed at the czar's court gave her too equivocal a rank to sign the marriage contract and to allow German protocol to accord her a place befitting her dignity as Czar Peter's spouse. She was then at Thorn in Polish Prussia. The czar first sent the newlyweds (January, 1712) off to Wolfenbüttel and shortly thereafter conducted the czarina back to Saint Petersburg as swiftly and as unostentatiously as usual.

Having arranged his son's marriage, he made a more solemn proclamation of his own, celebrating it in Saint Petersburg (February 19, 1712). The ceremony was as majestic as it could be in a newly created land, and at a period when finances were unbalanced by the war waged against the Turks and the war they were still fighting against the king of Sweden. The czar singlehandedly organized the festivities, working on them in person as he was wont to do. And so Catherine was publicly acknowledged as czarina, as a reward for having saved her husband and his army.

The acclamations that greeted the marriage in Saint Petersburg were sincere, and yet a subject's applause for the actions of an absolute monarch is always suspect. But the applause was confirmed by every sensible person in Europe, who observed with pleasure on the one hand the heir to that vast monarchy, with no reputation save that of his birth, married to a princess, and on the other—practically at the same time—a victorious legislator publicly sharing his bed and his throne with a nobody taken prisoner at Marienburg, who possessed nothing but her own merit. That approbation has become more general as we have become more enlightened through the wholesome philosophy that has taken such strides during the last forty years, a sublime and circumspect philosophy that teaches us to show only outward deference to every kind of greatness and power, reserving true respect for ability and services rendered.

I must now faithfully relate what I find concerning this marriage in the dispatches of Count Bassevitz, Aulic Councilor at Vienna[4] and long ambassador of Holstein to the court of Russia. He was a worthy man, upright and guileless, whose memory is still cherished in Germany. This is what he says in his letters: "The czarina had been indispensable not only to Peter's fame but also to the preservation of his life. The monarch was unhappily subject to painful convulsions, which were thought to be the effects of a poison given him in his youth. Catherine alone had discovered the secret of alleviating his sufferings by the painstaking care and infinite solicitude of which she alone was capable, and she devoted herself exclusively to the preservation of Peter's health, which was as precious to the state as it was to herself. As a result, the czar, unable to live without her, made her the companion of his bed and his throne." I confine myself to citing Count Bassevitz's own words.

Fortune, which in that part of the world produced so many scenes extraordinary to our eyes, and which raised the empress Catherine from degradation and hardship to the highest degree of eminence, once again served her in a remarkable fashion several years after the celebration of her marriage.

Here is what I find in the curious manuscript of a man then in the service of the czar, who speaks as an eyewitness:

An envoy from King Augustus to the czar's court, returning to Dresden through Courland, overheard in a tavern an apparently poverty-stricken man getting the insulting reception which this state all too often evokes from others. The irritated stranger said that they wouldn't treat him this way if he could contrive to be presented to the czar, in whose court he would possibly find more powerful protectors than one might think.

King Augustus's envoy, overhearing this speech, was interested enough to question the man, and, on receiving several vague replies, looked at him more attentively and believed that he discerned in his features some resemblance to the empress. When he was back in Dresden, he could not refrain from writing about this to one of his friends in Saint Petersburg. The letter fell into the hands of the czar, who instructed Prince Repnin, governor of Riga, to try and discover the man mentioned in the letter. Prince Repnin dispatched a confidential agent to Mitau in Courland. The man was found. His name was Karl Skavronsky, and he was the son of a Lithuanian gentleman killed in the Polish wars, leaving two infants—a boy and a girl—in the cradle. Neither of them had had any education, except such as may be received from nature during a period of universal neglect. Skavronsky, separated from his sister in his earliest childhood, knew only that she had been captured at Marienburg in 1704 and believed her to be still with Prince Menshikov, in whose company he thought that she had done fairly well for herself.

Prince Repnin, obeying his master's orders to the letter, had Skavronsky brought to Riga on some trumped-up charge or other. A form of legal proceeding was instituted against him, and he was sent closely guarded to Saint Petersburg, with instructions that he was to be well looked after en route.

When he reached Saint Petersburg, they took him to the house of one of the czar's majordomos, named Sheplev. The majordomo, who had been rehearsed in the role he was to play, acquired a good deal of information about the man's condition in life, telling him at last that the charge brought against him at Riga was very serious, but that he would get a fair hearing, that he would have to present a petition to His Majesty, that this petition would be drawn up in his name, and that arrangements would be made for him to deliver it in person.

The following day, the czar went to dine at Sheplev's house, and Skavronsky was presented to him. Peter asked him a lot of questions and was finally convinced, because of the artlessness of his answers, that he was the czarina's own brother. Both of them had been in Livonia during their childhood. All of Skavronsky's replies to the czar's questions were consistent with what his wife had told him of her birth and the misfortunes of her early life.

The czar, no longer in any doubt as to the truth of the matter, suggested to his wife the next day that she should have dinner with him at Sheplev's house. On rising from the table, he sent for the man he had questioned the day before, who came in the clothes he had worn on his journey, since the czar did not want him to appear in a different state from that to which his ill luck had accustomed him.

Peter questioned the man again, in his wife's presence. The manuscript relates that finally he spoke these very words to her: "This is your brother; come along, Karl, kiss the Empress's hand, and then embrace your sister."[5]

The author of the story adds that the empress swooned, and that when she had regained consciousness the czar said: "It's all perfectly simple; this gentleman is my brother-in-law. If he is deserving, we'll make something of him; if he isn't, we won't."

It is my opinion that these words reveal as much greatness as simplicity, and that such greatness is exceedingly uncommon. The author tells us that Skavronsky stayed with Sheplev a long while, that he was awarded a considerable pension, and that he lived a very secluded life. He does not pursue the story of this adventure, which serves simply to disclose Catherine's ancestry. However, it is known from other sources that Skavronsky was created a count, married a girl of good family, and had two daughters who were married to leading Russian noblemen. I leave it to the few persons who may be cognizant of these details to unravel the truth of the tale from what may have been added to it. The author of the manuscript does not appear to have narrated these facts with a view to spinning marvelous fictions for his readers, since his memoir was not intended to see the light of day. He writes naïvely to a friend what he claims to have seen. He may be mistaken as to certain particulars, but the basic narrative rings very true, for if Skavronsky had known that he was the brother of so eminent a personage, he would never have waited so many years to reveal himself. The actual recognition, strange though it may appear, is not so extraordinary as the rise of Catherine. Both are striking affirmations of destiny, and may well serve to make us suspend our judgment when we label as legends so many events of ancient times, events which are perhaps less contrary to the common run of things than the entire history of the empress of Russia.

The festivities held by Peter for his son's marriage and his own were not ephemeral entertainments that drain the treasury and are soon forgotten. He completed the cannon foundry and the admiralty offices; highways were improved; new ships were built and canals were dug; the stock exchange and state warehouses were finished, and the maritime commerce of Saint Petersburg began to flourish. He commanded that the Senate of Moscow be transferred to Saint Petersburg, which was accomplished in the month of April, 1712. The new city became ipso facto the capital of the empire. Several Swedish prisoners were employed in embellishing the city, whose foundation was the fruit of their defeat.

Chapter 4
Capture of Stettin. Invasion of Finland.
Events of 1712.

Peter was happy in his domestic affairs, his administration, his wars with Charles XII, and his negotiations with the sovereigns who wished to drive the Swedes from the Continent and contain them forever in the Scandinavian peninsula. Forgetting the Sea of Azov and the Black Sea, he now concentrated exclusively on the western coasts of northern Europe. The keys of Azov, which had long been denied the pasha who was supposed to enter the fortress in the name of the Grand Seignior, had at last been given up, and in spite of all Charles XII's efforts, in spite of all the machinations of his supporters at the Ottoman court, in spite even of several indications that a new war might break out, Russia and Turkey were at peace.

Charles XII still stayed obstinately on at Bender, letting his fortune and his hopes depend upon the whim of a Grand Vizier, while the czar threatened all his provinces, armed Denmark and Hanover against him, had Prussia on the verge of declaring against Sweden, and reawakened Poland and Saxony.

Charles now displayed against his distant enemies, united to crush him, the same unbending pride he used in his dealings with the Porte, on which he was dependent. From the depths of his retreat in the Bessarabian wilderness, he defied the czar, the kings of Poland, Denmark, and Prussia, the elector of Hanover—soon to become king of England[1]—and the Austrian Emperor, to whom he had so often given offense when passing through Silesia as a conqueror. The Emperor took his revenge by abandoning Charles to his adversity and by affording no protection to the territories Sweden still possessed in the Empire.

It would have been an easy matter to disperse the league being formed against him. He had merely to cede Stettin to Frederick, elector of Brandenburg and first king of Prussia, who had a very legitimate claim to this part of Pomerania, but Charles did not consider Prussia to be a leading power. Neither he nor anyone else could have foreseen that the Electorate of Brandenburg and the little kingdom of Prussia, which was practically uninhabited, would one day become formidable. He refused to agree to any setlement, and, determined to break rather than bend, ordered resistance on all sides, by land and sea. His territories were virtually drained of men and money, and yet he was obeyed. The Senate at Stockholm fitted out a fleet of thirteen men-of-war, the local militias were armed, and every citizen became a soldier. Charles XII's courage and pride seemed to invigorate all his subjects, who were almost as badly off as their master.

It is hard to believe that Charles had any methodical policy. He still had a following in Poland, which, with the aid of the Crimean Tartars, was capable of devastating that unhappy country, though not of restoring King Stanislas to the throne. His hopes of inciting the Ottoman Porte to uphold this faction and of proving to the Divan that it ought to send two hundred thousand men to his aid on the grounds that the czar was defending his ally Augustus in Poland were chimerical.

He was still in Bender, awaiting the outcome of his many fruitless schemes, while the Russians, Danes, and Saxons were already in Pomerania. Peter took his wife with him on this campaign. The king of Denmark had taken possession of Stade, a coastal city of the Duchy of Bremen (September, 1712), and the Russian, Saxon, and Danish armies were besieging Stralsund.

It was at this point (October, 1712) that King Stanislas, seeing the lamentable state of so many provinces, the impossibility of his ever reascending the Polish throne, and the utter confusion caused by Charles XII's obdurate absence, summoned the Swedish generals defending Pomerania with Sweden's last and only resource in the area, an army of ten or eleven thousand men.

He proposed an accommodation with King Augustus, and offered himself as a sacrifice. He addressed the generals in French. Here are his very words, for he left behind a copy of the text signed by nine of them, one of whom happened to be a Patkul and first cousin to the unfortunate Patkul broken on the wheel by Charles's command:

"I have till now served as an instrument of the glory of Swedish arms; I do not intend to be the fatal cause of their ruin. I declare my readiness to sacrifice my crown^2 and my own interests to preserve the sacred person of King Charles, since I can see no other human means of inducing him to leave the place where he now resides."

When he had made this announcement, Stanislas prepared to leave for Turkey, in the hope of swaying his obdurate benefactor, and of touching him by his sacrifice. His ill luck caused him to arrive in Bessarabia at precisely the same time that Charles, who had promised the sultan that he would leave his refuge and who had accepted the money and escort necessary for his return home, instead persisted in remaining and defying the Turks and Tartars. Against an entire army, aided only by his household staff, he fought that ill-starred Battle of Bender where the Turks, who could easily have killed him, contented themselves with taking him prisoner. Stanislas, arriving at this curious conjuncture, was himself arrested, and so two Christian kings were at one and the same time held captive in Turkey.

At this point, when all Europe was in a turmoil and France was concluding, against one part of Europe, a no less murderous war to place Louis XIV's grandson on the Spanish throne, England made peace with France, and Marshal de Villars's victory at Denain in Flanders saved the state from its other enemies. For a century, France had been Sweden's ally; it was essential that her ally not be deprived of her possessions in the Empire. Charles, too far away in Bender, did not yet know what was happening in France.

The regency in Stockholm ventured to ask the impoverished French for money at a time when Louis XIV lacked the wherewithal to pay even his own household. The regency dispatched a Count Sparre on a mission which was doomed to failure. Sparre came to Versailles and put it to the marquis de Torci that his government was quite unable to pay the small Swedish army that Charles XII still had in Pomerania—an army about to disperse for want of money—that France's sole ally was on the point of losing territories whose preservation was vital to the general balance of power, that the victorious Charles XII had, to be sure, overly neglected the king of France, but that Louis XIV's magnanimity was as great as Charles's present misfortunes. The French minister pointed out to the Swede France's inability to help his master, and Sparre lost all hope of success.

A private citizen of Paris accomplished what Sparre had despaired of achieving. There was a Parisian banker named Samuel Bernard who had amassed a colossal fortune, as much from government remittances to foreign countries as from his other enterprises. He was a man intoxicated by a kind of pride most uncommon in one of his profession. He had a passion for everything prestigious, and knew that sooner or later France paid back with advantage what had been hazarded in its behalf. Sparre went to dine with him and flattered him, and on rising from the table the banker handed him six hundred thousand francs, after which Bernard went to the marquis de Torci and told him: "I have given Sweden two hundred thousand crowns[3] in your name; pay me back when you can."

Count Stenbock, commander of Charles's army in Pomerania, did not expect such relief. He saw his troops on the verge of mutiny, and, with nothing but promises to give them, watching the storm gathering about him and fearing encirclement by three armies of Russians, Danes, and Saxons, he requested a truce. He judged that Stanislas was about to abdicate, that he could sway the imperious Charles XII, and that at the very least he must gain some time and save his troops by negotiations. He accordingly sent a courier to the king at Bender to describe the deplorable condition on his finances, his affairs, and his troops and to inform him that Stenbock was compelled to seek this armistice and would be fortunate to obtain it. The courier had only been gone three days, and Stanislas had not yet left Pomerania, when Stenbock received the two hundred thousand crowns from the Parisian banker (December 9, 1712), in those days a stupendous treasure for a bankrupt nation. Fortified by this universal remedy, he found himself in command of twelve thousand soldiers,[4] and, rejecting any notion of a truce, now wanted only to fight.

It was Stenbock who, after the defeat at Poltava in 1710, had taken Sweden's revenge on Denmark during a Danish incursion into Scania. He had counterattacked with simple militiamen who had only ropes for bandoliers and had won a total victory. Like all of Charles XII's generals, he was energetic and bold, but his valor was tarnished by his ferocity. It was he who, after an action fought against the Russians, gave orders that all prisoners were to be killed, then caught sight of a pro-czarist Polish officer clinging to King Stanislas's stirrup. That monarch had flung his arms around the Pole in order to save his life, but Stenbock killed him with a pistol shot even as Stanislas was holding him, as is related in my life of Charles XII,[5] and King Stanislas has told this author that had he not been restrained by respect and gratitude toward the king of Sweden, he would have cracked Stenbock's skull.

General Stenbock, then, advanced along the Wismar road against the combined forces of the Russians, Saxons, and Danes. He found himself face to face with the Danish and Saxon armies, while the Russians were still three leagues behind them. The czar dispatched three couriers one after the other to the king of Denmark, begging him to wait and warning him of the risk he would run if he fought the Swedes without superior numbers. The king of Denmark was reluctant to share the honors of a victory that he believed assured. He advanced on the Swedes and attacked them near a place called Gadebusch. The intense natural hostility between the Swedes and Danes was once more seen that day. The officers of the two nations fought one another relentlessly and fell dead, riddled with wounds.

Stenbock gained the victory before the Russians could come within range of the battlefield. A few days later, he received a reply from his royal master condemning any idea of a truce. Charles wrote that he would forgive this disgraceful step only in the event that it was atoned for, and that, strong or weak, Sweden must either conquer or perish. Stenbock had already anticipated this order by his victory.

However, it was similar to the one which had momentarily consoled King Augustus when, in the course of his own calamities, he defeated the Swedes—victorious everywhere else—at the Battle of Kalicz. The victory of Kalicz served only to aggravate Augustus's woes, and the

Battle of Gadebusch merely postponed the ruin of Stenbock and his army.

On learning of Stenbock's victory, the king of Sweden believed that his affairs were restored; he even deluded himself that he could persuade the Ottoman Empire, which was again threatening the czar with war, actually to go to war, and in this hope ordered General Stenbock to move into Poland, still in the belief that at the smallest success the time of Narva—when he was dictating terms—would come again. Such notions were shortly afterward dispelled by the Bender affair and his imprisonment among the Turks.

The single outcome of the victory of Gadebusch consisted in reducing to ashes one night the little city of Altona, with its population of tradesmen and manufacturers, a defenseless city that, never having taken up arms, ought not to have been sacrificed. It was totally destroyed. Several of its citizens perished in the flames, while others, who had escaped naked from the fire—old men, women, and children—expired of cold and exhaustion at the gates of Hamburg.[6] Such has frequently been the fate of thousands of people through the quarrels of two men. This dreadful advantage was Stenbock's sole gain. The Russians, Danes, and Saxons pursued him so hotly after his victory that he was forced to ask for asylum for himself and his army in the fortress of Tønning in Holstein.

Holstein was then one of the most devastated countries in the North, and its sovereign one of the most unfortunate of princes. He was Charles XII's own nephew, and it was for the sake of his father, the king's brother-in-law, that Charles had carried the war right into Copenhagen before the Battle of Narva and had made the Treaty of Travendal, by which the dukes of Holstein regained their rights.

Part of this land is the cradle of the Cimbrians and of those ancient Normans who conquered Neustria in France[7] as well as the whole of England, Naples, and Sicily. In our day, it would be impossible to find a nation less likely to make conquests than this part of the ancient Cimbrian Chersonesus. It comprises two small duchies: Schleswig, which belongs to the king of Denmark and the duke of Holstein in common; and Gottorp, which belongs to the duke alone. Schleswig is a sovereign principality; Holstein is part of the Austrian Empire, which we term the Roman Empire.

The king of Denmark and the duke of Holstein-Gottorp were kinsmen, but the duke, Charles XII's nephew and heir presumptive, was the born enemy of the king, who persecuted the youth. The bishop of Lübeck, administrator of the hapless ward's domains and one of his father's brothers, found himself between the Swedish army, which he dared not assist, and the menacing Russian, Danish, and Saxon armies.

Nevertheless, he had to attempt to save Charles XII's troops without displeasing the king of Denmark, now master of Holstein, whose resources he was eating up.

The bishop-regent of Holstein was completely under the influence of the famous Baron von Görtz,[8] the most subtle and enterprising of men and possessor of an all-embracing and highly resourceful intellect, who never found anything either too daring or too difficult. He was as ingratiating a diplomat as he was audacious a schemer, pleasing and persuasive and able to sweep people along by the warmth of his genius after winning them over by his smooth eloquence. He later gained over Charles XII the same ascendancy that kept the bishop-regent of Holstein in thrall, and we know that the honor he enjoyed of managing the most inexorably self-willed sovereign who ever sat on a throne ultimately cost him his head.[9]

Görtz had secret talks with Stenbock[10] at Husum and promised him that he would hand over the fortress of Tønning without compromising his master the bishop-regent (January 21, 1713). At the same time, he gave assurances to the king of Denmark that it would *not* be surrendered. Nearly all diplomacy is conducted in this fashion, affairs of state being of a different order from those of private citizens. The honor of ministers consists solely in success, while that of individuals lies in keeping their word.

Stenbock appeared in front of Tønning, and the commandant of the garrison refused to open the gates for him. The king of Denmark was thus in no position to complain of the bishop-regent, while Görtz issued an order in the name of the duke—then a minor—to let the Swedish army enter Tønning. The cabinet secretary, one Stamke, signed the duke of Holstein's name, and Görtz thereby merely compromised a child who did not as yet have the power to issue orders in his own name. At one and the same time he was serving the king of Sweden, on whom he wanted to make a good impression, and his master the bishop-regent, who ostensibly had not consented to the admission of the Swedish army. The commandant of Tønning, who was easily won over, surrendered the town to the Swedes, and Görtz vindicated himself as best he might with the king of Denmark, protesting that everything had been done over his objections.

The Swedish army,[11] part of which had withdrawn within the city and the rest beneath the city's guns, was not saved for all of that. General Stenbock was obliged to surrender together with eleven thousand men, just as some sixteen thousand had surrendered after Poltava.

It was stipulated that Stenbock, his officers and men could be either ransomed or exchanged, Stenbock's ransom being assessed at eight thousand Imperial crowns. This is no very great sum, yet it could not be found, and Stenbock remained in captivity in Copenhagen until his death.

The state of Holstein was left at the mercy of an angry victor. As a reward for Görtz's misuse of his name, the young duke was subjected to the king of Denmark's vengeance. Charles XII's ill luck afflicted his entire family.

Görtz, seeing his projects melt away, but still busily playing a major role among the confusion, returned to his original idea of establishing neutrality in those Imperial territories held by Sweden.

The king of Denmark was about to enter Tønning. George, elector of Hanover, wanted the duchies of Bremen and Verden, together with the city of Stade. Frederick William, the new king of Prussia, was casting an eye on Stettin. Peter I was making ready to take over Finland. All of Charles XII's possessions outside Sweden were prizes that his adversaries were planning to divide up among themselves. How were so many special interests to be reconciled with neutrality? Görtz carried on simultaneous negotiations with all the monarchs who had a stake in the division of spoils, dashing day and night from one province to the next. He urged the governor of Bremen and Verden to arrange for the elector of Hanover to sequester these two duchies to prevent the Danes from seizing them. He worked to such good purpose that he induced the king of Prussia to assume joint responsibility with Holstein for the sequestration of Stettin and Wismar, in return for which the king of Denmark would leave Holstein in peace and not enter Tønning. Putting Charles's strongholds into the hands of those who might well keep them forever was, to be sure, a strange way of rendering him a service, but Görtz, by delivering these cities as hostages, compelled them to neutrality, at least for some time. His hope was that he would later be able to make Hanover and Brandenburg declare in favor of Sweden. He won agreement with his views from the king of Poland, whose ruined domains needed peace. In a word, he desired to make himself indispensable to every monarch. He disposed of Charles XII's possessions like a guardian sacrificing part of a ruined and incapable ward's property in order to save the rest. And all this without any authority, with no other guarantee for his conduct than plenipotentiary powers granted by a bishop of Lübeck, who himself had not the slightest authorization from Charles XII.

Such was Görtz, who till now has been insufficiently known. We have seen prime ministers of great nations, an Oxenstierna, a Richelieu, or an Alberoni, cause upheavals in various parts of Europe; but that on his own authority the privy councilor of a bishop of Lübeck should have accomplished as much as they is something unheard of.

To begin with, he was successful. He made a treaty with the king of Prussia (June, 1713), whereby that monarch undertook, while keeping Stettin sequestered, to preserve the rest of Pomerania for Charles XII. Under the terms of this treaty, Görtz proposed to Governor Meyerfeld of Pomerania that he should yield the fortress of Stettin to the king of Prussia for the good of the peace, thinking that the Swedish governor of Stettin might be as easy to deal with as the Holsteiner governor of Tønning. But Charles XII's officers were not in the habit of obeying such orders. Meyerfeld replied that Stettin would be entered only over his dead body and its own ruins, and informed his master of this strange proposal. The messenger found Charles XII a captive at Timurtash after his adventure at Bender. It was not then known whether Charles would remain a prisoner of the Turks all his life, or if he would be exiled to some island of the Archipelago[12] or of Asia Minor. From his prison, Charles sent Meyerfeld the same instructions he had sent Stenbock, namely that he must die rather than give way to the enemy, and he ordered him to be as unyielding as he was himself.

Görtz, who saw the governor of Stettin upsetting his plans by refusing to listen to any talk of neutrality or sequestration, took it into his head to sequester not only the city of Stettin, but Stralsund as well, and he found a way to conclude with the king of Poland and elector of Saxony the same agreement for Stralsund that he had made with the elector of Brandenburg for Stettin. He saw clearly that the Swedes were powerless to hold on to these places without money and without an army, while their king was a prisoner in Turkey, and he expected to remove the scourge of war from the whole of the North by means of these sequestrations. Denmark itself finally became a party to Görtz's diplomacy. He completely won over Prince Menshikov, the czar's general and favorite, and persuaded him that Holstein could be ceded to his master. He delighted the czar with the notion of digging a canal from Holstein to the Baltic—an idea thoroughly in keeping with that founder's own inclinations. Peter was particularly taken with the idea of obtaining new power by consenting to become one of the princes of the Austrian Empire, and by acquiring at the Diets of Ratisbon the right to vote, which could always be upheld by the right of arms.

No one could be more pliant in more ways, assume more different shapes, or play more roles than this determined diplomat. Görtz went so far as to incite Prince Menshikov to destroy the city of Stettin, which he wanted to save, by shelling it, so as to force Commandant Meyerfeld to place it in sequestration, and he thus dared to outrage the king of Sweden, whom he wished to please, and whom indeed—unfortunately for himself—he afterward pleased only too well.

When the king of Prussia saw a Russian army bombarding Stettin, he was afraid that the city was lost to him and would now belong to Russia, which was precisely when Görtz pounced on him. Prince Menshikov was short of money; Görtz persuaded the king of Prussia to lend him four hundred thousand crowns. Next he sent word to the governor of Stettin. The message read: "Would you rather see Stettin in ashes and under Russian control, or would you rather entrust it to the king of Prussia, who will return it to your royal master?" The commandant was finally prevailed upon to surrender. Menshikov entered the stronghold and, on payment of the four hundred thousand crowns, handed it over, along with all the territory adjoining, to the king of Prussia, who, for the sake of form, permitted two Holsteiner battalions to enter it, but never returned this part of Pomerania to Charles XII.

Subsequently, the second king of Prussia, successor to a weak and spendthrift monarch, laid the foundations of the greatness that his country later attained thanks to military discipline and frugality.

Baron von Görtz, who pulled so many strings, was unsuccessful in persuading the Danes either to pardon the province of Holstein or to relinquish possession of Tønning. He failed in what was ostensibly his prime objective but was successful in everything else, and particularly in becoming a person of consequence in the North, which was in fact his principal goal.

The elector of Hanover had already made sure of Bremen and Verden, of which Charles XII had been dispossessed; the Saxons were encamped in front of his city of Wismar; Stettin was in the king of Prussia's hands (September, 1713); the Russians were about to besiege Stralsund in company with the Saxons, and the latter were already on the Isle of Rügen. In the middle of all these negotiations, the czar had invaded Finland, while elsewhere everyone was arguing about neutrality and partition. Having personally trained his artillery on Stralsund and left the rest up to Prince Menshikov and his allies, he had embarked in the month of May on the Baltic Sea, and, boarding a fifty-gun ship built by himself at Saint Petersburg, he set sail for Finland, followed by ninety-two galleys and one hundred and ten half-galleys, which were carrying sixteen thousand soldiers.

The incursion took place at Helsingfors (May 22, 1713), in the southernmost region of that cold and barren land, on the sixty-first degree of latitude.

The invasion succeeded despite every obstacle. The Russians made a feint at one spot and came ashore at another. Troops were disembarked and the city was taken. The czar took possession of Borgå and Turku[13] and gained control of the entire coastline. The Swedes were apparently at the end of their resources, for it was at that very moment that the Swedish army commanded by Stenbock was taken prisoner.

All of these disasters suffered by Charles XII were followed, as we have seen, by the loss of Bremen, Verden, Stettin, and part of Pomerania, and, to crown everything, King Stanislas and Charles himself were prisoners in Turkey. Nevertheless, Charles still clung to the idea of returning to Poland at the head of an Ottoman army, of restoring Stanislas to the throne, and of making all his enemies tremble.

Chapter 5
Peter the Great's Triumphs.
Charles XII's Return.

As was his wont after winning victories, Peter improved his naval establishment, settled twelve thousand families in Saint Petersburg, and kept all his allies loyal to his fortunes and to himself personally, despite their varied interests and opposing viewpoints. His fleet was even then threatening the entire Swedish coastline along the Gulfs of Finland and Bothnia.

One of his army commanders, Prince Golitsyn, who had been trained by Peter as they all had, advanced from Helsingfors, where the czar had disembarked, into the hinterland, toward the township of Tavastehus, an outpost protecting Bothnia. A few Swedish regiments, with eight thousand militiamen, were defending it. Battle was unavoidable, and the Russians won a total victory (March 13, 1714). They routed the Swedish force and pushed on as far as Vaasa, with the result that they now controlled eighty leagues of territory.[1]

The Swedes still maintained a fleet at sea. For a long while Peter had been eager to draw attention to the navy he had created. He set out from Saint Petersburg and assembled a fleet of sixteen ships of the line plus one hundred and eighty galleys suitable for maneuvering through the rocks around the Isle of Åland and the other Baltic islands not far from the Swedish coast, near which he encountered the enemy squadrons. The Swedish force was superior to the Russians in large men-of-war but had fewer galleys. It was better suited to fighting in the open sea than in rocky waters. Here was an advantage that Peter owed to his own unaided genius. He was serving in the fleet with the rank of rear admiral, subordinate to Admiral Apraxin. Peter wanted to seize the Isle of Åland, a mere twelve leagues from Sweden. It was necessary to sail past in full view of the Swedish ships. This daring maneuver was executed with the galleys opening the way under the enemy guns, which were unable to fire at so low an angle. The Russians landed on Åland, and as the coast is practically an unbroken chain of reefs, the czar had eighty small galleys portaged across a spit of land and refloated in the sea called the Hango, where his large vessels were waiting. Ehrenskjöld, the Swedish rear admiral, believed that he could easily capture or sink these eighty galleys and sailed up to reconnoiter, but he came under such a withering fire that nearly all his soldiers and sailors were killed. His galleys and praams[2] were captured, and so was his flagship. He made his escape in a longboat, but was wounded. Eventually he was obliged to surrender and was taken on board the galley commanded by the czar himself (August 8). The remainder of Ehrenskjöld's squadron sailed back to Sweden. There was consternation in Stockholm, where nobody thought himself safe.

At the very same time, Colonel Shuvalov Neushlov attacked the only fortress still holding out on the west coast of Finland and, in spite of the most stubborn resistance, captured it for the czar.

The battle of Aland[3] was, after Poltava, the most glorious victory of Peter's career. Master of Finland, where he left Prince Golitsyn behind as governor, vanquisher of all the Swedish naval forces, and more respected than ever by his allies, he returned to Saint Petersburg (September 15) when the weather, which had turned stormy, no longer permitted him to stay in Finnish and Bothnian waters. As an additional stroke of good luck just as he was arriving in his new capital, the czarina gave birth to a princess, who died a year later. He instituted the Order of Saint Catherine in his wife's honor and celebrated the birth of his daughter by a triumphal entry, which was, of all the celebrations to which he had accustomed his people, the one of which they had grown fondest. The fete was opened by bringing into the port of Kronslot nine Swedish galleys, seven bargeloads of prisoners, and Rear Admiral Ehrenskjöld's flagship.

The Russian flagship was laden with all the cannon, flags, and standards seized during the conquest of Finland. All of these spoils were brought to Saint Petersburg, which the Russians entered in battle array. A triumphal arch designed—as usual—by the czar himself was decorated with the emblems of all his victories, and the victors marched beneath it with Admiral Apraxin at their head, followed by the czar in his capacity of rear admiral and all the other officers in order of rank. They were presented to Viceroy Romodanovsky, who, in ceremonies of this kind, deputized for the master of the empire. The vice-czar distributed gold medals to every officer, while the common soldiers and ordinary seamen received silver ones. The Swedish prisoners passed beneath the triumphal arch, and Admiral Ehrenskjöld came directly after the victorious czar. When they reached the vice-czar's throne, Admiral Apraxin presented Rear Admiral Peter, who requested promotion to vice admiral in recognition of his services. A vote was taken, and we may well believe that every vote was in favor.

After this ceremony, which overjoyed all the bystanders and inspired everyone with emulation, love of country and of glory, the czar delivered a speech worthy of passing down to the most distant posterity:

My brothers, is there one among you who would have believed, twenty years ago, that he would be fighting at my side on the Baltic Sea in ships built by yourselves, or that we would be occupying countries conquered by our own exertions and courage? . . . The ancient seat of learning is ascribed to Greece. It then removed itself to Italy, and from Italy knowledge was diffused into every corner of Europe. Now it is our turn, if you will support my designs by joining studiousness to obedience. The arts circulate throughout the world like blood in the human body, and perhaps they will establish their empire among us on their way back to their former motherland, Greece. I venture to hope that one day we will make the most civilized nations blush because of our labors and our well-deserved glory.

This is an authentic summary of an oration worthy of a founder. It has been emasculated in all the translations, but the supreme merit of this eloquent address is that it was delivered by a victorious monarch, the founding father and lawgiver of his empire.

The older boyars listened to the speech with more regret for their ancient ways than admiration for their master's glory, but the young ones were moved to tears.

The times were likewise noteworthy because of the return of the Russian ambassadors from Constantinople bearing the ratified treaty with the Turks (December 15). Some time previously, a Persian ambassador had arrived in the name of Shah Hussein,[4] bringing the czar an elephant and five lions. At the same time he received an embassy from the khan of the Uzbeks, Mehemet Bahadir, who asked for his protection against the other Tartars. From deepest Asia and from Europe alike, all paid homage to his fame.

The regency at Stockholm, in despair over the lamentable state of affairs and the absence of the king, who had abandoned all responsibility for his country, had finally resolved to consult him no more and, immediately following the czar's naval victory, had asked the victor to issue a passport to an officer empowered to make peace proposals. The passport was sent, but in the meantime Charles XII's sister, Princess Ulrica-Eleanora, received word that her royal brother was finally making ready to leave Turkey to come home and defend himself. And so they dared not send the czar the secretly appointed negotiator. They put up with their misfortune and waited for Charles XII to appear and set things right.

And in fact, after a stay of five years and some months, Charles left Turkey toward the end of October, 1714. We know that he traveled in the same eccentric manner characteristic of all his actions. He reached Stralsund on November 22, 1714. No sooner was he there than Baron von Görtz presented himself. Görtz had been partly instrumental in Charles's troubles, but he vindicated himself so adroitly and filled the king with such high expectations that he won his confidence, just as he had won that of all the ministers and monarchs with whom he had negotiated. He gave him reason to hope that he would detach the czar from his allies and that they could then make an honorable peace, or at least fight on equal terms. From that moment on, Görtz enjoyed far more ascendancy over Charles than Count Piper ever had.

The first thing Charles did on his arrival in Stralsund was to ask the citizens of Stockholm for money. The little that they had, they sent him; it was impossible to refuse anything to a monarch who asked only in order to give, who lived as hard a life as his own common soldiers, and who risked his life as they did. Swedes and foreigners alike were moved by his misfortunes, his captivity, and his return. One could not refrain from censuring or from admiring him, from pitying him or from helping him. His fame was diametrically opposed to Peter's. It did not consist in promoting the arts, nor in legislation, nor in politics, nor in commerce. It went no further than his own person. His merit lay in a valor above and beyond ordinary courage; he fought for his domains with a greatheartedness equal to that intrepid valor, and it was enough for nations to be struck with respect for him. He had more admirers than allies.

Chapter 6
Europe at Charles XII's Return.
Siege of Stralsund, Etc.

When Charles XII finally returned to his kingdom at the end of 1714, he found Christian Europe in a very different state from that in which he had left it. Queen Anne of England had died after making peace with France, and Louis XIV was securing Spain for his grandson by forcing both the Austrian emperor Charles VI and Holland to subscribe to an unavoidable peace. All the affairs of Southern Europe were thus assuming a new complexion.

The affairs of the North were even more changed; Peter had now become their arbiter. The elector of Hanover, summoned to the throne of England, desired to enlarge his territories in Germany at the expense of Sweden, which had only acquired its German lands through the conquests of the great Gustavus Adolphus. The king of Denmark had aspirations to take back Scania, Sweden's finest province, which had formerly belonged to the Danes. The king of Prussia, heir to the dukes of Pomerania, intended to retrieve at least part of that province. On the other hand, the House of Holstein, which was oppressed by the king of Denmark, and the duke of Mecklenburg, who was almost openly at war with his own subjects, were imploring Peter I to protect them. Augustus, king of Poland and elector of Saxony, wanted Courland to be annexed to Poland, and so from the Elbe to the Baltic Peter was the protector of every monarch, whereas Charles had been their bane.

Since Charles's return, there had been much diplomacy but no progress. He believed he could acquire sufficient warships and privateers to nullify the czar's new naval power. As for land warfare, he was relying on his own courage, and Görtz, who had at one fell swoop become his prime minister, convinced him that he could defray expenses with a prodigy in the history of government, namely, a copper currency whose value was fixed at ninety-six times its real worth. But as early as April, 1715, Peter's ships captured the first Swedish privateers to put to sea, and a Russian army marched into Pomerania.

The Prussians, Danes, and Saxons joined forces before Stralsund. Charles XII perceived that he had returned from his prisons at Timurtash and Demotica on the Black Sea only to be besieged on the shores of the Baltic.

We have already seen, in the history of his life, with what proud and tranquil valor he defied in Stralsund all his foes together. I shall now simply add one minor detail that clearly delineates his character. Nearly all of Charles's senior officers having been killed or wounded during the siege, Colonel Baron von Reichel, worn out with sleepless nights and tribulations, threw himself down on a bench to take an hour's rest after a long day's fighting. He was summoned to mount guard on the ramparts, where he dragged himself, cursing the king's stubbornness and all these utterly intolerable and futile hardships. The king, overhearing him, ran up, took off his own cloak, and spread it out in front of Reichel, saying: "You are all in, my dear Reichel; I have slept for an hour, I am fresh, I will mount the guard for you. Go to sleep, I will wake you up when it's time." After these words, he wrapped him up despite his protests, let him go to sleep, and went off to mount guard.

It was during the siege of Stralsund (October, 1715) that the elector of Hanover, now king of England, bought from the king of Denmark the province of Bremen and Verden, together with the city of Stade, which the Danes had taken from Charles XII. King George paid eight hundred thousand Imperial crowns. Charles's states were thus bought and sold while he was defending Stralsund inch by inch. Eventually, when the city was no more than a heap of ruins, his officers forced him to leave (December). When he was safely away, General Dücker surrendered the ruins to the king of Prussia.

Some time later, when Dücker presented himself to Charles XII, the king upbraided him for capitulating to the enemy. Dücker replied: "I loved Your Majesty's reputation too much to do it the affront of holding out in a city from which Your Majesty had departed." Besides, the stronghold only remained in Prussian hands until 1721, when it was restored by the Peace of the North.[1]

During the siege of Stralsund, Charles endured another vexation, which would have been more grievous still had his heart been as susceptible to friendship as it was to glory. His prime minister, Count Piper, celebrated throughout Europe and ever faithful to his king (no matter what so many indiscreet authors may have written on the authority of a single misinformed colleague), Piper, I say, was his victim after the Battle of Poltava. As the Russians and Swedes had no agreement for the exchange of prisoners, Piper remained imprisoned in Moscow, and although he was not sent to Siberia like so many others, his state was a pitiable one. The czar's finances were not at that time administered as carefully as they ought to have been, and all his new institutions demanded expenditures that he had difficulty in meeting. He owed the Dutch quite a considerable sum in the matter of two of their merchantmen that had been burned off the coast of Finland. The czar claimed that it was for the Swedes to pay this amount and tried to urge Count Piper to assume responsibility for the debt. He was brought from Moscow to Saint Petersburg and offered his freedom in exchange for obtaining about sixty thousand crowns in letters of credit from Sweden. They say that he actually drew upon his wife in Stockholm for the sum, that she was neither in a position nor perhaps of a mind to give it, and that the king of Sweden took no initiative whatever to pay it. Be that as it may, Count Piper was locked up in the fortress of Schlüsselburg, where he died the following year at the age of seventy. His body was returned to the king of Sweden, who gave him a magnificent state funeral, a melancholy and vain reward for so many sorrows and such a deplorable end!

Peter was well pleased to have Livonia, Estonia, Carelia, and Ingria, which he regarded as Russian provinces, and pleased to have annexed almost the whole of Finland as well, which served as a surety in the event that a peace agreement might be forthcoming. He had married a niece to Charles-Leopold, duke of Mecklenburg, in April of the same year, with the result that all the northern princes were either his allies or his creatures. In Poland he kept King Augustus's enemies in check; one of his armies, approximately eighteen thousand strong, effortlessly dispersed all those confederacies which are constantly reviving in that land of liberty and anarchy. The Turks, finally abiding by the treaties, gave the fullest scope to his power and designs.

In this flourishing state of affairs, almost every day was marked by new institutions for the navy, the army, commerce, and legislation. He personally composed a set of military regulations for the infantry.

He founded (November 8, 1715) a naval academy at Saint Petersburg. Langa, responsible for promoting trade, departed for China by way of Siberia. Engineers were making maps all over the empire; a country house was under construction at Peterhof, and during the same period forts were erected along the Irtysh River; the freebooting of the peoples of Bukhara was checked, and in another region the Kuban Tartars were subjugated.

It seemed to be the pinnacle of good fortune that a son was born to him of his wife Catherine in the same year as an heir to his domains in the person of Prince Alexei's newborn son. But the child given him by the czarina soon died, and we shall see that Alexei's destiny was too cruel for the birth of that prince's son to be regarded as a blessing.

The czarina's confinement interrupted the journeys which she constantly made with her husband both on land and sea, but no sooner was she up and about again than she accompanied him on new travels.

Chapter 7
Wismar Captured. New Travels of the Czar.

All of the czar's allies were then besieging Wismar. This city, which should by rights belong to the duke of Mecklenburg, is situated on the Baltic seven leagues from Lübeck, whose extensive trade it might well rival, since it was formerly one of the most prosperous of the Hanseatic towns. The dukes of Mecklenburg exercised their right of patronage in Wismar far more than they did that of sovereignty. It was yet another of those German territories that had become Swedish through the Treaty of Westphalia. Wismar, like Stralsund, was finally forced to surrender. The czar's allies hurried to occupy it before his troops arrived, but Peter, having come to the place in person (February, 1716) after the capitulation, which had been effected in his absence, took the garrison prisoner. He was indignant that his allies had presented the king of Denmark with a city which should belong to a prince who had married Peter's niece,[1] and the subsequent cooling of relations, of which Prime Minister Görtz speedily took advantage, was the foundation of his proposed treaty between the czar and Charles XII.

As of that moment, Görtz gave the czar to understand that Sweden had been sufficiently humbled, and that Denmark and Prussia must not be excessively exalted. The czar agreed with his views; he had only ever waged war for political reasons, whereas Charles XII had fought purely for the sake of fighting. From that time on, Peter's actions against Sweden were merely halfhearted, while Charles XII, unlucky everywhere in Germany, determined, in one of those desperate gambles that success alone can justify, to carry the war into Norway.

Meanwhile, the czar wanted to take a second trip to Europe. He had made the first as a man desirous of learning the useful arts; he undertook the second as a monarch seeking to probe the inner workings of every European court. He took his wife to Copenhagen, Lübeck, Schwerin, and Neustadt; he met the king of Prussia in the little town of Auersberg; from there they went on to Hamburg and the city of Altona, which the Swedes had burned and which was being rebuilt. Going down the Elbe to Stade, they passed through Bremen (December 17, 1716), where the burgomaster put on a fireworks display and an illumination whose design formed in a hundred places the words: "Our liberator is coming to see us." Lastly, he revisited Amsterdam and the little cottage at Saardam where some eighteen years earlier he had learned the craft of shipbuilding. He found the cottage transformed into a pleasant and comfortable home, which stands to this day and is named the Prince's House.

We may guess with what idolatry he was received by a people of tradesmen and seafarers whose comrade he had been. They believed they saw in the victor of Poltava their former pupil, who had founded commerce and seamanship in his own country and had learned how to win naval battles in theirs; they regarded him as one of their fellow citizens who had become an emperor.

Everything about the life, travels, and deeds of Peter the Great—like those of Charles XII—appears alien to our perhaps slightly too effeminate ways, and it is for that very reason that the history of these two famous men excites our curiosity to such a degree.

The czar's spouse stayed behind in Schwerin. She was indisposed, far along in her latest pregnancy, and yet as soon as she was able to leave she wanted to rejoin the czar in Holland. Labor pains overtook her in Wesel, where (January 14, 1717) she gave birth to a prince who lived only one day. Among us it is not customary for a sick woman to travel immediately after her confinement, but six days later the czarina reached Amsterdam. She wished to see the cottage at Saardam where Peter had worked with his own hands. They went together, with no ceremony and accompanied only by two servants, to dine with a wealthy Saardam shipwright named Kalf, the first foreign trader to reach Saint Petersburg. His son had just come back from France, which was Peter's destination. The czarina and he listened with pleasure to this young man's adventure, which I would never relate did it not familiarize us with manners radically different from our own.

Kalf the shipwright had sent his son to Paris to learn French. Wanting the young man to maintain a respectable appearance, his father ordered him to take off the extremely plain garments worn by every citizen of Saardam and to incur in Paris expenses more in keeping with his fortune than his upbringing, knowing his son well enough to believe that the change would not corrupt his frugality or his wholesome nature.

In every Northern language, Kalf means "calf";[2] in Paris the traveler assumed the name "du Veau," lived in quite a magnificent style, and formed some connections. Nothing is more common in Paris than to lavish the titles of *marquis* and *count* on those who do not even possess a seignorial estate, and who are scarcely gentlemen. This ridiculous practice has always been tolerated by the government, so that with social distinctions becoming more blurred and the aristocracy brought lower, society might henceforth be secure from the once frequent outbreak of civil wars. The title of *high and mighty lord* has been usurped by persons raised to the peerage and by commoners who have paid large sums for government appointments. In brief, the names *marquis* and *count* unaccompanied by either marquisate or county—like a knight who belongs to no order of chivalry or an abbot without an abbey—are of no consequence whatever in our nation.

Kalf's friends and domestics always called him the count du Veau. He supped with princesses and played cards at the duchess of Berry's; few foreigners were more lionized. A young marquis who had participated in all his amusements promised to visit him in Saardam, and kept his word. There he found a shipwright's workshop and young Kalf dressed like a Dutch sailor, axe in hand, supervising his father's business. Kalf welcomed his guest with all the old-fashioned artlessness which he had resumed and from which he never again deviated. The wise reader may forgive this short digression, intended as it is simply to reprove vanity and to praise principle.

The czar stayed in Holland for three months. During his visit, more serious things occurred than Kalf's adventure. Since the Treaties of Nijmegen, Ryswick, and Utrecht,[5] The Hague had preserved its reputation as the center of European diplomacy. This small town, or rather village—the most agreeable in the North—was mainly populated by ministers from every nation and by travelers who came to receive instruction at their school. At that time, the foundations of a mighty European upheaval were being laid. The czar, apprised of the gathering storm, prolonged his stay in the Netherlands in order to be within sight of what was hatching in both North and South, and to make preparations for the course he himself would adopt.

Chapter 8
Continuation of Peter the Great's Travels. Görtz's Conspiracy. Peter's Reception in France.

Peter realized how jealous his allies were of his might, and how we often have more trouble with our friends than with our enemies.

Mecklenburg was one of the principal causes of those almost inevitable altercations between neighboring sovereigns dividing up conquered territories. Peter had not wanted the Danes to take Wismar for themselves, still less that they should dismantle its fortifications, and yet they had done both.

He was openly protecting the duke of Mecklenburg, his niece's husband, whom he treated as his son-in-law, against that country's nobility, who enjoyed the patronage of the king of England. And he was finally beginning to lose patience with the king of Poland, or rather with his prime minister, Count Flemming, who wished to throw off the yoke of dependence imposed by Russian assistance and power.

The courts of England, Poland, Denmark, Holstein, Mecklenburg, and Brandenburg were shaken by intrigues and cabals.

During the last part of 1716 and the beginning of 1717, Görtz, who, according to Bassevitz's memoirs, was tired of being merely a Holstein councilor and Charles XII's secret plenipotentiary, was the instigator of most of these intrigues, and he determined to exploit them in order to shake up Europe. His plan was to reconcile Charles XII and the czar, not only to put an end to the war, but to unite them, to restore Stanislas to the Polish throne, and to take Bremen and Verden—and the English crown as well—away from King George I of England, so as to leave him in no position to appropriate for himself what had been taken from Charles.

It so happened that there was at the same time another minister of Görtz's way of thinking, whose design was to overthrow both England and France. This was Cardinal Alberoni, then more dominant in Spain than Görtz was in Sweden, a man as audacious and enterprising as himself, but far more powerful, because he was at the head of a wealthier kingdom and did not pay his hirelings in copper coin.

From the shores of the Baltic, Görtz soon formed ties with the court of Madrid. Alberoni and he were equally in collusion with all the wandering Englishmen who favored the House of Stuart.[1] Görtz hurried to every nation where enemies of King George might be found, to Germany, Holland, Flanders, Lorraine, and, finally, toward the close of the year 1716, to Paris. Cardinal Alberoni began by sending one million francs to him in Paris to touch off the powder magazine, as Alberoni himself put it.

Görtz wanted Charles to make many concessions to Peter so that he could take back everything else from his enemies, and would have a free hand to invade Scotland while the Stuart faction in England showed their colors to some effect, after their many unavailing efforts. To execute these designs, it was necessary to remove the reigning king of England's greatest support, namely, the regent of France.[2] It was an extraordinary thing to see France allied with an English king against Louis XIV's grandson, placed by France herself on the Spanish throne at the cost of her own blood and treasure,[3] and in the teeth of the many enemies in league against her. But now everything had left its accustomed path, and the regent's interests were not those of the kingdom. From that time on, Alberoni organized a conspiracy in France against the regent. The groundwork of the whole vast enterprise was laid almost as soon as the plan had been conceived. Görtz was Alberoni's first co-conspirator, and was supposed to go next to Italy, in disguise, to hold talks with the Pretender near Rome. From there he was to hurry back to The Hague to see the czar and make all the final arrangements with the king of Sweden.

The author of this present history is particularly well informed about his subject matter, since Görtz proposed that he accompany him on his travels, and since, despite his extreme youth at the time,[4] he was one of the earliest eyewitnesses of a major part of these intrigues.

Görtz had returned to Holland at the end of 1716, furnished with letters of credit from Alberoni and with plenipotentiary powers from Charles. It is beyond doubt that the Pretender's party was to rebel while Charles was invading northern Scotland from Norway. The monarch who had been unable to retain his own territories on the Continent was going to attack and overthrow those of another, and might well have left his prison at Timurtash in Turkey and the ashes of Stralsund to crown James II's son in London, just as he had crowned Stanislas in Warsaw.

The czar, who was partly informed of Görtz's venture, was waiting for it to develop without actually entering into any of his plans or knowing all about them. Peter loved what was great and extraordinary as much as Charles XII, Görtz, and Alberoni, but he loved it as the founder of a nation, a legislator, and a true statesman, whereas Alberoni, Görtz, and indeed Charles himself may have been restless men aiming for high stakes rather than shrewd ones adopting prudent measures. It is possible, however, that their lack of success has caused them to be accused of recklessness.

When Görtz reached The Hague, the czar did not see him. It would have given too much offense to his friends in the States General, who were adherents of the king of England. His ministers saw Görtz only in secret, taking the strictest precautions. They had orders to listen to every proposal and to raise his hopes without committing themselves in any way or compromising the czar. In the meantime, the clearsighted were well aware, from Peter's inaction at a time when he could have invaded Scania with his own and the Danish fleet, from his coolness toward his allies and the complaints emanating from their courts, and lastly from his journey itself, that there had been a drastic reversal in policy that would not remain a secret much longer.

In the month of January, 1717, a Swedish packet carrying mail to Holland was forced by stormy weather to put into a Norwegian port, where the mail was seized. Enough was found in the letters of Görtz and some other ministers to put the authorities on the alert regarding the incipient revolution. The Danish court conveyed the letters to the Court of Saint James, and Gyllenborg, Swedish ambassador in London, was immediately arrested. His papers were seized, and among them was discovered a part of his correspondence with the Jacobites.

King George wrote forthwith to Holland (February), demanding that, pursuant to the mutual security pacts linking England and the States General, Baron von Görtz be arrested. That minister, who had agents everywhere, was forewarned of the warrant for his arrest and departed posthaste. He was already on the frontier, at Arnhem, when the pursuing law officers, having hastened after him with a speed quite out of the ordinary for that part of the world, arrested him, manhandled him, and took possession of his papers. His secretary Stamke, the man who had forged the duke of Holstein's signature during the Tønning incident, was treated more roughly still. To conclude, Count von Gyllenborg, the Swedish envoy to England, and Baron von Görtz, the bearer of credentials naming him Charles XII's minister plenipotentiary, were interrogated like criminals, the former in London, the latter in Arnhem. Every sovereign's ambassador raised an outcry that international law had been violated.

This law, more often invoked than clearly understood, whose limit and scope have never been defined, has at all times come under heavy attack. Ambassadors have been expelled from the courts to which they were accredited and on more than one occasion have been arrested, but never till now had they been questioned as though they were subjects of the countries in which they were resident. The Court of Saint James and the States General went beyond all the rules in view of the peril threatening the House of Hanover, but when all is said and done, no sooner was the danger discovered than it ceased to be a danger, at least under the present circumstances.

The historian Nordberg must either have been sadly misinformed, most unworldly, thoroughly blinded by partiality, or at least a very self-conscious courtier to presume to persuade us that the king of Sweden was scarcely implicated in the plot at all.

The affront offered his ministers strengthened Charles's determination to stop at nothing to dethrone the king of England. Meanwhile, for once in his life he was obliged to dissimulate, and to disavow his ministers to the regent of France, who was paying him a subsidy, and to the States General, whom he wished to humor. He gave less satisfaction to King George. Görtz and Gyllenborg, his ministers, were detained for almost six months, and the duration of the outrage reinforced in him all his designs for vengeance.

Amidst so many alarums and so much mutual mistrust, Peter, totally uncommitted, waited for time to settle everything and, having organized his vast domains so well that he had nothing to fear from within or without, resolved at last to go to France. He did not understand French, and consequently lost the greatest advantage to be gained from his journey, but he thought there was much to be seen and wanted to find out at first hand what terms the regent of France was on with England and whether or not the regent was securely in power.

Peter the Great was received in France as he deserved to be. To begin with, Marshal de Tessé, with a large retinue of noblemen, a squadron of guards, and the royal carriages, was sent to meet him. As usual, Peter had traveled so fast that he was already at Gournay when the carriages arrived at Elbeuf.[5] On the road, he was feted to his heart's content. His first accommodations were at the Louvre, where the state apartments had been made ready for him and others set aside for his entourage, Prince Kurakin and Prince Dolgoruky, Vice-Chancellor Baron Shafirov, and Ambassador Tolstoy, who had endured so many breaches of international law in Turkey. The regent had intended that this entire court be sumptuously housed and served, but Peter, having come to France to see what might be useful and not to put up with futile ceremonies that inconvenienced his simplicity and wasted precious time, took lodgings that very evening at the other end of the city, in the palace or townhouse of Lesdiguières, which belongs to Marshal de Villeroi. There he was just as lavishly entertained as he would have been at the Louvre. The following day (May 8, 1717), the regent of France came to pay his respects at this mansion; the day after that they brought Peter the little king,[6] conducted by his tutor Marshal de Villeroi, whose father had been Louis XIV's tutor. The czar was artfully spared the pains of returning the call immediately. There was an interval of two days, then he received the homage of the city corporations, and that same evening visited the king. The royal household was on parade, and the young monarch was brought to the czar's carriage. Peter, astonished and dis-

turbed by the crowd thronging around the boy king, picked him up and
carried him in his arms for a while.

Some diplomats, more subtle than sagacious, have written that when
Marshal de Villeroi tried to take the king of France's hand so that the
king might take precedence, the emperor employed the above stratagem
to disrupt the ceremonial with an air of kindliness and sensibility. Such
an idea is absolutely false. French politeness, as well as what was owed
to Peter the Great, would never have permitted the honors paid him to
be turned into aversion. Etiquette consisted in doing for a great
sovereign and a great man everything he would have wished for himself,
had he taken any heed of such details. The visits to France of the
Emperors Charles IV, Sigismund, and Charles V[7] were far from enjoying a celebrity comparable to that of Peter the Great's stay. These
emperors came for purely political reasons, and did not appear at a time
when the improved state of the arts could have ensured that their journeys would be epoch-making events. But when Peter went to dine with
the duke d'Antin at the Palace of Petitbourg three leagues outside Paris
and saw, at the end of the repast, his freshly painted portrait suddenly
placed in the banqueting hall, he realized that the French knew better
than any people on earth how to entertain so worthy a guest.

The czar was even more surprised when he went to watch medals
being struck in the long gallery of the Louvre, where all the king's
artists are honorably lodged. A newly minted medal fell on the ground,
and, hastening to pick it up, he saw engraved thereon, with an emblem
of Fame placing one foot on the globe on the reverse, these words from
Virgil, so suitable to Peter the Great: *vires acquirit eundo.*[8] The allusion
was as delicate was it was noble, and equally appropriate to his travels
and his fame. He himself and all his retinue were presented with these
gold medals. Whenever he visited artists, they laid their masterpieces at
his feet and begged that he would deign to accept them; when he went
to see the Gobelin tapestry-makers, or the carpets of the Savonnerie, the
studios of the royal sculptors, painters, and goldsmiths, or the manufacturers of mathematical instruments—everything which seemed to merit
his approval was offered him by the king.

Peter was a mechanician, an artist, and a geometer. He went to the
Academy of Sciences, which paraded all its rarest treasures for him, but
there was nothing there as uncommon as himself. With his own hand,
he corrected several geographical errors in the Academy's maps of the
Russian empire, especially in that of the Caspian Sea. Finally, he conde-
scended to become a member of the Academy, and later kept up an
uninterrupted correspondence on experiments and discoveries with
those whose simple confrère it pleased him to be. We must go back to
the days of Pythagoras and Anacharsis to find such travelers, and they
had not left an empire behind in order to acquire instruction.

At this point, I cannot refrain from once more bringing to the reader's attention how enraptured Peter was at the sight of Cardinal de Richelieu's tomb. He was not so much impressed by the beauty of this sculptural masterpiece as by the image of a minister who had become famous throughout Europe by keeping it unsettled, and who had restored to France the renown she had lost after the death of Henry IV.[9] We know that he embraced the statue and cried: "Great man, I would have given you half of my empire to learn from you how to govern the other half." Finally, before his departure, he wanted to see the celebrated Madame de Maintenon, whom he knew to be in fact the widow of Louis XIV, and whose life was then drawing to its close. The ostensible similarity between Louis XIV's marriage and his own aroused his curiosity, but between the king of France and himself there was this difference: Peter had publicly married a heroine, while Louis XIV had merely possessed in secret an amiable spouse. The czarina did not accompany Peter on this visit, because he had been overly fearful of the constraints of protocol and the curiosity of a court which was little accustomed to appreciate the merit of a woman who, from the banks of the Pruth to the shores of Finland, had faced death at her husband's side, on both land and sea.

Chapter 9
Return of the Czar to His Empire.
His Policies and Pursuits.

The advances made him by the Sorbonne when he visited Cardinal de Richelieu's mausoleum merit separate treatment.

Certain Sorbonne theologians wanted the glory of reconciling the Greek and Latin churches. Students of the ancient world know well enough that Christianity came to the West by way of the Greeks of Asia Minor; that it was born in the East, and that the first Fathers, the first Councils, the first liturgies, the first rites are all Eastern in origin; that we do not possess a single term designating an ecclesiastical dignity or office that is not Greek, bearing witness to this day to the source from which we derived everything. After the division of the Roman Empire[1] it was impossible that there not be two religions sooner or later, just as there were two empires, and that there not arise between the Christians of the East and the West the same type of schism separating the Osmanlis and the Persians.

This was the schism that some doctors of the University of Paris believed they could repair at one fell swoop by submitting a memorandum to Peter the Great. Pope Leo IX and his successors failed to solve the problem with the aid of papal legates, Councils, and even money. The theologians ought to have known that Peter the Great, as head of his own church, was not likely to recognize the pope. In vain did they speak in their memorandum of the freedoms enjoyed by the Gallican Church,[2] which was of small concern to the czar; in vain did they write that popes must be answerable to Councils, and that a pope's ruling is not a dogma. Their document succeeded merely in incurring the high displeasure of the Holy See, without pleasing either the emperor of Russia or the Russian church.

There were in this oecumenical scheme political objectives beyond their comprehension and controversial points that they claimed to understand but that each sect explains to its own satisfaction. It was a matter of the Holy Spirit, who proceeds from both the Father and the Son according to the Latins, but who nowadays proceeds from the Father *through* the Son according to the Greeks, after long proceeding solely from the Father. They cited Saint Epiphanius, who says that "the Holy Spirit is not the Son's brother, nor the Father's grandson."

However, on his departure from Paris the czar had other concerns than to verify passages from Saint Epiphanius. He accepted the doctors' memorandum graciously, whereupon they wrote to a number of Russian bishops, who replied politely, although the majority of them were indignant at the proposal.

It was to dispel fears concerning this reconciliation that Peter shortly afterward instituted the comic Festival of the Conclave, when he had driven the Jesuits out of his empire in 1718.

There was at his court an old jester named Zotov, who had taught Peter to read and fancied that he had earned the most important dignities thanks to this service. Peter, who sometimes relieved the vexations of ruling by jokes befitting a people whom he had not yet entirely reformed, promised his writing-master that he would give him one of the highest ranks in the world. He created him knes papa—prince-pope—with a stipend of two thousand rubles, and assigned him a house in the Tartar section of Saint Petersburg. Zotov was ceremoniously installed by buffoons and harangued by four stammerers. He appointed cardinals and marched in procession at their head. The whole Sacred College was drunk on brandy. After Zotov's death, an officer named Buturlin was named prince-pope. Moscow and Saint Petersburg have three times seen the revival of this ceremony, whose absurdity seems pointless, but which did have the effect of confirming Russian aversion to a church with pretensions to supreme power and whose heads had anathematized so many kings. The czar's mirth avenged twenty Holy Roman Emperors, ten kings of France, and a host of other sovereigns. Such was the entire fruit garnered by the Sorbonne from its impolitic notion of reuniting the Greek and Latin churches.[3]

The czar's journey to France proved more useful through his union with this mercantile kingdom and its industrious population than through the would-be reconciliation of two rival churches, one of which will always maintain its ancient independence and the other its recent superiority.

Peter took several French artisans into his employ, just as he had done in England, for every nation he visited was proud to further his intention of bearing all the arts and crafts to a new homeland, and to participate in this type of creation.

He then and there drafted a trade agreement with France, which he put into the hands of his ambassadors to Holland as soon as he had returned to that country. It could not be signed by Châteauneuf, French ambassador at The Hague, until August 15, 1717. This treaty dealt not only with commerce, but also with peace in the North. The king of France and the elector of Brandenburg accepted the role of mediators that Peter assigned them. This sufficed to make the king of

England aware of the czar's displeasure with him, and it gratified the hopes of Görtz, who from that moment on used every possible means to unite Peter and Charles, to stir up new enemies for George, and to lend a helping hand to Cardinal Alberoni all over Europe. Baron von Görtz now saw the czar's ministers at The Hague publicly, assuring them that he was fully empowered to conclude a treaty with Sweden.

The czar let Görtz prepare all their batteries without touching them off, ready to make peace with the king of Sweden, but also ready to carry on the war. He still maintained links with Denmark, Poland, and Prussia, and even, ostensibly, with the elector of Hanover.

It seems obvious that he had no predetermined plan other than to take advantage of the various contingencies. His chief goal was to improve all his new institutions. He realized that the negotiations and interests of sovereigns, their leagues, alliances, suspicions, and enmities, undergo almost annual vicissitudes, and that often no trace remains of a host of diplomatic initiatives. A single well-established manufacture is sometimes more beneficial to the commonweal than a score of treaties.

After he rejoined his wife, who was waiting for him in Holland, Peter continued his travels in her company. They crossed Westphalia and reached Berlin without any pomp. The new king of Prussia[4] was no less inimical to the vanities of ceremonial and splendor than the Russian monarch. A king who never used any armchair other than a wooden one, who always dressed like a private soldier, and who had forgone all the refinements of the table and all the comforts of life would have been an edifying sight for the etiquette of Vienna and Spain, for the *puntiglio* of Italy, and for the dominant taste for luxury in France.

The life of the czar and czarina was just as simple and just as hard, and if Charles XII had happened to be with them, four crowned heads could have been seen together accompanied by less ostentation than a German bishop or a Roman cardinal. Never have luxury and indolence been opposed by such noble examples.

It must be confessed that any of our fellow citizens would earn our respect and be regarded as a prodigy if once in his lifetime, out of pure curiosity, he accomplished one-fifth of the traveling Peter undertook for the welfare of his states. From Berlin he went with his wife to Danzig; at Mitau he set himself up as the protector of his widowed niece, the duchess of Courland. He visited all his recently conquered territories, issued new regulations in Saint Petersburg, went to Moscow, and there ordered the rebuilding of some dilapidated private houses. He then proceeded to Tsaritsyn on the Volga, to halt the incursions of the Kuban Tartars; he constructed lines of fortifications between the Volga and the Don, erected forts at regular intervals from one river to the other, and simultaneously published the military code he himself had drafted. A special court of justice was established to examine the conduct of his ministers and to restore order to the Treasury. He pardoned some culprits and punished others. Prince Menshikov himself was one of those greatly in need of Peter's clemency, but a stricter judgment that he believed it his duty to pass on his own son filled his most glorious life with bitterness.

Chapter 10
Condemnation of Prince Alexei Petrovich.

In 1689, Peter the Great, aged seventeen, had married Evdokiya-Theodora or Fedorovna[1] Lopukhina, brought up with all the prejudices of her nation and, unlike her husband, incapable of rising above them. The strongest objections he encountered when he tried to create an empire and educate his people came from his wife. She was ruled by superstition, so commonly associated with the female sex. In her eyes, every useful innovation was sacrilegious, and every foreigner employed by the czar to execute his great designs a corrupter.

Her public complaints encouraged the factious and upholders of the old ways. Furthermore, her conduct did not compensate for such serious acts. Finally, in 1696, the czar was obliged to repudiate her and to confine her in a convent at Suzdal, where she was made to take the veil under the name of Helena.

The son she had given him in 1690 was, unhappily, born with his mother's temperament, reinforced by his earliest upbringing. My sources inform me that this was entrusted to superstitious folk who ruined his mind forever. In vain did Peter think that he could correct these first impressions by giving his son foreign tutors. Their very quality as foreigners repelled Alexei. He was not born lacking intelligence. He both spoke and wrote German; he could draw; he learned a little mathematics: but the same documents that have been entrusted to my care affirm that the reading of ecclesiastical books was his undoing. The youthful Alexei believed he could see in these works the reprobation of all his father's deeds. There were priests at the head of the malcontents, and it was by priests that he let himself be governed.

They persuaded him that the whole nation was appalled by Peter's endeavors, that the czar's frequent illnesses did not augur a long life, and that his son could only hope to please his people by showing his aversion to innovation. This whispered advice did not constitute an overt faction or conspiracy, but everything seemed to be tending toward one, and minds were inflamed.

Peter's marriage to Catherine in 1707 and the children he had by her consummated the young prince's embitterment. Peter tried every means at his disposal to win him back, even making him head of the regency council for a year. He sent him abroad, and in 1711, at the close of the Pruth campaign, he married him to the princess of Wolfenbüttel, as I have already related. It was a most unhappy marriage. Alexei, aged

202

twenty-two, indulged in every kind of youthful debauchery and in all the grossness of the old ways of which he was so fond. His profligacy turned him into a brute. His wife, spurned, ill-used, lacking the bare necessities, and deprived of all consolation, pined away in sorrow and at last died of grief on November 1, 1715.

She left Prince Alexei a newborn son, who according to the natural order of things should one day have inherited the empire. Peter felt with anguish that when he was dead all his labors would be destroyed by his own descendants. After the death of the princess, he wrote his son a letter equally moving and ominous. It concluded with the following words: "I will wait a little longer to see if you are willing to mend your ways. If not, know that I will deprive you of the succession as one cuts off a useless limb. Do not suppose that I merely wish to intimidate you; do not rely upon your rank as my only son, for if I do not spare my own life for my country and the welfare of my people, how could I spare yours? I would rather bequeath my empire to a deserving stranger than to my own unworthy son."

This is a father's letter, but still more a lawmaker's. Moreover, it shows that the order of succession was not immutable in Russia, as it is in other kingdoms by virtue of those fundamental laws that deprive fathers of the right to disinherit their sons, and the czar believed that he possessed a special prerogative to dispose of an empire he himself had founded.

At precisely the same time, the empress Catherine gave birth to a prince, who died later, in 1719. Whether this news disheartened Alexei, or whether he was imprudent or ill-advised, he wrote his father that he was giving up the crown and all hope of reigning. "As God is my witness," he said, "I swear on my soul that I will never claim the succession. I place my children in your hands, and ask for nothing but my subsistence for the duration of my life."

His father wrote him a second time. "I observe," he said,

that in your letter you speak only of the succession, as if I needed your consent. I have pointed out to you the sorrow your conduct has occasioned me for so many years, yet you say nothing of this. Paternal exhortations do not move you in the least. I have made up my mind to write you for the last time. If you scorn my advice while I am still alive, how much will you value it after my death? Even if you now have the desire to keep your promises, the long beards[2] will be able to twist you any way they please, and force you to break them. . . . You are the only hope of these people. You have no gratitude at all toward your father. Have you been assisting him at his labors since you came of age? Do you not find fault with, do you not loathe all my efforts for the welfare of my people? I have reason to believe that if you survive me you will destroy my work. Mend your ways, make yourself worthy of the succession, or else become a monk. Reply either in writing or in person; if not, I will deal with you as I would with any malefactor.

This letter was harsh. It would have been an easy matter for the prince to reply that he would change his ways, but he contented himself with answering his father, in four lines, that he wanted to enter a monastery.

Such a decision did not appear natural, and it is strange that the czar was willing to travel while leaving behind in his empire so discontented and so obstinate a son. However, his very journey proves that the czar feared no conspiracy on his son's part.

He went to see Alexei before leaving for Germany and France. The prince, who was ill or pretending to be ill, received him while in bed, and confirmed, with the strongest oaths, his wish to retire to a cloister. The czar gave him six months to think it over, and then set off with the czarina.

No sooner was he in Copenhagen than he learned what he might well have assumed—that Alexei was seeing no one but malcontents who were indulging him in his vexations. Peter wrote that he must choose between the cloister and the throne, and that if he wanted to succeed him one day, he must come to him in Copenhagen.

The prince's confidants persuaded him that it would be dangerous for him to be so far away from all his counselors, caught between an angry father and a cruel stepmother. Accordingly, he made a pretense of going to see his father in Copenhagen, but instead set out for Vienna, where he threw himself on the mercy of his brother-in-law, the Emperor Charles VI,[3] expecting to stay with him until the czar's death.

It was more or less the same escapade as Louis XI's when, still only dauphin, he left the court of his father, Charles VII, and took refuge with the duke of Burgundy.

The dauphin was far more to blame than the czarevich, since he had married against his father's wishes, had raised troops, had sought asylum with a prince who was Charles VII's natural enemy, and had never returned to his father's court despite the king's urgent appeals.

Alexei, on the other hand, had married only at the czar's behest, had not rebelled at all, had levied no troops, did not withdraw to a hostile court, and returned to his father's feet [sic] at the first letter he received from him. For as soon as Peter found out that his son had been in Vienna, had withdrawn to the Tyrol and then to Naples, which then belonged to the Emperor Charles VI, he dispatched Captain of the Guards Rumyantsov and Privy Councilor Tolstoy, bearing a letter written in his own hand and dated from Spa, July 21, 1717, new style. They found the prince at Naples, in the Castel Sant'Elmo, where they handed him the letter, which was worded as follows:

> . . . I am writing you for the last time to tell you that you are to carry out my wishes, which Tolstoy and Rumyantsov will announce to you in my name.

If you obey me, I assure you and swear to God that I will not punish you, and that if you return I will love you more than ever; but if you do not, I give you, by virtue of my God-given power as your father, my eternal malediction, and as your sovereign I promise you that I will easily find ways to punish you, in which matter I trust that God will assist me and take up my righteous cause.

Moreover, bear in mind that I have in no way offered you violence. Was I obliged to leave you a free choice in the decision you were to make? Had I wanted to compel you, did I not have the power at hand? I had but to command, and I would have been obeyed.

The viceroy of Naples easily persuaded Alexei to return to his father. Here was indubitable proof that the Emperor of Austria was reluctant to make any commitment to the young prince that might subsequently give the czar grounds for complaint. Alexei had traveled with his mistress Efrosinia, and he came back with her too.

He might have been regarded as an ill-advised young man who had gone to Vienna and Naples instead of Copenhagen. Had this been his only fault, common to so many young men, it would have been easy to forgive. His father had taken God to witness that not only would he forgive him, but he would love him more than ever. Alexei set off on the strength of this assurance, but to judge from the instructions of the two envoys who brought him back and from the czar's own letter, it would seem that the father demanded that his son disclose the names of his advisors and that he carry out his pledge to renounce the succession.

It is difficult to reconcile this disinheritance with the second oath sworn in the czar's letter, to love his son more than ever. Perhaps the father, torn between paternal affection and the interests of the state, was content to love his son when he retired to a monastery; perhaps he yet hoped to recall him to his duty and to make him worthy of that succession by making him realize what it meant to lose a crown. In such unusual, difficult, and distressing circumstances, we may readily believe that neither the father nor his equally troubled son was in the first place at peace with himself.

On February 13, new style, the prince reached Moscow, where the czar was then in residence. That same day he went down on his knees before his father and had a very long conversation with him. The rumor immediately spread throughout the city that father and son were reconciled and that all was forgotten, but at dawn on the following day the Guards Regiments were stood to arms and the great bell of Moscow was tolled. The boyars and privy councilors were summoned to the Kremlin, while the bishops, archimandrites, and two Basilian monks—professors of theology—assembled in the cathedral church. Alexei, like a prisoner without his sword, was led into the fortress to stand before his father. He prostrated himself in the czar's presence, and, weeping, handed him a document in which he confessed his faults, declared himself unworthy of the succession, and implored him only to spare his life.[4]

After raising him to his feet, Peter took Alexei into a small room where he asked him several questions. He told him that if he concealed anything concerning his escape, he was risking his head. Next, the prince was taken back to the hall where the council was assembled, and there the czar's proclamation, already drawn up, was publicly read.

In this document, the father upbraided his son with all the matters we have enumerated: his lack of diligence in his studies, his relations with the partisans of the old ways, and his disgraceful behavior toward his wife. "He has violated," said Peter, "conjugal fidelity by forming an attachment with a girl of the humblest extraction while his wife was still alive." It is true that Peter had repudiated his own wife in favor of a captive, but that captive was of superior merit, and he was rightly dissatisfied with his wife, who was one of his subjects. Alexei, on the other hand, had neglected his wife for a young nobody whose sole asset was her beauty. Thus far, we can see only the peccadilloes of a young man, which a father is obliged to admonish, but which he may excuse.

He was then taken to task for having gone to Vienna to seek refuge with the Emperor. Peter said that Alexei had slandered his father by giving the Emperor Charles VI to understand that he was being persecuted and forced to renounce his heritage, and that finally he had begged the Emperor to protect him by armed might.

I fail to see first of all how the Emperor could have made war on the czar on such grounds, and how he could have interposed anything other than his good offices between the angry father and the wayward son. Charles VI had therefore been content to grant the prince a place of refuge, and sent him away again when the czar, having discovered his retreat, had asked to have him back.

Peter adds, in this terrible document, that Alexei had convinced the Emperor that his life would not be safe if he returned to Russia. Condemning Alexei to death after his return, and particularly after promising to pardon him, in a sense vindicated Alexei's complaints, but we shall see the czar's reasons for subsequently pronouncing this memorable sentence. In brief, what could be seen in this great assembly was an absolute monarch pleading against his own son.

"This," he said,

is the manner in which our son has returned home, and although he has deserved death for running away and for his calumnies, nevertheless our paternal affection pardons his crimes. However, taking into consideration his unworthy and dissolute conduct, we cannot in good conscience allow him to succeed to the throne, foreseeing only too clearly that after our death his depravity would destroy the national renown and bring about the loss of many territories won back by our armies. Above all, we would pity our subjects if by leaving them such a successor we threw them back into a condition far worse than their previous one.

And so, by our paternal authority, by virtue of which the laws of our empire permit any man—even a subject—to disinherit a son as it pleases him, and by virtue of our rank as sovereign, and bearing in mind the welfare of our domains, we deprive our son Alexei of the succession to our throne of Russia, because of his crimes and unworthiness, even though not one member of our family should survive us.

And we constitute and proclaim successor to the aforementioned throne after us our second son, Peter,[5] although he is still young, having no other successor.

We give our aforesaid son Alexei our paternal malediction if, at any time whatsoever, he lays claim to or seeks the aforesaid succession.

We desire also of our loyal subjects of the ecclesiastical, secular, and other estates, and of the entire nation, that, according to this enactment and in accordance with our will, they recognize and consider our aforesaid son Peter, appointed by us to the succession, as the legitimate successor, and that in conformity with this present enactment they ratify the whole by oath sworn before the sacred altar, on the holy Gospels, while kissing the cross.

And any person or persons who oppose our will at any time whatsoever, and who from this day forward dare consider our son Alexei as successor or assist him to this end, we proclaim traitors to ourselves and to the fatherland. And we have commanded that these presents be published everywhere, so that no one may plead ignorance thereof. Given at Moscow, February 14, new style. Signed by our hand and sealed with our seal.

It appears that these documents had been prepared in advance, or else that they were drawn up with extreme dispatch, since Prince Alexei had returned on the thirteenth and his disinheritance in favor of Catherine's son is dated the fourteenth.

For his part, the prince signed the renunciation of the succession.

"I acknowledge," he said, "that this exclusion is just; I have merited it by my unworthiness, and I swear to Almighty God in the Trinity to submit in all things to my father's will, etc."

When the instruments had been signed, the czar walked to the cathedral, where they were read a second time, and all the churchmen gave their approval and affixed their signatures to the foot of another copy. There are many nations where such a document would have no force whatsoever, but in Russia, as in ancient Rome, every father had the right to deprive his son of his inheritance, and this right was stronger in a sovereign than in a subject, and especially in a sovereign like Peter.

However, the fear remained that one day the very people who had incited the prince against his father and advised him to flee might attempt to annul a renunciation imposed under duress, and to return to the firstborn the crown that had been transferred to the younger son, born of a second marriage. In this eventuality, Peter foresaw civil war and the inevitable destruction of all his great and beneficial achievements. He had to choose between the interests of the nearly eighteen million souls who then comprised the population of Russia, and one individual who was incapable of ruling them. It was consequently important to know the identities of the malcontents, and the czar once again threatened his son with death should he conceal anything from him. As a result, the prince was juridically interrogated by his father, and then by the czar's commissioners.

One of the charges that served to convict him was a letter from an Imperial Resident named Pleyer,[6] written from Saint Petersburg after the prince's flight. This letter stated that there was mutiny in the Russian army stationed in Mecklenburg; that several officers were talking of sending the new czarina Catherine and her son to the prison that housed the repudiated czarina[7] and of putting Alexei on the throne as soon as he could be found. There was indeed a mutiny in that army at the time, but it was quickly put down. The officers' vague remarks came to absolutely nothing. Alexei could not have encouraged such talk; a foreigner spoke about it as a piece of news. The letter was not addressed to Prince Alexei, who possessed only one copy, sent him from Vienna.

A more serious charge was a draft in his own handwriting of a letter written from Vienna to the Russian senators and archbishops. Its language was blunt: "The constant and undeserved ill-treatment I have undergone has compelled me to run away; I was within an ace of being put in a monastery. Those who imprisoned my mother wanted to treat me the same way. I am under the protection of a great monarch; I implore you not to forsake me now." The word *now*, which could be considered seditious, had been struck out, then replaced in his own hand, then struck out again, which indicates a troubled young man giving way to his resentment and repenting it almost in the same breath. Only the draft of these letters was found; they had never reached their destination, and the court of Vienna had not forwarded them, which is fairly strong evidence that the Emperor had no wish to fall foul of Russia or to lend armed support to the son against his father.

The prince was confronted with several witnesses. One of them, named Afanasiev,[8] claimed that he had once heard him say: "I will say something to the bishops, who will repeat it to the parish priests, and the priests to the parishioners, and they will make me czar even against my wishes."

His own mistress, Efrosinia, testified against him. None of the charges was very specific; there was no well-thought-out scheme, no sustained intrigue, no conspiracy or confederacy at all, and still less any preparation. There was simply a young man of high rank, discontented and profligate, complaining about his father, running away from him, and wishing he would die; but this particular young man of rank was heir to the most immense monarchy in our hemisphere, and in his situation and his position there was no such thing as a minor fault.

Already accused by his mistress, he was again accused with respect to his mother, the former czarina, and her sister Maria.[9] He was charged with having consulted his mother about his flight and of having spoken of it to Princess Maria. The bishop of Rostov, confidant of all three, was arrested and testified that the two princesses imprisoned in a convent had hoped for a change that would restore them to freedom, and had by their advice incited the prince to run away. The more natural their resentment, the more dangerous it was. We shall see at the end of this chapter what sort of man this bishop was and how he had comported himself.

Alexei at first denied several actions of this nature, and by that very fact exposed himself to the death penalty with which his father had threatened him in the event that he did not make a full and sincere confession.

Finally, he confessed to the charge of having made some disrespectful remarks about his father, and excused himself on the grounds of anger and drunkenness.

The czar personally drafted some new articles of interrogation. The fourth was worded as follows:

"When you saw from Pleyer's letter that there was a mutiny in the army stationed in Mecklenburg, you were delighted. I believe you had some scheme in mind, and that you would have declared for the rebels even though I was still alive."

This was tantamount to interrogating the prince about his innermost feelings, which may be confessed to a father whose advice corrects them, but withheld from a judge who pronounces sentence based only on established evidence. The hidden feelings of the heart are not subject to criminal proceedings. Alexei could easily have denied them or disguised them; he was not obliged to bare his soul. Nevertheless he replied in writing: "If the mutineers had called on me during your lifetime, I would probably have joined them, provided they were strong enough."

It is unthinkable that he would have made this reply of his own volition, and it would also be extraordinary, at least by European standards, for him to be condemned for admitting to an idea that he might possibly have had one day, during a situation that never arose.

To this strange avowal of his most secret thoughts, which had always remained locked deep within himself, were added proofs that in more than one country are not admissible at the bar of human justice.

The prince, overcome, beside himself, and scrutinizing his innermost thoughts with that ingenuity born of fear for anything which might serve to destroy him, finally admitted that during confession he had accused himself before God to the archpriest Jacob of having wished that his father might die, and that his confessor Jacob had replied: "God will forgive you; we wish for the same thing."

Any evidence obtained from confession is inadmissible according to the canons of our church; it is a secret between God and the penitent. The Greek Church, in common with the Latin, holds that this intimate and sacred communication between the sinner and the Deity does not fall within the province of human justice, but this was an affair of state and of its ruler. The priest Jacob was put to the question and admitted what the prince had revealed. It was an unusual thing in this trial to see the confessor accused by his penitent and the penitent by his mistress. We may further add to the uniqueness of this episode that the archbishop of Ryazan had become implicated in the accusations because he had once, during the czar's first outburst of indignation against his son, preached a sermon that was too favorable to the young czarevich. The prince admitted under interrogation that he had been counting on the prelate, and this same archbishop of Ryazan was, as we shall shortly see, the senior ecclesiastical judge consulted by the czar concerning the criminal proceedings.

There is an essential observation to be made on this strange trial, most ineptly summarized in the crude *History of Peter I* by the self-styled Boyar Nestesuranov. Here is that observation.

Among Alexei's responses to his father's first cross-examination was the acknowledgment that when he was in Vienna—where he did *not* see the Emperor—he appealed to the chamberlain, Count von Schönborn,[10] who told him: "The Emperor will not forsake you, and when the time comes, after your father's death, he will help you ascend the throne by force of arms." "I replied," added the accused, "that I was not asking for that; I wanted no more than the Emperor's protection." This deposition is simple, natural, and has a strong ring of truth about it, for it would have been the height of folly to ask the Emperor for troops to dethrone his father, and no one would have dared to make so absurd a proposal, either to Prince Eugene[11] or to the council or to the Emperor himself. This statement was made in the month of February, and four months later, on July 1, near the close of the proceedings, the czarevich is made to say in his final written responses:

Being unwilling to imitate my father in anything, I sought to obtain the succession by any means whatsoever, *except the right one*. I wanted to get it by foreign assistance, and if I had been successful and the Emperor had kept his promise to procure the crown of Russia for me even by force of arms, I would have spared no pains to get my hands on the succession. For example, if the Emperor had asked in return for Russian troops to fight in his service against any of his enemies or if he had asked for large sums of money, I would have done anything he wanted, and I would have given lavish presents to his ministers and generals. I would have maintained at my own expense the auxiliary troops given me to put me in possession of the crown of Russia, and, to put it briefly, I would have stopped at nothing to accomplish my purposes.

This final statement of the prince appears extremely unnatural; he seems to be going out of his way to have himself believed guilty. What he says is even quite untrue in one essential point. He states that the Emperor had promised to procure him the crown by force of arms, which was false. Count von Schönborn had given him cause to hope that one day, after the czar's death, the Emperor would help him uphold his birthright, but the Emperor had made him no promises. And finally there was no question of rebelling against his father, but of succeeding him after his death.

In this last interrogatory he is telling what he believed he would have done had it been necessary to fight for his inheritance, an inheritance that he had not legally renounced before his journey to Vienna and Naples. And so he is again making a statement not about actual deeds, which are subject to the rigor of the law, but about what he supposes he *might* have done one day, which consequently does not seem to fall within the jurisdiction of any tribunal whatsoever. Here he accuses himself for the second time of secret thoughts which he might possibly have conceived in some future eventuality. Never before, anywhere on earth, had there been the spectacle of a man judged and sentenced for vain ideas that came into his mind but were communicated to no other person. No court in Europe would listen to a man accusing himself of a criminal thought, and it is claimed that God Himself only punishes such thoughts when they are accompanied by a firm intent.

One might respond to these very natural reflections that Alexei had justified his father's punishment of him by his reticence concerning several of the accomplices to his flight. His pardon was contingent upon a full confession, which he made only when it was too late. To conclude, after so much commotion it did not seem humanly possible that Alexei might one day forgive the brother in whose favor he had been disinherited, and it was said to be preferable to punish one guilty person rather than to risk the whole empire. The harshness of justice coincided with the state's interest.

We must not form an opinion of the customs and laws of one nation by comparing them with those of others. The czar possessed the fatal but actual right to inflict the death penalty on his son merely because he had run away. In his proclamation to the judges and bishops he explains himself thus:

In obedience to every divine and human law, and especially those of Russia, which among private citizens exclude the intervention of any judicial agency between a father and his child, we possess a sufficiently abundant and absolute power to judge our son as befits his crimes, in accordance with our will, without taking counsel of anyone. However, since no one is as clear-sighted in his own affairs as in those of others, and as even the most expert physicians do not venture to treat themselves, but consult others when they themselves are sick, fearing to burden my conscience with some sin, I hereby make known my situation to you and ask you for the remedy. For I dread eternal death if, ignorant perhaps of the properties of my ailment, I try to cure myself alone, principally because I have sworn by the judgments of God and promised in writing to pardon my son, and later confirmed this by word of mouth, in the event that he told me the truth.

Although my son has broken his promise, nevertheless, so as not to deviate from my obligations in any way, I beg you to give thought to the matter and to examine it with the closest attention to see what he has deserved. Do not delude me; if he deserves only a mild punishment and you judge this to be the case, do not be apprehensive that it will be unpalatable to me, for I swear by Almighty God and his judgments that you have absolutely nothing to fear.

Have no misgivings over the fact that you are to judge your sovereign's son, but, without consideration for my person, let justice be done, and do not condemn either your souls or mine to perdition. In a word, may our consciences have nothing to reproach us with on the dreadful day of judgment, and may our fatherland come to no harm.

The czar made an almost identical pronouncement to the clergy, and so everything took place with the utmost legitimacy, and Peter displayed in all his proceedings an openness indicative of a deep-seated conviction of the justice of his cause.

The criminal trial of the heir to this immense empire lasted from the end of February until July 5, new style. The prince was interrogated several times and made the confessions demanded of him; we have reported the most crucial of these.

On July 1 the clergy submitted its opinion in writing. The czar was in effect asking only for its opinion, and not for a sentence. The preamble is worthy of Europe's attention.

"This affair," said the bishops and archimandrites, "in no way falls within the province of ecclesiastical jurisdiction, and the absolute power established in the Russian Empire is by no means subject to the judgment of its citizens, but the sovereign has the authority to act as he sees fit, without the intervention of any subordinate."

After this introduction, they cited the Book of Leviticus, where it is said that he who has cursed his father or his mother will be punished by death. They also cited the Gospel according to Saint Matthew, which refers to Leviticus's stern precepts. Following several other citations, they concluded with these most remarkable words:

> If His Majesty wishes to punish the transgressor according to his actions and in proportion to his crimes, he has before him examples from the Old Testament. If he wishes to be merciful, he has the example of Jesus Christ Himself, who welcomes back the repentant prodigal son, who frees the woman taken in adultery who had merited stoning to death according to the Mosaic Law, and who prefers mercy to sacrifice. He has the example of David wishing to spare his son and persecutor Absalom, for David told his captains who wanted to fight him: Spare my son Absalom. His father wanted to spare him, yet divine justice did not spare him.
>
> The czar's heart is in God's hands; may the czar take the course toward which God's hand shall direct him.

This opinion was signed by eight bishops, four archimandrites, and two doctors of theology. As we have previously mentioned, the metropolitan of Ryazan—with whom the prince had been in collusion—was the first to sign.

The clergy's opinion was forthwith presented to the czar. It is plain to see that the clergy wanted to incline him toward clemency, and there is perhaps nothing more beautiful than this contrast between the mildness of Jesus Christ and the harshness of the Judaic Law when brought to the attention of a father prosecuting his own son.

On the same day, they interrogated Alexei for the last time, and he put his final confession in writing. In it, he accuses himself "of having been overly zealous in his youth,[12] of having frequented priests and monks, of having drunk with them, of having received from them impressions which filled him with abhorrence for the duties of his rank and even for the person of his father."

If he made this confession spontaneously, it proves that he was ignorant of the recommendation for mercy made by the very clergy he was accusing. It proves even more conclusively how greatly the czar had changed the ways of his country's priests, who from brutish ignorance had in so short a time attained the power to compose a document whose wisdom and eloquence would not have been disavowed by the most illustrious Fathers of the Church.

It is in these final admissions that Alexei declares what we have already reported, namely, that he wanted to attain the succession "by any means whatsoever, except the right one."

It would appear, from this last confession, that he was afraid he had insufficiently accused and incriminated himself in the earlier ones, and that by calling himself ill-natured and vicious, and by imagining what he would have done had he been the master, he was painstakingly trying to justify the death sentence that was about to be pronounced. And this sentence was in fact handed down on July 5. It may be found in un-abridged form at the end of this history.[13] I will confine myself here to observing that it opens—like the clergy's written opinion—by declaring that a judgment of this kind has never rested with subjects, but only with the sovereign, who is answerable to God alone. Then, after setting forth all the charges against the prince, the judges express themselves as follows: "What are we to think of his scheming to rebel, unparalleled in the history of mankind, in addition to plotting an abominable double parricide against his sovereign, both as father of his country and as his natural father?"

Perhaps these words were poorly translated from the transcript of the trial printed by order of the czar, for there have assuredly been greater rebellions in the history of mankind, and it cannot be seen from his actions that the czarevich ever conceived the design to kill his father. Perhaps by the word *parricide* was meant the admission made by the prince that he had one day confessed his wish that his royal father were dead. Nevertheless, the secret avowal, during confession, of a secret thought is *not* a double parricide.

Be that as it may, the death sentence was unanimous, without specifying the manner of his death. Out of a hundred and forty-four judges, not a single one even thought of a lesser penalty. An English publication that made a great stir at the time states that if such a case had been judged by the English Parliament, not one judge would have been found out of a hundred and forty-four who would have pronounced even the mildest sentence.

Nothing could be more revealing of the differences between times and places. Manlius[14] might himself have been sentenced to death by English law for killing his son, and yet he was respected by the austere Romans. In England the laws do not punish a prince of Wales for running away, since as a peer of the realm he is free to go wherever he chooses. Russian law does not permit the sovereign's son to leave the realm against his father's wishes. A felonious thought that is not acted upon may not be punished in either England or France, whereas in Russia it may. Among us, long-drawn-out, categorical, and repeated disobedience is merely misbehavior that must be repressed, but it was a capital offense in the heir to a vast empire whose ruin would have been brought about by this very disobedience. In brief, the czarevich was guilty toward the entire nation for wishing to plunge it back into the darkness from which his father had rescued it.

Such was the acknowledged power of the czar that he could have had his son put to death for disobedience without consulting anyone, yet he left it up to those who represented the nation; and so it was the nation itself that condemned the prince, and Peter had so much confidence in the equity of his behavior that by having the account of the proceedings printed and translated he placed himself before the bar of world opinion.

History has not permitted me either to disguise or to soften anything in the account of this tragic episode. In Europe it was not known who was more to be pitied, a young prince accused by his father and condemned to death by those who should one day have been his subjects, or a father who believed himself obliged to sacrifice his own son to the well-being of his empire.

Several books were published stating that the czar had sent to Spain for the records of the trial of Don Carlos, who was condemned to death by Philip II,[15] but it is untrue that Don Carlos was ever brought to trial. Peter I's conduct was totally unlike that of Philip II. The Spaniard never let it be known why he had his son arrested, nor how the prince had died. He wrote absolutely contradictory letters on the subject to the pope and the Empress. Prince William of Orange publicly accused Philip of sacrificing his son and his wife to his own jealousy and of being less a strict judge than a jealous and cruel husband and an unnatural and parricidal father. Philip suffered these accusations in silence. Peter, on the contrary, did everything in broad daylight, openly proclaimed that he preferred his nation to his son, left the matter in the hands of the clergy and the great magnates, and made the entire world not only their judge, but his too.

Another extraordinary aspect of this tragic affair was the fact that the czarina Catherine, who was hated by the czarevich and openly threatened with the most wretched of fates should that prince ever come to power, nevertheless had absolutely nothing to do with his misfortune, and was neither accused nor even suspected by any foreign ambassador resident at Saint Petersburg of having taken the slightest action against a stepson from whom she had everything to fear. It is true that no one says that she interceded for him, but contemporary memoirs, especially those of Count Bassevitz, unanimously affirm that she was sorry for the unhappy Alexei.

I have in my possession the memoirs of a government official in which I find the following: "I was present when the czar told the duke of Holstein that Catherine had begged him to prevent the sentence from being read to the czarevich: 'Be content,' she said to me, 'to have him enter a monastery, because the infamy of a public sentence of death will be on your grandson's head.' "

The czar did not give in to his wife's entreaties. He believed that it was important for the sentence to be read publicly to the prince, so that after this solemn act Alexei would never be able to repudiate a decree in which he himself had acquiesced and which, by making him legally dead, would forever ensure his total incapacity to claim the crown.

However, if after Peter's death a powerful faction had arisen in favor of Alexei, would this civil death have prevented him from reigning?[16]

The sentence was read to the prince. My sources inform me that he fell into convulsions at the words: "The divine, ecclesiastical, civil, and military laws condemn to death without mercy those whose crimes against their father and sovereign are manifest." They say his convulsions turned into a stroke, from which he was brought round with difficulty. He recovered his senses a little, and in this intermediary stage between life and death begged that his father come to him. The czar came; tears flowed from the eyes of the father and his unhappy son. The condemned man asked for pardon, and his father publicly granted it. The last sacraments were solemnly administered, and Alexei died in the presence of the entire court the day after this fatal decree. His body was first taken to the cathedral and laid in an open coffin, where it remained for four days exposed to the public gaze, and was finally interred in the chapel of the citadel beside Alexei's wife. The czar and czarina attended the ceremony.

I am here unavoidably obliged to imitate, if I may venture to say so, the conduct of the czar; i.e., to submit to public scrutiny all the facts I have just related with the most scrupulous fidelity, and not those facts only, but the rumors that circulated and everything published about this melancholy affair by the most reputable authors. Lamberti, the most impartial of all and the most accurate, who confined himself to citing original and authentic documents concerning European affairs, seems in this instance to stray from his characteristic detachment and perceptiveness. He expresses himself in the following terms:

> The czarina, still fearful for her son's sake, knew no relief until she had induced the czar to put his elder son on trial and have him sentenced to death. The curious fact is that the czar, after personally knouting him, which is a form of torture, also personally cut off his head. The czarevich's body was put on public display with the head joined to the body so that no one could tell it had been separated. Some time later it happened that the czarina's son died, to the great sorrow of both herself and the czar. The latter, who had beheaded his firstborn with his own hand, reflecting that he now had no successor, became irascible. He received information at that time that the czarina was engaged in clandestine and unlawful intrigues[17] with Prince Menshikov. This, added to the thought that the czarina was responsible for his having sacrificed his elder son, led him to contemplate shaving her head and confining her in a convent, as he had done with his first wife, who was still there. The czar was in the habit of jotting down his daily thoughts in notebooks, which he did with his aforementioned plans for the czarina. She had bribed some of the pages who had the entrée to the czar's bedchamber. One of them, who regularly removed the notebooks from beneath the dressing table to show them to the czarina, took those contain-

ing the czar's latest intention. No sooner had the empress glanced at the plan than she informed Menshikov, and a day or two later the czar fell violently ill of a mysterious and fatal malady. The sickness was attributed to poison, since it was perfectly obvious that it was so acute and unexpected that it could only come from such a source, said to be fairly common in Muscovy.

These charges, recorded in Lamberti's *Memoirs,* got abroad in Europe. There still exist large numbers of printed works and manuscripts capable of transmitting these opinions to the most distant posterity.

I believe it my duty at this point to state what has come to my knowledge. To begin with, I attest that the person who told Lamberti the strange anecdote he relates was, to be sure, born in Russia, but was not of Russian stock, nor was he domiciled in the empire at the time of the czarevich's tragedy, having been absent for several years. I met him once; he saw Lamberti in the little town of Nyon, which I have often visited and where that writer was living in retirement. The same man admitted to me that he had only spoken to Lamberti about rumors current at the time.

Let it be seen from this example how much easier it used to be for one man to stigmatize another's memory before the invention of printing. Manuscript histories, possessed by few, were neither exposed to the light of day nor rebutted by contemporaries, nor were they within reach of general criticism, as they are nowadays. A single line of Tacitus or Suetonius, or even the fabricators of legends, sufficed to make a ruler hateful to the world and to perpetuate his infamy from one age to the next.

How could the czar possibly have cut off his son's head with his own hand, when extreme unction was being administered in the presence of the entire court? Was Alexei headless when they poured the holy oil on his head? At what time was it possible to sew his head back onto his body? The prince was not left alone for an instant between the reading of his sentence and his death.

The anecdote in which Alexei's father used a sword nullifies the one in which he used poison. It is certainly most unusual for a young man to die of a sudden convulsion brought on by the reading of a death sentence, and particularly a sentence he was expecting, but, after all, physicians admit that such a thing is possible.[18]

If the czar had indeed poisoned his son, as so many writers have given out, he would by that very fact have lost the fruits of everything he had done during this fateful trial to convince Europe of his right to punish him. All the reasons for Alexei's condemnation would have been suspect, and the czar would have condemned himself. If he had desired his son's death, he would have had the sentence carried out. Was he not the absolute master? Does a prudent man, a monarch on whom the whole world has its eye, resolve to poison in cowardly fashion someone he can put to death by the sword of justice? Does a man want to blacken his reputation among generations yet unborn with the name of poisoner and parricide when he can instead so easily assume that of a severe judge?

It clearly follows from everything I have related that Peter was more king than father and that he sacrificed his son to the interests of the founder and legislator and to the nation, which, but for this unhappy act of severity, would have relapsed into the state from which he had rescued it. It is manifest that he did not immolate his son to a cruel stepmother and to his male child by her, since he often threatened to disinherit Alexei before Catherine gave him this son, whose frail infancy was threatened by a premature death, and who in fact died shortly afterwards. If Peter had created such a scandal solely to gratify his wife, he would have been weak, foolish, and cowardly, which he most assuredly was not. He foresaw what would happen to his institutions and his nation if his designs were carried through after his death. All of his projects have been brought to perfection just as he predicted. His country has become famous and respected throughout Europe, from which it was formerly separated, whereas if Alexei had reigned, everything would have been destroyed. In a word, when considering this catastrophe sensitive souls shudder and austere ones approve.

This great and terrible event is still so fresh in the memory of mankind, and is spoken of so often with astonishment, that it is absolutely essential to examine what contemporary authors had to say about it. One of those penurious scribblers who impudently usurp the title of historian has this to say in his book dedicated to Count von Brühl, prime minister to the king of Poland, whose name might serve to lend weight to his theory: "All Russia is persuaded that the czarevich died solely because of the poison prepared by the hand of a cruel stepmother." This accusation is nullified by the czar's admission to the duke of Holstein that czarina Catherine had advised him simply to confine his condemned son in a monastery.

As for the poison later given by the empress to her husband Peter, the fable is demolished by the mere recounting of the adventure of the page and the notebooks. Does a man really take it into his head to write himself a memorandum: "I must remember to have my wife locked up"? Are these details that can be forgotten and must be noted down? If Catherine had poisoned her stepson and her husband, she would have committed other crimes. Not only was she never blamed for any act of cruelty whatsoever, but she was particularly celebrated for her mildness and indulgence.

It is necessary at this point to disclose the primary cause of Alexei's conduct, his flight, his death, and the death of the accomplices who perished at the hands of the executioner. It was the abuse of religion, it was the priests and monks, and this source of countless misfortunes is indicated clearly enough in some of Alexei's admissions reported by myself, and especially in the expression used by Czar Peter in a letter to his son: "Those long beards will be able to twist you any way they please."

Here, almost word for word, is how the memoirs of an ambassador to Saint Petersburg explain the czar's language: "Several churchmen," he writes,

who were attached to their time-honored barbarism, and still more so to their own authority, which they were progressively losing as the nation grew more enlightened, were longing for the reign of Alexei, which promised to plunge them back into their dear barbarity. Among their number was Dositheus, bishop of Rostov, who fabricated a vision of Saint Dmitry. The saint had appeared to him and assured him, in the name of God, that Peter had not three months to live; that Evdokiya, confined in the convent at Suzdal under the name of Sister Helena, together with the czar's half-sister, Princess Maria, was to ascend the throne and rule conjointly with her son, Alexei. Evdokiya and Maria were foolish enough to believe this imposture, and were so convinced by it that in her convent Helena removed her nun's habit, resumed the name of Evdokiya, had herself styled Your Majesty, and caused the name of her rival Catherine to be struck out of public prayers. She now always appeared clad in the traditional ceremonial robes worn by czarinas. The convent's treasurer declared her opposition to this usurpation. Evdokiya replied in no uncertain terms, "Peter punished the Streltsi, who insulted his mother; my son Alexei will punish anyone who insults his." She then had the treasurer locked in her cell. An officer named Stepan Glebov was brought into the convent. Evdokiya made him the instrument of her designs, and won his attachment by granting him her favors. Glebov circulated Dositheus's prediction in the little town of Suzdal and its environs. Meanwhile, the three months elapsed, and Evdokiya berated the bishop because the czar was still alive. "My father's sins are responsible," Dositheus replied. "He has informed me that he is in purgatory." Evdokiya immediately had a thousand requiem masses said, and Dositheus assured her that they were having the desired effect. A month later he came to tell her that his father's head was already out of purgatory, and the following month the deceased was only waist-deep in it. Finally, he was attached to purgatory only by his feet, and when his feet were released—which was the hardest part—the czar would not fail to die.

Princess Maria, convinced by Dositheus, put herself in his hands on condition that the prophet's father leave purgatory without further ado and that the prediction be fulfilled. Meanwhile Glebov continued his relationship with the former czarina.

It was mainly on the strength of these prophecies that the czarevich fled abroad to await his father's death. All this was soon discovered. Dositheus and Glebov were arrested; Princess Maria's letters to Dositheus and Helena's to Glebov were read in the open Senate. Princess Maria was confined at Schlüsselburg and the ex-czarina transferred to a different convent, where she was kept under guard. Dositheus and Glebov and all their accomplices in this futile and superstitious intrigue were put to the question, as were those privy to Alexei's flight. His confessor, his tutor, and the marshal of his household were all executed.

We therefore see what a high and fatal price Peter the Great paid for his people's happiness, how many obstacles—both public and secret—he had to overcome in the middle of a long and hard-fought war, with enemies outside Russia and rebels within, half his own family up in arms against him, the majority of the clergy doggedly opposed to his projects, practically the entire nation long incensed over its own felicity, which it did not as yet perceive, prejudices to be destroyed among the people and discontent to be calmed in their hearts. It required a new generation, molded by his care, finally to embrace the notions of happiness and glory that its fathers had been unable to endure.

Chapter 11
Public Works and Institutions Founded in and about the Year 1718.

During this horrible catastrophe, it became evident that Peter considered himself solely as father of his country, and his nation as his only family. The punishments he had been obliged to inflict upon that part of Russia which wanted to prevent the other part from enjoying happiness were sacrifices offered up to the common weal by grievous necessity.

It was in the year 1718, the period of his elder son's disinheritance and death, that he procured the most benefits for his subjects, through comprehensive civil administration, hitherto unknown in Russia; through manufactures and industries of all kinds, which Peter either founded or improved; through the new branches of commerce that were beginning to flourish; and through those canals which connect rivers, seas, and peoples separated by nature. Nothing will be found here concerning those striking events that delight the common run of readers, those court intrigues that divert malice, or those great revolutions that interest the vulgar curiosity of mankind. Here are instead the authentic wellsprings of public felicity, which philosophic eyes love to contemplate.

The czar accordingly appointed at Saint Petersburg a lieutenant general in charge of imperial civil administration to be head of a tribunal responsible for maintaining order from one end of Russia to the other. Luxurious clothes and games of chance, more dangerous than luxury itself, were strictly prohibited. Schools of arithmetic, already decreed in 1716, were established in every city in the empire. Orphanages and foundling homes, which had already been started, were completed, endowed, and occupied.

We will include here all the useful institutions planned earlier and finished some years later. All the major cities were rid of an abuse too long tolerated in other countries, the odious throng of beggars unwilling to practice any trade save that of importuning those who do practice one, who drag out—at the expense of others—a wretched and shameful existence.

In Saint Petersburg, the well-to-do were obliged to build houses of approved design, in keeping with their means. It was an excellent regulation to have all the materials brought free of charge to Saint Petersburg in every boat and wagon returning empty from the neighboring provinces.

221

Weights and measures were determined and standardized, as were the laws. This uniformity, which has been so greatly desired, but to no avail, in nations long since civilized, was established in Russia without any difficulty or grumbling, while we think that among us such a salutary set of rules would be impracticable. The prices of necessary commodities were controlled; streetlights, which Louis XIV was the first to install in Paris and which are still unheard-of in Rome, illuminated the city of Saint Petersburg. Fire pumps, barriers in the well-paved streets, every measure conducive to safety, cleanliness, and order, facilities for internal trade, privileges awarded to foreigners, as well as ordinances preventing the abuse of these privileges, all imposed a modern aspect on Saint Petersburg and Moscow.

More than ever before, armament factories were improved, especially the one built by the czar some ten miles outside Saint Petersburg. He was its first superintendent, often with a thousand workmen laboring before his eyes. He would give orders in person to all the contractors operating the flour, gunpowder, and saw mills, as well as the managers of the rope and sailcloth factories, the brickworks, tile kilns, and textile mills. Many workers in every trade came to him from France, which was one advantage derived from his travels there.

He founded a commercial court whose members were half Russian nationals and half foreigners, so that all manufacturers and artists would receive equally favored treatment. A Frenchman built a manufactory of very fine mirrors in Saint Petersburg with the help of Prince Menshikov. Another Frenchman set people to work making high-warp tapestries modeled on those of the Gobelins, and this industry receives much state support to this day.[1] A third Frenchman built thriving gold and silver wire-drawing establishments, and the czar commanded that in this particular industry, only four thousand marks[2] of gold or silver were to be used per annum, so as not to deplete the stock available in his domains.

He awarded thirty thousand rubles, i.e., one hundred and fifty thousand francs, with all necessary materials and equipment, to those who undertook to manufacture bunting[3] and other woolen stuffs. This profitable liberality enabled him to outfit his troops in cloths manufactured in Russia, whereas such materials had previously been obtained from Berlin and other foreign countries.

In Moscow they made linens as fine as those of Holland, and at the time of Peter's death there were already fourteen linen mills and hemp mills in Moscow and Jaroslaw.

In the old days, when silk was worth its weight in gold in Europe, no one would have dreamed that one day, beyond Lake Ladoga in a frozen waste of trackless marshes, there would arise an opulent and magnificent city where Persian silk would be produced just as fine as that of Isfahan. Peter set out to do it, and succeeded. Iron mines were worked more efficiently than ever before; some gold and silver mines were discovered, and a mining commission set up to determine whether the workings would yield a profit greater than their operating costs.

In order to make this multitude of industries, crafts, and enterprises flourish, it was not enough to sign letters patent and appoint inspectors. In the early days, Peter had to see to everything for himself, and even work at everything with his own hands, as he had earlier built, rigged, and navigated ships. When it came to cutting canals through muddy and almost unworkable ground, he could sometimes be seen taking charge of the workmen, digging up the earth, and carting it away himself.

During the year 1718 he planned the Ladoga Canal and locks. It was a matter of linking the Neva to another navigable river in order to bring merchandise to Saint Petersburg easily, without making a wide detour through Lake Ladoga, which was too subject to gales and frequently impassable for small craft. He personally surveyed the terrain; the instruments he used to break and carry away the earth are still preserved. His example was followed by all his courtiers, thus expediting a task previously deemed impossible. It was completed after his death, for not one of his projects recognized as feasible has been abandoned.

The great Kronstadt Canal, which can easily be drained so that warships may be careened and their hulls repaired, was also begun at the very moment of his son's trial.

That same year he built the new town of Ladoga. Shortly after, he dug the canal that joins the Caspian Sea to the Gulf of Finland and the Atlantic Ocean. Boats that have sailed up the Volga first navigate the two rivers he connected. From these rivers, they pass through another canal into Lake Ilmen, finally entering the Ladoga Canal, where goods can be transported over the high seas to every corner of the world.

Even as he was busy with these labors, carried out under his personal supervision, he turned his attention to far-off Kamchatka, in the most distant reaches of the Orient, and had two forts built in that land so long unknown to the rest of the world. Meanwhile, surveyors from his naval academy, founded in 1715, were already proceeding throughout the empire to make accurate maps and to bring to the notice of all mankind the vast expanse of territories that Peter had organized and enriched.

Chapter 12
Trade.

Trade with the outside world had dwindled almost to nothing before Peter's time, but he revived it. It is fairly well known that world commerce has changed its direction on several occasions. Southern Russia was, before Tamerlane, the emporium of Greece and indeed of India, with the Genoese acting as principal middlemen. The Don and Dnieper were laden with the products of Asia. But when, near the end of the fourteenth century, Tamerlane conquered the Chersonesus Taurica, later called the Crimea, and the Turks were masters of Azov, this major branch of world trade was annihilated. Peter had tried to revive it by seizing control of Azov. The ill-starred Pruth campaign lost him the city, and with it all his plans for trading by way of the Black Sea.[1] A no less extensive trade route through the Caspian Sea remained to be opened up. Already in the sixteenth century, and again at the beginning of the seventeenth, the English, who had started the Archangel trade, had attempted to do the same thing on the Caspian, but all their efforts came to nothing.

I have already told how Peter the Great's father had a Dutchman build him a ship for trading out of Astrakhan along the Persian coast. The vessel was burned by the rebel Stenka Razin, and so all hopes of trading directly with the Persians evaporated. The Armenians, who are the middlemen of this part of Asia, were welcomed into Astrakhan by Peter the Great. It was necessary to deal through them and to leave them all the profits. In India the Banians[2] are utilized in the same way, as are the Jews in Turkey and in many Christian states, for those who have only one resource at their disposal invariably become highly competent at the profession which is indispensable to them. Other nations voluntarily become dependent upon an ability which they themselves lack.

Peter had already remedied this disadvantage by concluding with the emperor of Persia a treaty by whose terms all silk not intended for Persian mills would be delivered to the Armenians of Astrakhan, to be transported by them to Russia.

Persia's domestic upheavals soon wrecked this arrangement. We shall later see how Hussein, the Persian shah or emperor, was persecuted by rebels and implored Peter's aid, and how Peter, after sustaining bitter wars against the Turks and Swedes, conquered three Persian provinces, but at this point we are dealing with commerce only.

Trade with China

The commercial venture with China seemed destined to be the most profitable. Two immense states with a common frontier, each possessing what the other lacked, were, to all appearances, in the fortunate position of needing to form useful connections, particularly since the solemn pact between the Russian and Chinese empires of the year 1689, according to our system of reckoning dates.[3]

The first foundations of this commerce had been laid as early as the year 1653. In Tobolsk, partnerships were formed by Siberians and families from Bukhara who had settled in Siberia. Their caravans passed through the Kalmuck plains and then crossed the deserts to Chinese Tartary,[4] making considerable profits, but the disorders that arose in Kalmuck territory and frontier disputes between Russians and Chinese upset these enterprises.

After the peace of 1689, it was natural for the two nations to agree on a neutral site to which merchandise could be taken. The Siberians, like every other tribe, needed the Chinese more than the Chinese needed them, and so the emperor of China was asked to grant permission for caravans to be sent to Peking, and this was readily obtained at the beginning of the present century.

It is highly noteworthy that the emperor K'ang-hsi had already authorized the construction in the outskirts of Peking of a Russian church served by Siberian priests, at the expense of the Chinese Imperial Treasury. K'ang-hsi had indulgently built this church for the benefit of several families from Eastern Siberia, some of whom had been taken prisoner before the peace of 1689, while the others were deserters. After the Treaty of Nerchinsk, none of them wanted to return home; Peking's climate, the pleasant Chinese way of life, and the ease of earning a comfortable livelihood by a modicum of work had made them all settle in China. Unlike Jesuit institutions, their little Orthodox church posed no threat to the empire's tranquility. Besides, the emperor K'ang-hsi favored freedom of conscience, a tolerant attitude that had existed since time immemorial throughout Asia, as it had throughout the world until the time of the Roman emperor Theodosius I.[5] These Russians, who intermarried with Chinese families, have since abandoned their Christianity, but their church still stands.

It was decreed that the Siberian caravans were to possess this church in perpetuity when they brought furs and other goods to Peking. The round trip took three years. Prince Gagarin, governor of Siberia, was in charge of this trade for twenty years. Sometimes the caravans were very big, and it was difficult to house the multitude of people comprising the largest of them.

The caravans passed through the territories of a lama, a kind of sovereign who resides on the Orhon River and is known as the Koutoukas. He is a deputy of the High Lama and has made himself independent by changing something in the country's religion, in which the ancient Indian belief in the transmigration of souls is predominant. One cannot do better than compare this priest with the Lutheran bishops of Lübeck and Osnabrück who have thrown off the yoke of the bishop of Rome. This Tartar prelate was affronted by the caravans, and so were the Chinese. Business was once again disturbed by their misconduct, and the Chinese threatened to forbid the caravans access to their empire if they did not put a stop to these disorders. The China trade was then very profitable for the Russians, who brought back gold, silver, and precious stones. The largest known ruby in the world was brought from China to Prince Gagarin, later found its way into Prince Menshikov's hands, and is at present one of the adornments of the imperial crown.

Prince Gagarin's provoking behavior greatly damaged the commerce that had enriched him, but in the long run it brought about his own downfall. He was indicted before the high court founded by the czar and beheaded one year after the condemnation of the czarevich and the execution of most of that prince's associates.

Meanwhile, the emperor K'ang-hsi, conscious that his health was failing and aware that European mathematicians were more knowledgable than those of China, believed that European physicians were also better than his own. He requested, through the ambassadors returning from Peking to Saint Petersburg, that the czar send him a doctor. There happened to be an English surgeon at Saint Petersburg who volunteered to play this role. He set off with a new ambassador and Laurents Langa, who has left us a description of this journey. The embassy was welcomed and its expenses defrayed in magnificent style. The English surgeon found the emperor in good health, and won a reputation as a most capable doctor. The caravan following in the embassy's train earned high profits, but committed new excesses and so antagonized the Chinese that they expelled Langa, then the czar's Resident at the Chinese imperial court, and with him all the Russian merchants.

The emperor K'ang-hsi died. His son Yung-cheng, who was as wise as his father but more resolute, being the same man who ousted the Jesuits from his empire as the czar himself had done in 1718, signed an agreement with Peter specifying that Russian caravans would henceforth do their trafficking only on the common frontier of the two empires. Only agents dispatched in the name of the emperor or empress of Russia are authorized to enter Peking, where they are lodged in an immense house which the emperor K'ang-hsi had originally assigned to the envoys of Korea. It has been a long time since either caravans or crown agents have been sent to the city of Peking. This branch of trade is languishing, but ready to recover.

Commerce at Saint Petersburg and the Other Ports of Europe

From then on,[6] more than two hundred foreign vessels berthed each year at the new imperial capital. This commerce increased daily, and has on more than one occasion yielded the Crown the equivalent of five million in French currency, i.e., far more than the interest on the capital laid out for establishing Saint Petersburg. This trade greatly diminished Archangel's, which was Peter's intention, because Archangel is too inaccessible and too distant from other nations and because business transacted under the supervision of a diligent sovereign is always more beneficial. The Livonia trade retained its original standing. All in all, Russian business has done well. Between one thousand and twelve hundred ships entered her harbors every year, and Peter contrived to combine profit with renown.

Chapter 13
Laws.

Good laws are known to be rare, and their implementation rarer still. The vaster a state is, and the more heterogeneous its peoples, the harder it is to unite them under the same jurisprudence. Czar Peter's father had a legal code drafted under the name of the *Ulozhenie;*[1] it had even been published, but it was far from adequate.

During his travels, Peter had amassed materials to reconstruct this great but rapidly crumbling edifice. He borrowed judicial procedures from Denmark, Sweden, England, Germany, and France, taking from those various nations what he deemed suitable for his own.

The court of final appeal was composed of boyars. Rank and ancestry were the qualifications for membership, whereas learning should have been. This court was dissolved.

Peter created the post of attorney general, with four deputies for each of the imperial provincial governments.[2] They were responsible for supervising the conduct of judges, whose sentences were reviewed by the Senate he founded. Each of these judges was furnished with a copy of the *Ulozhenie,* with the necessary addenda and emendations, until such time as it would be possible to draw up a comprehensive juridical code.

He forbade all judges, under pain of death, to accept what we call *douceurs.*[3] Among us, they are only modest, but it would be a good thing if they were nonexistent. The major costs of our justice are the salaries of underlings, the proliferation of documents, and above all that onerous practice whereby lawyers compose lines three words in length and, as a result, bury citizens' fortunes beneath an immense heap of papers. The czar saw to it that costs were moderate and justice prompt. Judges and clerks of the court received stipends from the public treasury and did not purchase their offices.

It was chiefly in the year 1718, while he was earnestly investigating his son's case, that Peter drew up these regulations. Most of the laws that he introduced were borrowed from Sweden, nor did he have the slightest objection to admitting as judges in Russian courts Swedish prisoners familiar with the jurisprudence of their homeland, who, having learned the language of the empire, wished to remain in Russia.

Private citizens' lawsuits came before the provincial government and its assessors. The next step was to appeal the verdict to the Senate. If anyone found guilty by the Senate then appealed to the czar himself and his appeal was unjust, he was pronounced worthy of death. However, in order to temper the severity of this law, Peter created a chief appellate judge[4] who received petitions from all those with cases before the Senate or the lower courts concerning which the law was not as yet sufficiently explicit.

At last, in 1722, he completed his new code, and forbade any judge, under pain of death, to deviate from it or to substitute his personal opinions for the law of the land. This formidable ordinance was widely publicized, and still is, in the imperial courts.

Peter created everything. Society itself was his work. He regulated rank according to men's occupations, from the admiral and the field marshal down to the ensign, without paying any heed to ancestry, never ceasing to bear in mind, and desirous of teaching his nation, that services rendered are better than noble birth. A hierarchy was established for women, too, and whoever, at a reception, usurped a place not assigned to her had to pay a fine.

By a more useful regulation, any soldier who became an officer was ennobled, while any boyar stigmatized by the law became a commoner.

Once these laws and regulations were drafted, increased trade, the growth of the cities and of private fortunes, the peopling of the empire, new ventures, and the creation of new positions inevitably brought in their wake a host of new legal business and unforeseen cases, all of which resulted from Peter's successful and comprehensive reforms. The empress Elizabeth[5] completed the corpus of laws begun by her father, and these laws reflect the mildness of her reign.

Chapter 14
Religion.

At the same time, Peter was working harder than ever on the reform of the clergy. He had abolished the patriarchate, an act of authority that had not endeared him to the churchmen. He wanted his imperial government to be all-powerful and the ecclesiastical administration to be respected but obedient. What he had in mind was the establishment of a permanent religious council dependent on the sovereign, and giving the church only such laws as were approved by the supreme master of the state, of which the church forms but one part. He was assisted in this venture by the archbishop of Novgorod,[1] one Feofan Prokop or Prokopovich, i.e., son of Prokop.

This prelate was a learned and judicious man. His travels to various parts of Europe had apprised him of the abuses prevalent there. The czar, who had witnessed them himself, possessed, in every one of his newly founded institutions, the great advantage of being able, without fear of contradiction, to select the useful and avoid the dangerous. He himself worked with the archbishop in 1718 and 1719. A perpetual synod was established, composed of twelve members, either bishops or archimandrites, all handpicked by the sovereign. This college was later increased to fourteen.

His reasons for founding the synod were explained by the czar in a preliminary address. The greatest and most noteworthy reasons are the following: "That there is no need to fear, under the administration of a college of priests, the disorders and disturbances that might arise under a single ecclesiastical head; that the common people, ever prone to superstition, on seeing a head of State on the one hand, and on the other hand a head of the Church, might suppose that there are indeed two powers." He cites with respect to this important point the interminable dissensions between the Empire[2] and the Church, which have drenched so many kingdoms in blood.

He thought and said publicly that the concept of the two powers, based upon the allegory of the two swords of the Apostles, was preposterous.

The czar conferred upon this tribunal the right to regulate all ecclesiastical discipline, to scrutinize the morals and abilities of those nominated to bishoprics by the sovereign, to be the final arbiters of religious cases in which appeals were formerly made to the Patriarch, and to be kept informed concerning monastery revenues and the distribution of alms.

This synod was called *Most Holy,* a title that had once been assumed by the Patriarchs. Thus the czar was in effect reestablishing the patriarchal dignity, now however divided among fourteen members, all dependent upon the sovereign and all taking an oath to obey him—an oath that the Patriarchs had not taken. The members of this sacred synod enjoyed the same rank as senators, but they too, like the senators, were subject to the monarch.

This new form of ecclesiastical administration and its new code did not come into effect or receive a standard format until four years later, in 1722. Peter first wanted the synod to present to him the men he would deem the most qualified to be prelates. The emperor would choose a bishop, and the synod would consecrate him. Peter frequently presided over the assembly. One day when the business in hand was the presentation of a new bishop, the synod noted that it still had only ignorant candidates for the czar. "Very well!" he said, "just choose the most honest man; he'll do as well as a learned one."

It is worthy of note that in the Orthodox Church there are no secular abbés, as we call them;[3] the clerical collar is known in Russia only for its absurdity, but, through a different kind of abuse, since in this world everything must be an abuse, their prelates are drawn from the monastic orders. The first monks were merely secular clergy, some devout, others fanatical, who withdrew into the deserts. They were eventually brought together by Saint Basil,[4] from whom they received a Rule. They took vows and were reckoned as the lowest order in the hierarchy, the starting-point in the rise to dignities. This is what has filled Greece and Asia Minor with monks. Russia was inundated with them; they were wealthy, powerful, and—though extremely ignorant—at Peter's accession almost the only people who could write, a skill they took advantage of in the early days of his reign, when they were so astonished and scandalized by Peter's innovations in every sphere. In 1703, he had been obliged to forbid monks the use of pen and ink. Express permission was required of the archimandrite, who was held accountable for those to whom he gave it.

Peter wished this edict to remain in force. At first he had wanted no one to enter a monastery before the age of fifty, but that was too late. The life of man is too short; there was not sufficient time to train future bishops. Through his synod he decreed that a man would be permitted to become a monk once he had passed thirty, but never before that. Military personnel and farmers were prohibited from ever entering a monastery without an express order from the emperor or the synod. A married man could never be accepted, even after divorce, unless his wife became a nun of her own free will and they had no children. Nobody in the service of the state may turn monk without special authorization. Every monk must labor at some trade with his own hands. Nuns must never leave their convent; they are tonsured at the age of fifty, as were the deaconesses of the early church, and if before receiving the tonsure they want to get married, they are not only allowed, but urged, to do so, an admirable regulation in a land where people are far more necessary than monasteries.

Peter's wish was that those unhappy girls whom God has created to people the state but who, thanks to a mistaken piety, entomb in the cloisters the race whose mothers they were intended to be, may at least be of some service to the society they are betraying. He commanded that they all be employed at some handiwork befitting their sex. The empress Catherine undertook to send for seamstresses from Brabant and Holland. She allocated them to various convents, where needlework was shortly produced with which Catherine and the ladies of the court bedecked themselves.

There is perhaps nothing in the world more sensible than these enactments, but the regulation personally devised and recommended to the synod by Peter in 1724 merits the recognition of all the ages. He was aided in this by Feofan Prokopovich. The ancient ecclesiastical institution is most learnedly analyzed in the document. Monkish idleness is forcefully attacked, manual labor being not only commended but commanded, and the principal occupation must be to serve the poor. Peter commands that disabled soldiers be distributed among the monasteries, that monks be appointed to take care of them, and that the sturdiest monks cultivate the fields belonging to the monasteries. The same orders apply to convents; the strongest nuns are to take care of the gardens, while the others must serve local sick women and girls brought to the convent. He goes into the minutest detail of these various services, and assigns some monasteries and convents to receive and bring up orphans.

One might think on reading this edict of Peter the Great's, dated January 31, 1724, that it was composed at one and the same time by a minister of state and a Father of the Church.

Nearly all the practices of the Russian Church are different from ours. Among us, as soon as a man becomes a sub-deacon he is forbidden to marry, and it is sacrilegious for him to serve in peopling his homeland. In Russia, on the contrary, a man is no sooner ordained sub-deacon than he is obliged to take a wife. He then becomes a priest or archpriest, but to become a bishop he must be either a widower or a monk.

Peter forbade all pastors to employ more than one of their own children in the service of the church, for fear that too numerous a family might tyrannize the parish, and they were permitted to use more than one of their offspring only when the parish itself requested this. We can see that in the smallest details of these ecclesiastical ordinances everything is aimed at the well-being of the state, and that every possible step is taken to ensure that priests may be respected without becoming dangerous, and that they become neither debased nor powerful.

I find in some curious memoirs written by an officer of whom Peter the Great was very fond that one day somebody was reading the sovereign the chapter in *The Spectator*[5] that contains a parallel between himself and Louis XIV. When he had listened to it, he said: "I don't think I deserve the favorable comparison they give me over the king, but I *have* been fortunate enough to be his superior in one essential respect: I have compelled my clergy to be obedient and peaceful, whereas Louis XIV allowed his to get the upper hand."

A ruler who spent his days amid the exertions of war and his nights in drawing up a multitude of laws, administering an enormous empire, and directing so many colossal undertakings spread out over a distance of two thousand leagues needed some relaxation. We could not expect the amusements of Peter's day to be as noble or as refined as they have become since, nor must we be shocked that Peter enjoyed his "cardinals' feast," which we have already mentioned, as well as certain other diversions of the same type. These were occasionally at the expense of the Roman Church, to which he had an aversion very pardonable in a monarch of the Greek rite who wished to be the master in his own house. He put on similar shows at the expense of Russian monks, but only the old-style monks whom he wished to ridicule while he was reforming the new ones.

We have already seen that, before promulgating his ecclesiastical laws, he created one of his court jesters pope and celebrated the Festival of the Conclave. The jester, whose name was Zotov, was eighty-four years old. The czar conceived the idea of marrying him to a widow as old as himself, and of solemnly celebrating the nuptials. The guests were invited by four stammerers; some decrepit old men escorted the bride, while four of the fattest men in Russia served as runners. The band was on a cart drawn by bears goaded with steel points, which, by their roaring, provided a bass worthy of the tunes being played on the wagon. The bride and groom were blessed in the cathedral by a blind and deaf priest wearing spectacles. The procession, the wedding ceremony, the nuptial feast, the disrobing of the bridal couple, and the ritual of putting them to bed were all equally appropriate to the buffoonery of the entertainment.

A festivity of this kind may strike us as being very odd, but is it any more so than our own carnival recreations? Is it a finer thing to see five hundred persons wearing hideous masks and ridiculous garments capering all night long in a large room without speaking to one another?

Were our own ancient All Fools' Day, our Feasts of the Donkey and of the Abbot of Cuckolds once celebrated in our churches any more stately? And did our comedy of the *Mère sotte* display any more genius?[6]

Chapter 15
The Aland Negotiations. Charles XII's Death.
The Treaty of Nystadt.

The czar's stupendous exertions, the administrative routine of the Russian empire, and the trial of the unhappy Prince Alexei were not the only matters that preoccupied him. He had to protect his flanks while setting the internal affairs of Russia in order. The war with Sweden still continued, though sluggishly and much slowed down by hopes of an early peace.

The fact remains that in the year 1717 Cardinal Alberoni, prime minister to King Philip V of Spain, and Baron von Görtz, who had gained a moral ascendancy over Charles XII, tried to change the map of Europe by reconciling Peter and Charles, by unthroning King George I of England, and by restoring Stanislas in Poland, while Alberoni was to give his master Philip the regency of France. As we have seen, Görtz had confided in the czar himself. Alberoni had entered into negotiations with Prince Kurakin, the czar's ambassador to The Hague, through the intermediary of the Spanish ambassador, Baretti Landi, who was, like the cardinal, an expatriate Mantuan.

They were foreigners who wished to overthrow everything for the sake of masters to whom they owed no natural allegiance, or perhaps rather for their own benefit. Charles XII lent himself to all of these schemes, while the czar was content to scrutinize them. Since the year 1716, he had attacked Sweden only halfheartedly, rather to force her to buy peace by ceding the territories he had conquered than to crush her once and for all.

Already the energetic Baron von Görtz had prevailed upon the czar to send plenipotentiaries to the Isle of Aland to negotiate this peace. The arrival at the conference of the Scotsman Bruce, commander of the Russian artillery, and the famous Osterman,[1] who was later at the head of affairs, coincided with the czarevich's arrest in Moscow. Görtz and Gyllenborg were already at the congress representing Charles XII, both impatient to reconcile the king with Peter and to be revenged on the king of England. The odd thing was that there was a peace conference but no armistice. The czar's fleet was still cruising along the Swedish coast, taking prizes. The intent of these hostile acts was to accelerate the conclusion of a treaty which was vital to Sweden and which would bring renown to her conqueror.

Already, in spite of the minor hostilities that were still going on, there was every indication of an early peace. The preliminaries were acts of magnanimity more effective than mere signatures. The czar released—without ransom—Marshal Rehnskjöld,[2] whom he himself had captured, and the king of Sweden reciprocated by freeing Generals Trubetskoy and Golovin, who had been prisoners in Sweden since the Battle of Narva.

The negotiations were making progress, and everything was about to change in the North. Görtz suggested that the czar acquire the duchy of Mecklenburg, whose duke, Charles, had married a daughter of Peter's elder brother Ivan. The noblemen of his country were up in arms against him. Peter had an army in Mecklenburg and took the side of the duke, whom he regarded as his son-in-law. The king of England, as elector of Hanover, championed the aristocracy. Securing Mecklenburg for Peter, already master of Livonia and about to become more powerful in the Empire than any elector, was yet another way of mortifying the king of England. In return, the duke of Mecklenburg was to be given the duchy of Courland and part of Prussia, at the expense of Poland, where Stanislas was to be restored. Bremen and Verden were to revert to Sweden, but could only be taken from King George I by force of arms. Görtz's plan, as I have already mentioned, was accordingly that Peter and Charles XII, united not only by peace but by an offensive alliance, should send an army to Scotland. After conquering Norway, Charles XII in person was to invade Great Britain, where he flattered himself he could make a new king, having already made one in Poland. Cardinal Alberoni promised to subsidize Peter and Charles. The ousted King George would probably drag down with him in his fall his ally the regent of France, who, deprived of all support, would be delivered into the hands of a triumphant Spain and a rebellious France.

Alberoni and Görtz believed themselves to be on the point of throwing all Europe into confusion, when a ball fired at random from a swivel gun on the ramparts of Fredrikshald in Norway reduced all their plans to nothing.[3] Charles XII was killed; the Spanish fleet was beaten by the English;[4] the conspiracy hatching in France was uncovered and dispersed; Alberoni was driven out of Spain; Görtz was beheaded in Stockholm; and out of all that formidable league, which had barely begun to move, the sole power remaining was the czar, who, not having compromised himself in any way, imposed his will on all his neighbors.

In Sweden everything changed after Charles XII's death. He had been a despot, but his sister Ulrica-Eleonora was elected queen only on condition that she would renounce despotism. He had wanted to join with the czar against England and her allies, while the new Swedish government joined with these allies against the czar.

The Congress of Aland was not in fact broken off, but Sweden, in league with England, hoped that an English fleet in the Baltic would procure more advantageous peace terms for her. Hanoverian soldiers entered the territories of the duke of Mecklenburg (February, 1719), but the czar's troops drove them out again.

Peter also maintained an army corps in Poland that overawed Augustus's and Stanislas's supporters simultaneously, and as for Sweden, he kept a fleet in readiness with the intent either of making an assault on the coast or of preventing the Swedish government from dragging out the Congress of Aland. This fleet consisted of twelve large ships of the line, several of the second class, plus frigates and galleys. The czar, still under the command of Admiral Apraxin, was vice admiral.

To begin with, a squadron from this fleet distinguished itself against a Swedish squadron and, after a stubborn fight, captured a ship of the line and two frigates. Peter, who encouraged the navy he had created by every possible means, gave the equivalent of sixty thousand francs to the officers of the squadron, as well as gold medals and, above all, tokens of honor.[5]

While this was going on, the English fleet, commanded by Admiral Norris, sailed into the Baltic to assist the Swedes. Peter had enough faith in his new navy not to allow the English to overawe him; he confidently remained at sea and sent word to the English admiral asking whether he had come merely as a friend of the Swedes or as an enemy of Russia. The admiral replied that he had as yet no definite orders. In spite of this equivocal response, Peter remained at sea.

The English had indeed come with the sole intention of encouraging the czar by a show of force to offer the Swedes acceptable peace terms. Admiral Norris sailed to Copenhagen, and the Russians made several landings in Sweden in the vicinity of Stockholm. They destroyed some copper works, burned nearly fifteen thousand houses (July, 1719), and did enough damage to make the Swedes long for peace to be concluded forthwith.

And in fact the new queen of Sweden urged that negotiations be revived. Osterman was even sent to Stockholm, and the situation remained unchanged throughout 1719.

The following year, the prince of Hesse, the queen of Sweden's husband, who had become king in his own right by his wife's abdication in his favor,[6] began his reign by sending an ambassador to Saint Petersburg to expedite the much-longed-for peace, but in the midst of these diplomatic initiatives the war still went on.

The English fleet joined the Swedish one, but without as yet committing any hostile acts, there being no open rupture between Russia and England. Admiral Norris offered King George's mediation, but offered it at gunpoint: that alone put a stop to the negotiations. The position of the Swedish coastline relative to Russia's new provinces on the Baltic is such that Sweden may easily be attacked, whereas the Russian territories are very difficult of access. This became apparent when Admiral Norris, having thrown off all pretense, made another[7] landing, in conjunction with the Swedes, on a small Estonian island called Narguen,[8] which belonged to the czar. They burned down a hovel (June, 1720), but at the same time the Russians descended upon Vaasa, where they burned forty-one villages and more than a thousand houses, inflicting indescribable damage throughout the area. Prince Golitsyn boarded and captured four Swedish frigates. The English admiral seemed to have come solely to see for himself how redoubtable the czar had made his navy. Norris hardly did anything but show himself in the same waters through which the four Swedish frigates were being taken in triumph to the port of Kronslot outside Saint Petersburg. It would appear that the English did too much for simple mediators, and too little for enemies.

Finally (November, 1720), the new king of Sweden asked for a cessation of hostilities, and, having been unsuccessful so far with English threats, he employed the mediation of the duke of Orleans, regent of France, who, as an ally of both Sweden and Russia, had the honor of reconciling them. The regent sent Campredon as plenipotentiary to Saint Petersburg, and from there to Stockholm (February, 1721). The negotiators convened in Nystadt, a small Finnish city, but the czar refused to grant an armistice until they were on the point of signing the treaty. He had an army in Finland ready to subdue the rest of that province, and his naval squadrons were an ever-present menace to Sweden. The only way to attain peace was by acceding to his wishes. Eventually, Sweden subscribed to all his demands, surrendering to him in perpetuity all the conquered territories, from the frontiers of Courland to deep within the Gulf of Finland, and beyond that again along the Kexholm region and the border of Finland itself that extends northward from the vicinity of Kexholm. And so Peter remained unchallenged sovereign of Livonia, Estonia, Carelia, the Viborg region, and the neighboring islands that guaranteed him the continued domination of the sea, for example, the isles of Usedom,[9] Dago, Møn, and many others. The whole covered an area of three hundred leagues in length and of varying widths, and constituted a great kingdom, Russia's reward for twenty years of hardship.

The Treaty of Nystadt was signed on September 10, 1721, new style, by Peter's minister Osterman and by General Bruce.

Peter's elation was all the keener since, finding himself relieved of the necessity of maintaining large armies on the Swedish front and of anxieties over England and his neighbors, he was now in a position to devote himself entirely to the reform of his empire, a reform already so auspiciously begun, and to foster the flowering of the useful arts and commerce introduced by his own unwavering and painstaking efforts.

In his first transports of delight, he wrote his plenipotentiaries: "You have drafted the treaty as if we had written it ourselves and sent it to you to have it signed by the Swedes. This glorious event will be forever preserved in our memory."

Celebrations of every kind manifested the pleasure of the citizens throughout the empire, and especially at Saint Petersburg. The triumphal ceremonies that the czar had displayed during the war were as nothing compared to the peaceful rejoicings that every Russian greeted with rapture. This peace was the noblest of his triumphs, and what gave him even more satisfaction than all the dazzling fetes was a total amnesty granted the convicts held in the prisons and the remission of all the taxes due the imperial treasury throughout the empire until the day when the peace was made public. The chains of a multitude of wretches were broken, the only exceptions being brigands, murderers, and perpetrators of high treason.

It was at this time that the Senate and the Holy Synod conferred upon Peter the titles of *the Great,* of *Emperor,* and of *Father of the Fatherland.* Chancellor Golovkin was the spokesman for all the estates of the realm in the cathedral church.[10] The senators then cried three times: "Long live our Emperor and Father!" and their acclamations were followed by those of the populace. The ambassadors of France, the Empire, Poland, Denmark, and Holland offered their congratulations that same day, addressed him by his newly awarded titles, and acknowledged as emperor the man who had already been publicly designated by that title in Holland since the Battle of Poltava. The names *Father* and *Great* were glorious ones, which no one in Europe could deny him; that of *emperor* was merely an honorific title bestowed by custom upon the Austrian emperor as titular king of the Romans, and these appellations require a certain time to be formally employed in the chancelleries, where protocol is not the same thing as renown. Shortly afterward, Peter was recognized as emperor throughout Europe, except by Poland—which was as ever racked by discord—and by the pope, whose approbation has become quite worthless since the Holy See has progressively lost its influence as nations have become more enlightened.

Chapter 16
Victories in Persia.

Russia's location is such that she has perforce to safeguard her interests among all the peoples who live near the fiftieth degree of latitude. When she was ill-governed, she was in turn the prey of the Tartars, the Swedes, and the Poles, while under a strong and vigorous government she became redoubtable to every other nation. Peter had inaugurated his reign by signing an advantageous treaty with China.[1] Later on, he fought the Swedes and Turks at one and the same time, and concluded his reign by leading armies into Persia.

Persia was beginning to fall into that deplorable state of affairs in which she still languishes to this day. Let us picture the Thirty Years' War in Germany, the period of the Fronde, the Saint Bartholomew's Day Massacre, King Charles VI and King John in France, the English Civil Wars, the long devastation of Russia by the Tartars, or the Tartar invasion of China, and we shall have some idea of the calamities that have ravaged Persia.[2]

All that is needed to plunge an entire kingdom into this abyss of disasters is a weak and negligent ruler and a powerful and ambitious subject. Hussein, the shah or shac or sophy of Persia, a descendant of the great Shah Abbas, was then on the throne. He gave himself up to ease and luxury, while his prime minister committed acts of injustice and cruelty tolerated by the indolent Hussein. Such were the origins of forty years of carnage.

Like Turkey, Persia has provinces that are governed in various ways. She has immediate subjects, vassals, tributary princes, and even some tribesmen who are themselves paid a tribute by the court in the name of a pension or subsidy. Such, for example, were the people of Daghestan, who live in the Caucasus Mountains to the west of the Caspian Sea. They were once part of ancient Albania,[3] for every nation has changed its name and its boundaries. Today these people are called Lesghians. They are highlanders who are rather under the protection than the dominion of Persia. They received subsidies to defend the frontier.

At the other end of the Persian empire, near India, lived the prince of Kandahar, who commanded the Afghan militia. This prince was a vassal of Persia, as the hospodars of Wallachia and Moldavia are vassals of the Turkish empire. This vassalage is not hereditary, but bears a perfect resemblance to the ancient fiefs established in Europe by the Tartar-like tribes who overturned the Roman Empire. The Afghan militia controlled by the prince of Kandahar consisted of those same Albani from the shores of the Caspian Sea adjacent to Daghestan, mixed with Circassians and Georgians—rather like the old Mamelukes who subjugated Egypt. Timur, whom we call Tamerlane, led this armed host into India, and it remained established in the province of Kandahar, which belonged now to India and now to Persia. The revolution started with the Afghans and Lesghians.

Mir Vais, or Mirivitz,[4] administrator of the province and appointed solely to collect tributes, murdered the prince of Kandahar, roused the militia, and remained master of Kandahar until his death in 1717. His brother succeeded him peacefully on payment of a modest tribute to the Persian Porte, but Mir Vais's son, born with his father's ambition, murdered his uncle and tried to become a conqueror. This young man was called Mir Mahmud, but in Europe he was known only by the name of his father, who had started the rebellion. Mahmud reinforced his Afghans with all the Ghebers he could collect. These were ancient Persians[5] formerly dispersed by Caliph Omar, but still devoted to the religion of the Magi, so flourishing in the days of Cyrus, and still secretly hostile to the new Persians.[6] Finally, he marched into the heart of Persia at the head of one hundred thousand fighting men.

At the same time, the Lesghians or Albani, who had not been paid their subsidies because of the troubled times, came down in arms from their mountains, so that the fire broke out and burned from both ends of the empire until it reached the capital.

The Lesghians ravaged all the land along the western shore of the Caspian Sea as far as Derbent, or the Iron Gate. In this devastated region, fifteen leagues from the sea, is the city of Shemakha. It is claimed to be the ancient residence of Cyrus, to which the Greeks gave the name Cyropolis—for we know the geographical locations and place names of the area only through the Greeks, and just as the Persians never had a king called Cyrus, still less did they have a city called Cyropolis. In the same way, the Jews, who dabbled in writing when they had settled in Alexandria, dreamed up the city of Scythopolis, built, they said, by the Scythians near Judaea, as though the Scythians and Hebrews were capable of giving Greek names to cities.

The city of Shemakha was wealthy. The Armenian neighbors of this part of Persia transacted an immense business there, and Peter had just established—at his own expense—a company of Russian merchants that was beginning to prosper. The Lesghians took the city by surprise, sacked it, slaughtered all the Russians trading there under the protection of Shah Hussein, and pillaged their shops, the loss from which was calculated at about four million rubles.

Peter demanded satisfaction from the emperor Hussein, who was still fighting for his crown. Hussein could not offer him redress, and

Mahmud would not. Peter determined to take the law into his own hands and to profit from Persia's troubles.

Mir Mahmud was still pursuing his victorious course in Persia. The sophy, on learning that the emperor of Russia was making preparations to enter the Caspian Sea and avenge the massacre of his subjects in Shemakha, secretly begged him, through an Armenian messenger, to come to the aid of Persia at the same time.

Peter had for a long while contemplated ruling the Caspian Sea with a powerful navy and diverting the trade of Persia and part of India through his own domains. He took soundings in the depths of this sea, studied its coastline, and made accurate charts. Accordingly, he set off for Persia on May 15, 1722. His wife accompanied him on this journey, as she always did. They sailed down the Volga as far as the city of Astrakhan. From there he hurried to restore the canals which were to link the Caspian, the Baltic, and the White Seas, a task partly completed during his grandson's reign.[7]

While he was directing operations, his infantry and supplies were already embarked upon the Caspian. He had twenty-two thousand infantrymen, nine thousand dragoons, and fifteen thousand Cossacks. Three thousand sailors capable of serving as marines during landings were working his ships. The cavalry took the overland route through deserts where water often runs short. After crossing these deserts, one has to get through the Caucasus Mountains, where three hundred men could hold up an entire army. However, in view of the prevailing lack of order in Persia, anything could be attempted.

The czar sailed about a hundred leagues southward from Astrakhan, as far as the small town of Andreihof.[8] We are surprised to find the name Andrew on the shores of the Hyrcanian Sea,[9] but certain Georgians, anciently a sort of Christians, had built the city, and the Persians had fortified it. It was captured with ease. Peter then continued his advance overland into Daghestan, where he distributed manifestoes in Persian and Turkish. It was necessary to deal tactfully with the Ottoman Porte, which included among its subjects not only the neighboring Circassians and Georgians, but also some great vassals who had only recently come under Turkey's protection.

Among others, there was an extremely powerful one named Mahmud of Utemish, who assumed the title of sultan and dared to attack the Russian emperor's troops. He was utterly defeated, and the contemporary account states that his land was turned into a bonfire.

Soon Peter reached Derbent (September 14, 1722), called Demircapi, the Iron Gate, by the Persians and Turks. It is so named because there was in fact an iron gate on the southern side.[10] It is a long, narrow city, one end of which touches a precipitous branch of the Caucasus, and whose walls are bathed at the far end by the waves of the sea, which during storms frequently rise higher than the walls themselves. These walls could well be regarded as a wonder of the ancient world. They are forty feet high and six feet thick, flanked by square towers at fifty-foot intervals; the wall appears to be all of a piece. It is built of sandstone and crushed seashells that serve as mortar, and the whole forms a mass harder than marble. The city may be entered from the sea side, but from the land side it appears impregnable. There are still some remains of an ancient wall, similar to the Great Wall of China, constructed during the remotest antiquity. It extended from the shores of the Caspian to those of the Black Sea, and was probably a rampart erected by the ancient kings of Persia against the innumerable barbarian hordes that dwelt between the two seas.[11]

Persian tradition has it that the city of Derbent was in part restored and fortified by Alexander. Arrian and Quintus Curtius say that Alexander did indeed rebuild the city. To be sure, they claim that it was on the banks of the Don, but the fact is that in their day the Greeks gave the name Don to the river Cyrus,[12] which flows near the city. It would be inconsistent for Alexander to have built the Caspian Gate on a river whose mouth is in the Black Sea.

There were once three or four Caspian Gates in different mountain passes, all very likely constructed for the same purpose, since the tribes to the east, west, and north of this sea have always been barbarians redoubtable to the rest of the world, and this was the principal point of departure for all those swarms of conquerors who subjugated Asia and Europe.

May I be permitted to observe at this point how much pleasure authors of every period have taken in deceiving people, and how much they have preferred empty rhetoric to the truth? Quintus Curtius puts into the mouths of some nondescript Scythians an admirable speech full of moderation and philosophy, as though the local Tartars had been so many sages and as though Alexander had not been the general named by the Greeks to lead them against the king of Persia, who was overlord of a great part of southern Scythia and India. The rhetoricians who fancied that they were imitating Quintus Curtius have done their utmost to make us view these savages of the Caucasian wilderness, hungering after rapine and bloodshed, as the most virtuous people in the world, and they have depicted Alexander, the avenger of Greece and conqueror of the man who wished to enslave her,[13] as a brigand who roamed the world to no purpose and with no justice.

No thought is given to the fact that these Tartars were never anything but destroyers, while Alexander built cities in their own land. This is a point of comparison, if I may venture to say so, between Peter the Great and Alexander. Peter was as energetic, as well disposed to the useful arts, and more diligent with respect to legislation. Like Alexander, he wanted to alter human relationships, and he built or restored as many cities as Alexander.

At the approach of the Russian army, the governor of Derbent did not attempt to withstand a siege, either because he believed that he could not defend himself or because he preferred the protection of the emperor Peter to that of the tyrant Mahmud. He brought out the silver keys of the city and citadel, and the army entered Derbent peacefully and encamped on the seashore.

The usurper Mahmud, already in control of a large part of Persia, tried in vain to forestall the czar and keep him from entering Derbent. He stirred up the neighboring Tartars and came hurrying up in person, but Derbent had already fallen.

Peter could not pursue his conquests any further at that time. The ships bringing fresh supplies, recruits, and horses had been lost near Astrakhan, and the season was far advanced. He returned to Moscow (January, 1723), where he made a triumphal entry. There, as was his wont, he gave a solemn account of his expedition to the deputy czar Romodanovsky, continuing to the end to play that singular comedy which, according to his eulogy at the Academy of Sciences in Paris, should have been performed before every monarch on earth.

Persia was still divided between Hussein and the usurping Mahmud, the former seeking a supporter in the emperor of Russia, the latter fearing in him an avenger who would snatch the fruits of rebellion from his grasp. Mahmud did everything in his power to incite the Ottoman Porte against Peter. He sent an embassy to Constantinople. The chieftains of Daghestan, who were under the protection of the Grand Seignior and who had been despoiled by Russian armies, demanded vengeance. The Divan was anxious about Georgia, which the Turks numbered among their possessions.

The Grand Seignior was ready to declare war, but the courts of Vienna and Paris stopped him. The Austrian Emperor let it be known that if the Turks attacked Russia, he would be obliged to defend her. The Marquis de Bonac, French ambassador to Constantinople, by his representations ably backed up the Imperial threats. He brought home the point that it was actually in the Porte's interest not to permit a usurping rebel from Persia to teach men how to unthrone sovereigns, and that the Russian emperor had merely done what the Grand Seignior should have done himself.

During these delicate negotiations, the rebel Mir Mahmud had advanced to the gates of Derbent. He devastated the surrounding countryside so that there would be nothing left for the Russians to subsist on. That part of ancient Hyrcania today called Gilyan was sacked, and its desperate inhabitants of their own free will placed themselves under the protection of the Russians, whom they regarded as liberators.

They imitated therein the example of the sophy himself. That unhappy monarch had sent an ambassador to Peter the Great solemnly imploring his aid. Hardly had the ambassador set out on his journey than the rebellious Mir Mahmud seized Isfahan, and with it the sophy himself.

The son of the dethroned and captive sophy, whose name was Tahmasp, eluded the tyrant, mustered some troops, and joined battle. He was no less eager than his father in urging Peter the Great to protect him, and sent the ambassador the same instructions already given by Shah Hussein.

Izmail Beg, the Persian ambassador, had not yet arrived, but his mission had already succeeded. He learned, on landing in Astrakhan, that General Matyushkin was about to leave with fresh troops to reinforce the Army of Daghestan. The city of Baku or Bachu, which gives the Caspian Sea its Persian name of Baku, had not as yet been captured. Izmail Beg gave the Russian general a letter for its citizens, in which he exhorts them in the name of the shah to submit to the emperor of Russia. The ambassador continued his journey to Saint Petersburg, and General Matyushkin went off to besiege the city of Baku. The ambassador arrived at the Russian court together with the news of the city's capture (August, 1723).

Baku is close to Shemakha, where the Russian factors had been butchered. It is neither so populous nor so prosperous as Shemakha, but is renowned for the naphtha with which it supplies all Persia. Never was a mission accomplished with more dispatch than Izmail Beg's (September, 1723). To avenge the deaths of his subjects and to aid the Sophy Tahmasp to fight the usurper, the Emperor Peter promised to march his armies into Persia, and the new sophy ceded to him not only the cities of Baku and Derbent, but also the provinces of Gilyan, Mazanderan, and Astrabad.

Gilyan, as we have already observed, is southern Hyrcania; Mazanderan, which adjoins it, is the land of the Mardi; Astrabad lies next to Mazanderan, and these were the three chief provinces of the ancient Medic kings. As a result, Peter found himself—thanks to the use of force and diplomacy—in control of Cyrus's original kingdom.

An observation not without interest is that the articles of this agreement regulated the prices of commodities to be supplied to the army. A camel was to cost only sixty francs (twelve rubles); a pound of bread came to less than five half-farthings, and a pound of beef to approximately six. These prices clearly demonstrate the area's abundance of real wealth, i.e., that which comes from the land, and its shortage of money, which is merely conventional wealth.

Such was the lamentable state of Persia that the unfortunate Sophy Tahmasp, a vagabond in his own kingdom pursued by the rebel

Mahmud, the murderer of his father and his brothers, was obliged to entreat both Russia and Turkey to be so kind as to take a portion of his kingdom, in order to retain the rest for himself.

The Emperor Peter, Sultan Achmet III, and Shah Tahmasp therefore agreed that Russia would keep the three provinces mentioned above, and that the Ottoman Porte would have Kasvin, Tauris, and Erivan, aside from what it would also take from Mir Mahmud. And so that beautiful realm was at one and the same time dismembered by the Russians, the Turks, and the Persians themselves.

Consequently, until his death the Emperor Peter reigned from the far-off Baltic to beyond the southern boundaries of the Caspian. Persia continued to be a prey to ruinous revolutions. The once wealthy and cultured Persians were plunged into destitution and barbarism, while Russia emerged from uncouth poverty to affluent urbanity. One individual, because he was of an active and resolute disposition, exalted his homeland, while another, because he was feeble and indolent, caused his country's downfall.

We are still very ill-informed regarding the particulars of all the woes that have so long beset Persia. It has been maintained that the hapless Shah Hussein was unmanly enough to place with his own hands his Persian miter—what we would call the crown—on the usurper Mahmud's head. Mahmud is said to have later gone out of his mind, and so a weakling and a madman settled the fate of countless thousands. It is also said that Mahmud, in a fit of insanity, personally killed all of Shah Hussein's sons and nephews, to the number of one hundred, and that he had the Gospel according to Saint John recited over his head in order to purify and heal himself. These Persian fables have been spread abroad and published in Paris by our own monks.

The tyrant who had murdered his uncle was eventually murdered in his turn by his nephew Ashraf, who was as cruel and as despotic as Mahmud had been.[14]

Shah Tahmasp continued to beg for Russian aid. He was the same Tahmasp or Thamas subsequently helped to recover his throne by the celebrated Quli Khan, only to be deposed by Quli Khan himself.[15]

These revolutions, the wars which Russia was later obliged to wage against the Turks, whom she defeated, and the evacuation of three Persian provinces, which cost Russia far more than they brought her, do not concern Peter the Great. They did not occur until several years after his death, and it suffices to say that he concluded his military career by adding three provinces to his empire in the vicinity of Persia, when he had just added three others near the frontiers of Sweden.

Chapter 17
Coronation of the Empress Catherine I.
Death of Peter the Great.

On his return from the Persian expedition, Peter found himself more than ever the arbiter of the North. He proclaimed himself protector of the family of that very Charles XII whose adversary he had been for eighteen years. He invited the king's nephew, the duke of Holstein, to Saint Petersburg, intending that he should marry his eldest daughter. From that time forward he took steps to uphold the duke's rights over his duchy of Schleswig-Holstein, and even formally pledged himself to this in a treaty of alliance concluded with Sweden (February, 1724).

He continued the public works already begun all over the empire, as far away as deepest Kamchatka. In order to direct these works more efficiently, he founded the Academy of Sciences at Saint Petersburg (February, 1724). The useful arts were everywhere flourishing; industries were fostered, the navy expanded, the army properly maintained, and the laws respected. He enjoyed his renown in peace, and wished to share it in a novel fashion with the woman who, by salvaging the disastrous Pruth campaign, had, as he put it, contributed to that very renown.

It was in Moscow that he had his wife crowned and anointed,[1] in the presence of the duchess of Courland, his elder brother's daughter,[2] and of the duke of Holstein, his future son-in-law. The proclamation he issued is worthy of note. It recalls how several Christian kings followed the practice of crowning their wives, and reminds us of the examples set by the emperors Basilides, Justinian, Heraclius, and Leo the Philosopher.[3] The emperor specifies the services rendered the state by Catherine, particularly in the Turkish war, when his army, as he says, reduced to twenty-two thousand men, was facing more than two hundred thousand foemen. Nothing was said in the decree about the empress's being named his successor, but he was getting the people of his empire used to the idea by means of this novel ceremony.

Something else that may have contributed to Catherine's being regarded as her husband's heir apparent is the fact that he himself walked before her on coronation day, in his capacity as captain of a new company created by him and named the Empress's Guards.

When they reached the church, Peter placed the crown on her head; she tried to embrace his knees, but he stopped her, and on leaving the cathedral had the orb and scepter borne before her. The ceremony was worthy in all respects of an emperor. Peter exhibited as much magnificence on brilliant public occasions as he did simplicity in his private life.

Having crowned his wife, he finally resolved to marry his eldest daughter, Anna Petrovna, to the duke of Holstein. The princess resembled her father in many ways, being tall, stately, and very beautiful. She was betrothed to the duke of Holstein (November 24, 1724), but with no elaborate ceremony. Peter already felt that his health was much impaired, and a domestic sorrow that may well have aggravated his last fatal illness made this final period of his life ill-suited to grandiose festivities.

Catherine had a young chamberlain[4] named Mons de la Croix,[5] born in Russia of a Flemish family. He was of distinguished appearance, and his sister, Madame de Balk, was lady-in-waiting to the empress. Together they ran her household. They were both denounced to the emperor, imprisoned, and put on trial for having accepted gifts. Since the year 1714, all persons holding official positions had been forbidden under pain of dishonor and death to accept presents, a prohibition that had been repeated on several occasions.

Both brother and sister were convicted. All those who had either purchased or rewarded their services were named in the sentence, with the exception of the duke of Holstein and his minister, Count von Bassevitz. It is even likely that the presents given by the duke to those who had helped arrange his marriage were not regarded as criminal.

Mons was sentenced to be beheaded, and his sister, the empress's favorite, to receive eleven strokes of the knout. The lady's two sons, one a chamberlain and the other a page, were stripped of their noble rank and sent off to the Army of Persia as private soldiers.

These drastic measures, so abhorrent to our way of thinking, were no doubt necessary in a land where upholding the law seemed to demand an appalling severity. The empress begged her husband to pardon her lady-in-waiting, but he angrily refused. In his fury he smashed a Venetian looking glass and said to his wife: "You see that it takes only one blow of my fist to return this glass to the dust from which it came." Catherine looked at him with affecting sorrow and replied, "Well, you have broken the most exquisite object in your palace, but do you believe that it will become more beautiful because of that?" These words appeased the emperor, but the only grace his wife could obtain from him was that her lady-in-waiting should receive five strokes of the knout instead of eleven.

I would not be reporting this incident were it not vouched for by an ambassador[6] who witnessed it, and who, having himself given presents to the brother and sister, was perhaps one of the chief causes of their tragedy. The affair emboldened those who judge spitefully of every-thing to spread the story that Catherine cut short the life of a husband who inspired her with more fear of his wrath than gratitude for his kindnesses.

These cruel suspicions were apparently corroborated by Catherine's alacrity in recalling her lady-in-waiting immediately after her husband's death, and in showering her with favors. It is the historian's duty to report the widespread rumors that break out in every age and in every land whenever a monarch dies an untimely death, as though unaided nature did not suffice to destroy us. However, that same duty requires the historian to demonstrate the recklessness and unfairness of these rumors.

There is an immense distance between the fleeting displeasure that may be caused by a strict husband and the desperate resolve to poison a lord and master to whom one owes everything. The risk of such an undertaking would have been as great as the crime itself. There was at that time a strong faction opposed to Catherine and in favor of the son of the ill-starred czarevich. Nevertheless, neither this group nor any other person at court suspected Catherine, and the vague rumors then current were merely the opinion of a few ill-informed foreigners indulg-ing, for no apparent reason, in the detestable pastime of attributing high crimes to those believed to have a motive for committing them. It was extremely doubtful indeed that Catherine possessed such a motive. There was no guarantee that she would succeed to the throne; she had been crowned, but solely in her capacity as the sovereign's consort, and not as his intended successor.

Peter had decreed this pageantry for purely ceremonial purposes, and not as conferring the right to reign. It was reminiscent of the precedent set by certain Roman emperors who had crowned their consorts, though not one of them ever became mistress of the empire. To con-clude, during Peter's last illness it was believed by some that Princess Anna Petrovna would succeed him conjointly with her husband the duke of Holstein, or that the emperor would name his grandson his successor. Consequently, far from Catherine's having anything to gain from the emperor's death, it was in her interest that he survive.

It was an acknowledged fact that Peter had long suffered from an abscess and from retention of urine, which caused him intense pain. The mineral waters of Olonets and others that he took afforded only minimal relief. Since the beginning of the year 1724, he had been visibly failing. His exertions, which he never abated, exacerbated his disease and hastened his end. His condition soon appeared to be critical, and he experienced attacks of burning fevers, which caused him to lapse into an almost ceaseless delirium. During a period of remission in his suffer-ings, he tried to write,[7] but his hand only formed illegible characters, of which all that could be deciphered were these words in Russian: "Give everything to . . ."

He cried out for Princess Anna Petrovna, to whom he wished to dictate something, but when she appeared at his bedside he had already lost the power of speech, and he sank into a death agony that lasted for sixteen hours. The empress Catherine had not left his bedside for three nights. At last he died in her arms, on January 28, at about four o'clock in the morning.

His body was carried into the great hall of the palace, followed by the entire imperial family, the Senate, personages of the highest distinction, and a throng of ordinary citizens. He lay in state, and everyone was free to approach him and kiss his hand, until the day of his funeral, which took place on March 10/21, 1725.[8]

It was both believed and published that his will named Catherine heiress to the empire, but the truth is that he never made a will, or at least that one was never found, a most astounding piece of negligence on the part of a lawmaker, and one which proves that he had not thought his illness to be fatal.

At the hour of his death no one knew who would occupy his throne. He was survived by his grandson Peter, son of the hapless Alexei, and his eldest daughter, the duchess of Holstein.[9] There was a sizable faction favoring the young Peter, but Prince Menshikov, the empress Catherine's perennial ally, forestalled the schemes of all other parties. Peter was at the point of death when Menshikov led Catherine into a room where their friends were already assembled. They had taken the crown jewels to the fortress[10] and secured the allegiance of the Guard. Prince Menshikov won over the archbishop of Novgorod,[11] and Catherine held a secret meeting with them and with a confidential secretary named Makarov,[12] a meeting attended by the duke of Holstein's ambassador.

On leaving this council, the empress returned to her dying husband, who breathed his last in her arms. Immediately, the senators and generals hurried to the palace, where the empress addressed them. Menshikov replied in their name, and for form's sake they deliberated in the empress's absence. Feofan, archbishop of Pleskov, declared that the emperor had said, on the eve of Catherine's coronation, that he was crowning her solely that she might reign after him. The whole assembly signed the proclamation, and Catherine succeeded her husband on the very day he died.[13]

Peter the Great was regretted in Russia by all those whom he had formed, and the next generation, which succeeded the partisans of the old ways, soon came to regard him as its father. When foreigners saw that all his institutions were stable, they conceived an unshakable admiration for him and admitted that he had been inspired by extraordinary wisdom rather than by a desire to perform astounding exploits.[14] Europe acknowledged that though he had loved fame, he had employed it in doing good, that his failings had never impaired his great qualities, and that, while the man had his blemishes, the monarch was invariably great. He coerced nature in every respect, in his subjects, in himself, on land and on sea, but he coerced it in order to embellish it. The arts, which he transplanted with his own hands into territories several of which were then untamed, have, by bearing fruit, testified to his genius and immortalized his memory. Nowadays they seem to have originated in the very lands to which he took them. Legislation, civil administration, diplomacy, military discipline, the navy, commerce and industry, the sciences and fine arts, everything has been brought to perfection as he intended, and, by an unprecedented and unique phenomenon, all his achievements have been perpetuated and all his undertakings perfected by four women who have succeeded him, one after the other, on the throne.

The palace has experienced revolutions since his death, but the state has not. The empire's splendor increased under Catherine I; under Anna Petrovna[15] Russia triumphed over the Turks and Swedes; under Elizabeth it conquered Prussia and part of Pomerania; and it has enjoyed peace and seen the arts flourish under Catherine II.[16]

It is for Russian historians to enter into all the details of the institutions, legislation, wars, and enterprises of Peter the Great. They inspire their fellow countrymen by extolling all those who aided that monarch in his martial and diplomatic exertions. It is enough for a foreigner, a disinterested lover of excellence, to attempt to show what that great man was like who learned from Charles XII to defeat him, who on two occasions left his domains the better to rule them, who to set an example for his people worked with his own hands at virtually all of the necessary arts, and who was both the founder and the father of his empire.

The sovereigns of nations long civilized will say to themselves: "If, in the frozen regions of ancient Scythia, one man, by his own unaided genius, has accomplished such great things, what should we not achieve, in kingdoms where the accumulated labors of several centuries have made everything easy for us?"

Letter from Voltaire to Ivan Shuvalov[1]
on the First Volume of *The History of Russia*

Ferney, June 11, 1761

Sir:

You have brought upon yourself the burden of importunity that my doubtless too frequent letters must be inflicting upon you. This is what comes of inspiring me with a passion for Peter the Great and for yourself; passions are somewhat loquacious.

Your Excellency will have received several notebooks that are mere rough drafts; I shall wait until you write in the margins a few words that will assist me in painting the real picture. The notebooks were written in haste. You will easily distinguish the copyist's mistakes from the author's, and everything will then be put exactly right. I simply wanted to sound you out on your preferences.

As soon as I was able to find a moment's leisure, I read the comments on the first volume, which you sent in duplicate but of which only one copy reached me, the other having apparently been lost with the rest of the papers entrusted to M. Pushkin.

I will make one general request, Sir, both of yourself and of those who wrote the comments, namely, that you be good enough to bear in mind that your secretary at Les Délices[2] is writing for the southern nations, who do not pronounce proper names at all as the northern nations do. I have already shared with you the honor of pointing out that there never was a king of Persia called Darius nor a king of India named Porus, also that the Euphrates, the Tigris, the Indus, and the Ganges were never so named by the native peoples, and that the Greeks Hellenized everything.

Graïs dedit ore rotundo
Musa loqui.[3]

In your country, Peter the Great is not called Peter; permit me, however, to continue calling him Peter, to name Moskva, Moscow and the Moskva River the Moska, etc.

I said that it would be possible for caravans, by making a detour through independent Tartary, to encounter scarcely one mountain between Saint Petersburg and Peking, which is the simple truth. If you cross the land of the Eluts,[4] the deserts of the Kotkos-Kalmucks, and the Koko Nor Tartar country,[5] there are mountains to your right and left, but to all intents and purposes you could certainly go to China without climbing one mountain, just as you could travel overland—and that very easily—from Saint Petersburg to the heart of France almost exclusively over level ground. This is a rather important observation in the realm of natural philosophy, since it serves to refute the theory, as false as it is famous, that ocean currents formed the mountains that cover the earth. Kindly note, Sir, that I do not say there are no mountains between Saint Petersburg and China; what I *do* say is that they may be avoided by taking the roundabout way.[6]

It is inconceivable to me how someone can tell me "that Black Russia is quite unknown." One has merely to open La Martinière's dictionary—not to mention nearly all the geographers—at the entry of *Russia* to find these words: "Black Russia, between Volhynia and Podolia," etc.[7]

I am also quite astonished to be informed that the city which you call Kiev or Kieff[8] was not originally named Kiovia. La Martinière is of my opinion, and if the Greek inscriptions have been destroyed, nevertheless they did once exist.

I am unaware if the person transcribing the documents sent to me by you, Sir, is a German; he writes *Iwan Wassiliewitsch,* whereas I write *Ivan Basilovitz.*[9] This has given rise to several misconceptions in the comments.

There is a particularly odd one with respect to the district of Moscow called the Chinese City. The author of the observations states that "this district was so called before anyone had the slightest knowledge of the Chinese and their wares." I appeal to Your Excellency: how can anything be termed Chinese when no one knows that China exists? Would we speak of Russian valor if there were no Russia?

Can such observations have possibly been made? I would have been most happy, Sir, had your important occupations allowed you to cast an eye over the manuscripts that you are pleased to forward to me. Their author is prodigal of German s's, c's, k's, and h's. The river that we call Véronise, a very euphonious name, is in the manuscripts called Woronetsch, and in the comments I am told that you pronounce it Voronège [Voronezh]. How do you expect me to get my bearings amidst all these vexations? I am writing in French; am I not to conform to the suavity of French pronunciation?

Why, when I meticulously followed your records, distinguished between the bishops' serfs and monastic serfs, and wrote that there were 721,500 monastic serfs, is it considered unworthy of notice that a zero was omitted when this figure was repeated on page 59, and that the error is entirely due to the bookseller, who has transcribed the figure incorrectly?

Why do people persist in reviving the disgraceful and barbaric fable about Czar Ivan Vasilievich,[10] who, they say, wanted to have the hat of an alleged English ambassador named Bèze nailed to the unfortunate ambassador's head? For what demented reason did this czar want oriental ambassadors to speak to him bareheaded? Is your critic unaware that throughout the Orient it is a breach of respect to remove one's hat? Ask the English minister, Sir, and he will assure you that there never was an Ambassador Bèze, the first English ambassador to Russia being Lord Carlisle.[11]

Why am I told that in the sixth century people in Kiev were writing on paper, which was not invented until the twelfth?

The most judicious observation I have come across is the one concerning the Patriarch Photius. It is certain that Photius died long before Princess Olga;[12] Polyeuctus should have been written instead of Photius, since Polyeuctus was Patriarch of Constantinople in Princess Olga's time. This is a copyist's error that I should have corrected on reading the proof sheets. I am guilty of this oversight, which anyone of good faith may easily rectify.

Do these comments actually inform me, Sir, that the patriarchate of Constantinople is the most ancient? Alexandria's was the oldest, and there were twenty bishops of Jerusalem before there was one at Byzantium.

It is truly a matter of the utmost importance to know whether a Dutch physician was named Vangad or Vangardt! Your manuscripts, Sir, call him Vangad, and your critic scolds me for having misspelled the name of this great personage. He would seem to have gone out of his way to discomfit me, to irritate me, and to discover—in a work composed under your patronage—mistakes that are not there.

I have also received, Sir, a memorial entitled *Abstract of Researches into the Antiquity of the Russians, taken from the full-length History now in progress.*

This peculiar work begins by saying "that the antiquity of the Slavs goes back as far as the Trojan War, and that their king Polimenes went with Antenor to the ends of the Adriatic Sea, etc." This was the kind of history we wrote a thousand years ago;[13] it was thus that we used to trace our descent from Hector by way of Francus, and it is apparently for this reason that someone wishes to denounce my preface, in which I point out what should be thought of these miserable fairy tales. You, Sir, have too much taste, too much good sense, and too much erudition to tolerate the flaunting of such absurdities in so enlightened an age.

I suspect the same German of being the author of the abovementioned memorial, for I see Ivanovitz and Basilovitz written as follows: Wanovitsch and Wassiliewitsch. I could wish that this man had more wit and less consonants.

Take my word for it, Sir, confine yourself to Peter the Great. I relinquish to you our Chilperics, Childerics, Sigiberts, and Chariberts,[14] and content myself with Louis XIV.

If Your Excellency thinks as I do, I beg Your Excellency to apprise me of the fact. I await the honor of your reply with my customary zeal and desire to please you, and shall ever think my time well spent if I have convinced you of the sentiments full of esteem and devotion in which I shall remain, Sir, my whole life long, Your Excellency's, etc.

Notes

A Note on Peter's Successors

Although Voltaire repeatedly refers to four empresses succeeding Peter, the facts are a little more complicated. His first successor was Catherine I, his widow, who reigned until her death in 1727. She was followed by Peter II, Alexei Petrovich's son (d. 1730), who was succeeded by Anna Ivanovna, Peter the Great's niece (and duchess of Courland), who reigned until her death in 1740. Anna's infant grandnephew, Ivan VI, was her nominal successor, but the throne passed to Elizabeth, daughter of Peter I and Catherine, in 1741. After Elizabeth's death, her nephew, Peter III, became czar. This Peter was, of course, the grandson of Peter and Catherine; his father, Duke Charles-Frederick of Holstein, was the nephew of Charles XII of Sweden and believed by many to be that monarch's rightful heir. Despite this heritage, Peter III did not long retain his throne. He married Sophia of Anhalt-Zerbst, who took the name Catherine and her husband's crown, reigning for thirty-four years as Catherine the Great. It is perhaps not surprising that Voltaire skips over Peter I's male heirs.

A Bibliographical Note

The following list includes probably the best-known and most widely available English-language biographies of Peter the Great. As regards the major events of Peter's life, there are, naturally, few disputes, but emphases, assessments of motives, opinions on the worth of various achievements, and so on vary perhaps even more widely than they would in several biographies of an American president. Kluchevsky's book deals at length with the internal administrative changes in Russia during Peter's reign; unfortunately, the general reader will find this translation less than satisfactory. De Jonge emphasizes what he perceives as Peter's essential "Russianness." Sumner provides a brief review of the facts of Peter's life. Grey's book, long the best academic biography of Peter, provides a more thorough treatment, as does Massie's long (834-page) Life.

De Jonge, Alex, *Fire and Water*. New York: Coward, McCann & Geoghegan, 1980.
Grey, Ian, *Peter the Great, Emperor of All Russia*. Philadelphia and New York: Lippincott, 1960.
Kluchevsky, Vasily O., *A History of Russia*, trans. C. J. Hogarth. New York: Russell & Russell, 1960 [1926]. 5 volumes; vol. 4 contains Peter the Great and his times.
Massie, Robert K., *Peter the Great, His Life and World*. New York: Knopf, 1980.
Sumner, Benedict H., *Peter the Great and the Emergence of Russia*. London: English Universities Press, 1960 [1951].

In the notes which follow, these biographies are referred to by their author's last name alone, obviating excessive repetition of bibliographical details.

Translator's Introduction

1. See A Bibliographical Note, above.
2. See Hywel Berwyn Evans, *A Provisional Bibliography of English Editions and Translations of*

Voltaire, in *Studies on Voltaire and the Eighteenth Century,* vol. 8, ed. Theodore Besterman (Geneva: Institut et Musée Voltaire, 1959).

3. See my translation, *Lion of the North: Charles XII of Sweden* (Rutherford, N.J.: Fairleigh Dickinson University Press; London and Toronto: Associated University Presses, 1981).

4. *Lion of the North,* 19.

5. *Lion of the North,* 131.

6. See Boswell's preliminary remarks on the obligations of the biographer in the Introduction to his *Life of Johnson.*

7. *Peter the Great,* Part II, ch. 8. Voltaire was twenty-two at the time.

8. Voltaire often makes use of rhetorical questions in *Peter the Great:* e.g., "the Streltsi provoked a new uprising, and—who would believe it?—the cause was religion, the cause was dogma" (Part I, ch. 5): "Who would believe that there was a university at Dorpat?" (Part I, ch. 13), and so on.

9. Cf., among passages too numerous to mention, ". . . it is evident that the first kings of China bore the same names as the ancient kings of Egypt, for in the name of the Yu dynasty may be found characters which, when arranged in a different order, form the word *Menes.* It is thus not to be doubted that the Emperor Yu took his name from King Menes of Egypt, and that the Emperor Ki is manifestly King Atoës if you change *K* to *A* and *i* to *toës*" (Preface).

10. "The hospodar or voivode chosen by the Porte to govern these provinces [Moldavia and Wallachia] is always an Orthodox Christian. By this choice, the Turks have displayed their tolerance, while our ignorant ranters berate them for their persecutions" (Part II, ch. 1). On the Asiatic practice, followed in Muscovy, of not wearing a sword in church or at court: "This is an oriental practice contrary to our own ridiculous and barbarous custom of conversing with God, kings, our friends, and women with a long offensive weapon trailing at our heels" (Part I, ch. 2).

11. Part I, ch. 1.

12. Historical and Critical Preface. Later, writing of Swedish atrocities perpetrated on the Ukrainian peasantry, Voltaire cites an approving passage from Nordberg containing Charles XII's instructions to put some Ukrainians on trial and *then* execute them. Voltaire continues: "Such are the sentiments of justice and humanity found in a royal confessor" (Part I, ch. 17).

13. Grey, p. 453, n. 3.

[The unattributed notes that follow are Voltaire's; the translator's notes are enclosed in brackets.]

Historical and Critical Preface

1. [Voltaire consistently omits the *Saint* from the city's name.—J.]
2. [Voltaire uses *arts* in its old connotation to comprise the useful as well as the fine arts.—J.]
3. [J.-J. Rousseau never fails to bring out the worst in Voltaire.—J.]
4. [Elizabeth Petrovna, 1709–62, empress from 1741 to 1762.—J.]
5. [I.e., Voltaire himself.—J.]
6. [Stanislas Leszczynski, 1677–1766.—J.]
7. [And who is, needless to say, Voltaire himself.—J.]
8. [First published in 1751.—J .]
9. [Troyes.—J.]
10. [The famous boulevard of the same name was constructed as recently as the 1860s.—J.]
11. [Small town on the Luxembourg border, about 120 miles northeast of Paris.—J.]
12. [In 1745, after the victory of Fontenoy.—J.]
13. [Voltaire naturally uses the French *église,* derived from the Greek *ekklesia.*—J.]
14. [Vanquisher of three Roman legions in the Teutoburgerwald during the reign of the emperor Augustus.—J.]

15. [Two distinguished French historians. Jacques-Auguste de Thou, 1553–1617; Paul de Rapin de Thoyras, 1671–1725.—J.]

16. [The first edition of *Peter the Great*, Part I, was printed in 1759 and published the following year.—J.]

17. [Fought in the times of Alexander the Great and Julius Caesar, respectively.—J.]

18. [Chaplain to King Charles XII of Sweden, and butt of Voltaire's irascible comments in numerous footnotes in his history of that king.—J.]

19. [Legendary deeds of Theseus.—J.]

20. [Anacharsis the Scythian was the friend of Solon of Athens, sixth century B.C. The modern Scythian, of course, is Peter the Great.—J.]

21. [Gaius Suetonius Tranquillus, fl. ca. 100 A.D., author of a rather scandalmongering work entitled *The Lives of the Twelve Caesars*.—J.]

22. [La Beaumelle, Laurent Angliviel de, 1726–73. The Nordberg of *The Age of Louis XIV*.—J.]

23. [Voltaire uses the word *prince* throughout his works in its old connotation as a generic term meaning *king, ruler, monarch*, etc., as does Machiavelli in *The Prince*.—J.]

24. [What Voltaire is denouncing here is the well-known French predilection for the *portrait physique et moral*, a psychological profile in addition to an actual description of the subject—or rather he is criticizing the *abuse* of the portrait, as may be deduced from what follows.—J.]

25. [An interminable romance—published 1654–60—by the celebrated *précieuse* Madeleine de Scudéry.—J.]

26. [Albrecht von Wallenstein, 1583–1634, the most celebrated Austrian general of the Thirty Years' War.—J.]

27. [1614–79. A flamboyant and somewhat erratic churchman and would-be statesman, much addicted to political intrigue; author of interesting *Memoirs*, filled with vivid and extremely subjective portraits of his contemporaries.—J.]

28. [Louis Maimbourg, 1610–86, author, *inter alia*, of a *History of the Holy League*. Voltaire's distaste for Maimbourg's work, already apparent in his use of "insipid hues," is further revealed in the terms "illuminates," i.e., as in a medieval manuscript—needless to say, anathema to Voltaire—and "historical romances." Voltaire's actual words are *histoires romanesques*—"romantic" histories, in other words, but one remove from pure fiction.—J .]

29. [Anne of Austria, Louis XIV's mother.—J.]

30. [Ivan III, Grand Duke of Moscow, ruled 1440–1505. His grandson Ivan IV (Ivan the Terrible) was actually the first to proclaim himself czar.—J.]

31. [The Holy Roman Emperor.—J.]

32. [The right of nations, i.e., international law.—J.]

33. [Louis XIV.—J.]

34. [Hubner's *Universal Geography* was published in French in translation in 1757.—J.]

35. [The Ob, located in the USSR east of the Urals, empties in fact not into the Black Sea, but into the Arctic, at the Gulf of Ob (a very pardonable error!).—J.]

Foreword

1. [See A Note on Peter's Successors. In addition to Peter's male heirs, Voltaire here somewhat ungraciously omits Catherine I, Peter's czarina and the only person capable of managing him, who succeeded him. Her wildly romantic and improbable career is, however, described at some length both in *Peter the Great* and *Lion of the North* (q.v., Book 5).—J.]

2. [Published 1731.—J.]

Part I, Chapter 1

1. [The league is not a fixed measurement, but varies, as used by Voltaire, roughly from 2.5 to 4.5 miles.—J.]

2. [Ivan and his younger half-brother, Peter, ruled as a kind of joint czar from 1682 until Ivan's death in 1696.—J.]

3. ["La dîme royale" was a form of combined poll tax and income tax suggested by Vauban in 1707.—J.].

4. [Voltaire says *Kiovie,* i.e., Kiev, capital of the Ukraine.—J.]

5. [Madyes the Scythian: ruler of Transcaucasian region in western Persia ca. 630 B.C.—J.]

6. [As in *Lion of the North,* Voltaire makes no concessions whatever to contemporary usage, but persists in using wherever possible the more mellifluous names dating back to antiquity. Here, the Dnieper reverts to the Greek *Borysthenes;* cf. the Letter to Count Shuvalov.—J.]

7. [The explanation that follows is rather pointless to the English-speaker, since it involves an apparent attempt to introduce into French the name *Russiens,* which, as Voltaire points out, could easily be confused with *Prussiens.* Hence his preference for *Russes,* the standard term used in modern French. I, however, shall naturally continue to write *Russians* (the usage of the language in which I am writing). The Roxolani mentioned in the paragraph were an ancient Sarmatian people dwelling north of the Black Sea.—J.]

8. [The celebrated Teutonic Knights, founded at Acre in 1190, and immortalized as the Nazi-like villains of Sergei Eisenstein's epic film *Alexander Nevsky.*—J.]

9. [The northernmost tip of Norway.—J.]

10. [Voltaire here takes no account of Peter's transferral of the capital to Saint Petersburg.—J.]

11. In Russian, *Moskva.*

12. [Voltaire's text says *Kremelin,* and his note explains "In Russian, *Kremlin."*—J.]

13. [Considering the almost total lack of paving in the streets even of major cities like Paris and London in the early seventeenth century, Moscow's must have been in a truly abominable state to have made such an impression on Lord Carlisle, unless he was an unusually fastidious person.—J.]

14. [Peter the Great had two half-brothers. Feodor reigned 1676–82; Ivan and Peter ruled jointly until the former's death in 1696.—J.]

15. M. de Shuvalov.

16. [Region north of the Black Sea; its inhabitants may have been ancestors of the Slavs.—J.]

17. [The Volkhov.—J.]

18. [Ivan III Vasilievich (the Great) was grand duke of Moscow 1462–1505; he subjugated Novgorod in 1478. Voltaire calls him *Ivan Basilovitz* and adds a note: "In Russian, *Ivan Vasilievich."* Voltaire frequently confuses this grand duke with his grandson, *Czar* Ivan Vasilievich (Ivan IV, the Terrible).—J.]

19. [Voltaire says *la Kiovie.*—J.]

20. [Voltaire had made almost exactly the same comment thirty years before, in *Lion of the North,* with respect to the Bug/Hypanis.—J.]

21. [Old name for the Crimea.—J.]

22. [In accordance with his practice, Voltaire persists in using the classical name: *Palus Méotides.*—J.]

23. [Voltaire calls it *Véronise,* but adds the note, "In Russia, it is spelled and pronounced *Voronezh."*—J.]

24. [West end of the Caucasus.—J.]

25. [Voltaire is apparently confusing the Yaik and the Ural; see n. 29 below.—J.]

26. [Captain John Perry, hydraulic engineer hired by Peter during his stay in England (1689) to dig a canal system between the Volga and the Don.—J.]

27. [Kipchak Khanate. Capital located near present-day Astrakhan.—J.]

28. [Voltaire says "Jean Basilidès, petit-fils d'Ivan Basilovitz." These are Ivan IV (the Terrible) and his grandfather Ivan III (the Great); cf. n. 18 above.—J.]

29. [Orenburg is actually located on the Ural River, in the southwest foothills of the Urals; the Caucasus Mountains are a good 750 miles southwest of the city.—J.]

30. [Modern Uzbek S.S.R..—J.]

31. From the *Memoirs* of Strahlenberg, corroborated by my Russian sources.

32. [Captured at Poltava.—J.]

33. [Again, Voltaire prefers the old classical name, the *Hyrcanian Sea.*—J.]

34. [Not the *North* Sea; the White Sea or Arctic Sea.—J.]

35. [Voltaire says *Mount* Taurus, but it's a range, not a peak.—J.]

36. [Voltaire says *Austral* Lands.—J.]

37. [By "northern Tartary," Voltaire apparently means the extreme western part of Siberia. "La mer Glaciale," here used for the White Sea, usually means the Arctic.—J.]

38. [Feodor I, son of Ivan the Terrible, reigned 1584–98.—J.]

39. [*Horizon* 18: 4 (Autumn 1976) contains an account of the discovery and conquest of Siberia by one Yermak or Ermak, starting in 1579.—J.]

40. Documents sent from Saint Petersburg.

41. Ibid.

42. [By Buffon.—J.]

43. [It is unclear whether Voltaire is using the term (which is in the singular) specifically to refer to the human species, or to the animal kingdom in general.—J.]

44. [Voltaire actually writes *Irtis*, adding the note, "In Russian, *Irtysh.*"—J.]

45. In Russian, *Tobolskoy.*

46. [Undoubtedly mammoth or mastodon.—J.]

47. [Tattooing?—J.]

48. [In Voltaire's time, *Germany* almost invariably meant the Holy Roman or Austro-Hungarian Empire, not the modern nation-state of Germany, which did not properly exist until the age of Bismarck.—J.]

49. [Like the Académie des Sciences, the Académie des Inscriptions is one of the five academies constituting the Institut de France. The Académie Française is the best-known outside of France.—J.]

50. [Presumably the whole of the Americas, North and South alike.—J.]

51. [The Kuril islands would seem to be the ones intended.—J.]

52. [Joseph Nicolas Delisle, 1688–1768; his brother Guillaume, 1675–1726, was a geographer.—J.]

53. [I.e., the Northeast Passage.—J.]

54. [Actually, Delisle died seventeen years after Bering.—J.]

55. [Voltaire's Burgundians he calls by the old generic term *Germains.*—J.]

Part I, Chapter 2

1. [See chapter 1, Description of Russia.—J.]

2. [Voltaire says *odonoskis.*—J.]

3. [The "Old Believers."—J.]

4. [In Voltaire's day, France still had the largest population of any single nation in Europe.—J.]

5. [Voltaire discreetly omits the term *vérole* (syphilis), since it is perfectly obvious from *la petite vérole* (smallpox) what he means. It was still a matter of faith in his day that venereal disease had been brought back to Europe from the Americas by Columbus's men in 1494, which is apparently when the first European outbreak occurred.—J.]

6. [This was an English ambassador in the preface.—J.]

7. [See above, preface.—J.]

8. [The Terrible. Voltaire persists in calling him *Jean ou Ivan Basilidès.*—J.]

9. [Which, needless to say, ceased to be a republic with the advent of the emperors.—J.]

10. [A little of Rousseau's "noble savage" appears to have crept into Voltaire's thought here.—J.]

11. [Princess Olga, wife of Prince Igor and mother of Svyatoslav I, was, according to tradition, converted in 955 in Kiev, or, according to another tradition, in 957 in Constantinople. Saint Clotilde (475?–545?) was the wife of Clovis the Great. Mieczylaw I was duke of Poland 962–92, converted in 966. The emperor Henry II (reigned 1002–24) is himself known as Saint Henry.—J.]

12. [*A Picture History of Russia*, ed. John Stuart Martin (New York: Bonanza Books, 1968), says it was the emperor Constantine Porphyrogenitus (reigned 913–59) who had his eye on her.—J.]

13. [She was Prince Igor's widow.—J.]

14. He was called Svyatoslav. [Svyatoslav actually reigned only ten years (962–72), his mother having served as regent during his minority.—J.]

15. [Vladimir I, reigned 980–1015, known variously as *the Great* and/or *Saint* Vladimir.—J.]

16. Taken from a privately owned manuscript entitled *Ecclesiastical Government in Russia*.

17. [I.e., in Turkish Constantinople/Istanbul.—J.]

18. [See next chapter.—J.]

19. [Zealous reformer (1605–81) and arch-opponent of the "Old Believers" or "Raskolniki."—J.]

20. [Cf., e.g., the Gnostics, "those who know."—J.]

21. [The Raskolniki sect was founded in reaction to the reforms of the Patriarch Nikon in the mid-seventeenth century.—J.]

22. [The histories all say the old style was with *two* fingers; Nikon introduced the three-fingered blessing.—J.]

23. [Voltaire calls it the *Pont-Euxin*.—J.]

24. [Wool was England's major source of wealth during the late Middle Ages.—J.]

25. [Plus ça change, plus c'est la même chose!—J.]

26. ["Enfin Pierre naquit, et la Russie fut formée." An Alexandrine consciously or unconsciously inspired by Boileau's *Art poétique:* "Enfin Malherbe vint, et le premier en France, / Fit sentir dans les vers une juste cadence." (Chant Ier, ll.131–32).—J.]

Part I, Chapter 3

1. The Russians spell it Romanow; the French have no *w*. It is also pronounced Romanof. [Voltaire himself had written *Romano*.—J.]

2. [Filaret's wife's name was Xenia, also known as Marta the Nun. Perhaps her surname was Sheremeteyeva; Voltaire calls Marshal Sheremeteyev *Sheremeto* on occasion.—J.]

3. [Sigismund III, reigned 1586–1632. Formerly king of Sweden as well, but deposed by Swedes because he was a Catholic, and succeeded in Sweden by his own uncle, Charles IX.—J.]

4. [Alexei's two czarinas were (1) Maria Miloslavskaya (d. 1669) and (2) Natalya Naryshkina, Peter the Great's mother.—J.]

5. [The hospodars were governors of Moldavia and Wallachia, and vassals of the sultan.—J.]

6. [John Sobieski, king of Poland (John III) 1674–96. The Generals of the Crown were two co-commanders-in-chief of the Polish army.—J.]

7. [Ladislas Jagello, grand duke of Lithuania and king of Poland, 1386–1434.—J.]

8. [Hugh Capet, reigned 987–96, founder of the Capetian dynasty. Louis VII (the Younger) reigned 1137–80.—J.]

9. [Actually Marta Apraxina; she was Matveyev's goddaughter. Voltaire writes *Mateona*. —J.]

10. [I.e., all the nations of Western Europe, especially France.—J.]

11. [Pulcheria, Byzantine empress 414–53 A.D., was sister of Emperor Theodosius II (reigned 408–50) and became regent in 414.—J.]

Part I, Chapter 4

1. Taken in its entirety from documents sent from Moscow and Saint Petersburg.
2. [I.e., his exclusion by Feodor, who named Peter. As it turned out, Ivan and Peter "ruled" as joint czars, while Sophia really ran the show from behind the scenes.—J.]
3. [Massie, p. 48, calls him Dr. Van Gaden; de Jonge (p. 49) refers to a Dr. Daniel whose son was killed by the Streltsi; Voltaire may have combined the two. For his final word on the subject, see the Letter to Shuvalov.—J.]
4. [Lucius Cornelius Sulla was all-powerful in Rome at the turn of the second and first centuries B.C. The two Triumvirates comprised: (1) Julius Caesar, Pompey the Great, and Marcus Licinius Crassus; and (2) Octavius Caesar (the future Augustus), Mark Antony, and Marcus Aemilius Lepidus. The old Roman Republic was overthrown and replaced by the monarchical empire as a direct result of the activities of these and other such men.—J.]
5. Or Matheeff; in our language it is Matthew. [Artemon Matveyev had been Czar Alexei's chief minister and had introduced him to his second wife, Natalya Naryshkina. Prince Michael Dolgoruky was son of the Streltsi commander.—J.]
6. [The Red Square.—J.]
7. [Voltaire does not distinguish between Germans and Dutchmen here.—J.]

Part I, Chapter 5

1. Based in its entirety on records sent from Saint Petersburg.
2. [*Ahasuerus* is the Hebrew form of the name *Xerxes:* see the story of Esther in the Old Testament.—J.]
3. ["But many that are first shall be last; and the last shall be first." Matthew 19:30. Also see Matthew 20:16.—J.]
4. [The expression has a figurative meaning, although in view of what had already transpired, here it's possibly meant to be taken literally.—J.]
5. [I.e., with no legalistic nonsense about a trial or anything like that.—J.]
6. [Prince Ivan Khovansky, "a braggart and an ambitious rogue," according to Grey, p. 41. Massie, p. 41, points out that Khovansky had helped to incite the Streltsi revolt.—J.]
7. [The famous Troitsa Monastery (= "of the Trinity") is the largest in Russia.—J.]
8. [In Italy (Monte Cassino), France (Corbie), and Germany (Fulda and Kempten).—J.]
9. [Possibly modern Kargopol (61:32 N).—J.]

Part I, Chapter 6

1. Documents from Saint Petersburg and Moscow.
2. [Lake Pleschev (Grey, p. 55).—J.]
3. ["Franz Lefort, who was the son of a prosperous Genevan merchant. . . . was pleasure-loving, high-spirited, but idle and irresponsible. . . . Lefort, then in his early thirties, cast a spell over Peter, who had met no one like him before." Grey, p. 69. Kluchevsky, p. 15, gives a similar assessment.—J.]
4. [It was long the headquarters of Calvinism, ever since Jean Calvin took up permanent residence there in 1541.—J.]
5. [King William III.—J.]
6. [Until the Revolution, the senior regiment of the Russian army.—J.]
7. [General Patrick Gordon, born Aberdeenshire, 1635, Catholic émigré, "an honorable, conscientious, and courageous Scot," to cite Grey, p. 68.—J.]

8. General Lefort's manuscripts.

9. [One of the most remarkable acts of toleration and statesmanship in the history of Europe. Promulgated by Henry IV in 1598 and guaranteeing freedom of worship to French Protestants, the edict was inexcusably revoked by Louis XIV in 1685.—J.]

10. Ibidem.

Part I, Chapter 7

1. Based on documents sent from China and Saint Petersburg, and on letters published in the *History of China* compiled by Duhalde.

2. [Again demonstrating his cavalier attitude toward foreign place names, Voltaire uses *la mer Glaciale* to refer to what in this context can only be the Arctic Ocean; in the previous chapter he had used precisely the same name to denote the White Sea.—J.]

3. [The Tartar Strait, joining the Sea of Okhotsk and Sea of Japan.—J.]

4. Memoirs of the Jesuits Pereira and Gerbillon.

5. [Voltaire calls it *Nipchou.*—J.]

6. 1689, September 8 (new style), Chinese archives.

Part I, Chapter 8

1. [Candia is Crete; the Peloponnese is now called the Morea.—J.]

2. [E.g., Germanicus, Scipio Africanus.—J.]

3. Sheremetow, or Sheremetof, or, according to another spelling, Czeremetoff. [Voltaire's obvious irritation at these preposterously un-French names is equaled only by that of the translator at Voltaire's own idiosyncratic orthography. The version of the name given in Voltaire's actual text is *Sheremeto.*—J.]

4. [Probably Jacob Jansen, a Dutchman (mentioned by Grey, p. 84).—J.]

5. [Old name for the Netherlands.—J.]

6. [Caffa is now Feodosiya; the Cimmerian Bosporus is the Kerch Strait.—J.]

7. Lefort's *Memoirs*.

8. [Ancient country on the eastern shore of the Black Sea, famous for the exploits of Jason and the Argonauts in search of the Golden Fleece, and of Medea.—J.]

9. General Lefort's manuscripts.

10. [Poland was unique in having an electoral monarchy while styling itself a republic.—J.]

Part I, Chapter 9

1. Records from Saint Petersburg and Lefort's *Memoirs*. [The Golovin of this embassy was actually Feodor Alexeevich, according to Massie, p. 169, and de Jonge, p. 104.—J.]

2. [Frederick I of Prussia, reigned 1701–13.—J.]

3. Manuscript memoirs of Lefort.

4. [Now Zaandam.—J.]

5. [I.e., in two or more sections.—J.]

6. [According to Sumner, this was Farquharson, a mathematician from Aberdeen.—J.]

7. [A rather unfair hit at the theory of vortices propounded by René Descartes, who had, after all, been dead since 1650, when Isaac Newton was eight.—J.]

8. [An allusion to the disedifying persecution of the great astronomer by the Church in the early

seventeenth century for daring to champion the Copernican heliocentric solar system to the disadvantage of the comfortably geocentric Ptolemaic arrangement.—J.]

9. [It was in fact the royal yacht, and was almost brand new.—J.]

10. [What the French nowadays call *capitaine de vaisseau*, i.e., full captain.—J.]

11. [It must be remembered that in Voltaire's day the Papal States were an independent power, which explains the distinction made here between Rome and Italy.—J.]

12. [I.e., "the inn." Voltaire naturally calls it *Wurtchafft*.—J.]

13. [Leopold's son and successor as emperor, Joseph.—J.]

14. [Mirza: a Persian title of honor.—J.]

15. Manuscripts from Saint Petersburg and Lefort.

Part I, Chapter 10

1. Lefort's papers.

2. Memoirs of Captain Perry the engineer, who was working for Peter the Great in Russia. The Lefort papers.

3. Lefort's papers.

4. [This was the Semyonovsky Regiment mentioned earlier.—J.]

5. [Voltaire here uses two expressions that are practically synonymous, *le droit du glaive* and *celui de condamner à des peines afflictives et à la mort*.—J.]

6. [Peter in other words adopted the Julian calendar, because the Gregorian, as Grey remarks (p. 163), "was suspect to Protestant and Orthodox alike as a papist invention; it was not adopted in England until 1752, and in Russia until 1918."—J.]

7. [Obscure. This may mean some individuals were still using scrolls.—J.]

8. [This rosy picture is contradicted by de Jonge (p. 129), who characterizes Peter's approach as a "mocking and sadistic brand of play . . . callous indifference to the fact that many of the persons whose beards he was now shearing believed that he might thereby be endangering their chances of entering paradise."—J.]

9. [Gala evening.—J.]

10. On September 10, 1698. I am consistently using the new style of dating.

Part I, Chapter 11

1. Nordberg, Charles XII's chaplain and confessor, says in his history "that he had the insolence to complain about grievances, and was sentenced to lose both his honor and his life." This is the language of a priest in the service of despotism. Nordberg should have known that it is impossible to deprive of his honor a citizen who does his duty.

2. See *The History of Charles XII*. [De Jonge (p. 150) attributes Peter's absence from the Battle of Narva to cowardice: "He displayed his occasional capacity for panic." Massie (p. 329) refutes this accusation.—J.]

3. [The Battle of Arbela marked the destruction of the Persian host of King Darius by the incomparably smaller army of Alexander the Great, 331 B.C.—J.]

4. [Actually, the prisoner was the son of Czar (or King) Mitelleski; according to *Lion of the North*, Book 2, the czarevich's name was Artfchelou.—J.]

5. Page 439, volume 1, quarto edition, The Hague.

6. Chaplain Nordberg claims that after the Battle of Narva the Grand Turk immediately wrote a congratulatory letter to the king of Sweden in the following terms: "The Sultan Pasha, by the grace of God, to King Charles XII, etc." The letter is dated from the era of the Creation.

7. It is printed in most contemporary newspapers and records, and may be found in *The History of Charles XII.*

Part I, Chapter 12

1. Taken in its entirety, as are the following chapters, from Peter the Great's journal sent to me from Saint Petersburg.
2. [Voltaire calls it the *Naiova* River.—J.]
3. [Viborg is actually on the Gulf of Finland, some fifty miles from the western shore of Lake Ladoga.—J.]
4. [Noteburg was on an island in the Neva where it empties into the lake, not on the lake proper.—J.]
5. [Presumably a namesake of the General Schlippenbach previously mentioned.—J.]

Part I, Chapter 13

1. Taken from Peter the Great's journal.
2. [Hydromel is unfermented mead.—J.]
3. May 27, 1703, Whitsunday, foundation of Saint Petersburg. [The longitude of Saint Petersburg is actually 30 degrees 20 minutes east.—J.]
4. The previous chapters, as well as all the following, are taken from Peter the Great's journal and from documents sent from Saint Petersburg and collated with all the other documents in my possession.

Part I, Chapter 14

1. [Small craft armed with mortars for bombarding shore positions.—J.]
2. [Voltaire calls it *Gémavershof, ou Gémavers.*—J.]
3. [Lithuanian lowlands.—J.]
4. [In Poland, fifty miles southwest of Grodno.—J.]

Part I, Chapter 15

1. [I.e., Blenheim, 1704.—J.]
2. Issued in the Ukraine, 1709.
3. [Stanislas was a former Count Palatine.—J.]
4. [Livonia, then a province of Sweden.—J.]

Part I, Chapter 16

1. [At Zholkva near Lvov; Voltaire says, "Yolkova's proposals to elect, etc."—J.]
2. [See *Lion of the North*, Book 3, for a full account of this incident.—J.]
3. [Brigadier Muhlenfeld was commander of the Grodno garrison (cf. Grey, p. 277).—J.]

4. In Russian, Bibich.
5. [Halberdiers of the Swedish royal bodyguard.—J.]

Part I, Chapter 17

1. [Voltaire calls it *Mohilou*, adding the note, "In Russian, *Mogilev*."—J.]
2. [Voltaire calls it *Sossa*, and notes "In Russian, *Sozh*."—J.]
3. Admitted by Chaplain Nordberg, vol. 2, p. 263.
4. Vol. 2, p. 279.
5. [Presumably Budis was a secretary.—J.]
6. See chapter 1, pp. 47–48.
7. [In the Ottoman Empire, the horse's tail was the official emblem of a pasha.—J.]
8. [About sixty miles.—J.]

Part I, Chapter 18

1. Or Psol.
2. In 1730 the *Memoirs of Peter the Great,* by the self-styled Boyar Ivan Nestesuranov, were published in Amsterdam. His *Memoirs* state that, before crossing the Dnieper, the king of Sweden sent a general to make peace terms with the czar. The four volumes of these *Memoirs* are a tissue of similar falsehoods and ineptitudes, or compilations from news sheets. [Massie (p. 490) puts the Swedish force at Poltava at 19,000 men, against 42,000 Russians.—J.]
3. This fact is also to be found in a letter printed in the introduction to *Les Anecdotes de Russie.*
4. [In the late 1750s.—J.]

Part I, Chapter 19

1. La Motraye, in the account of his travels, publishes a letter from Charles XII to the Grand Vizier, but the letter is false, as are most of the tales of that mercenary traveler, and Nordberg himself admits that the king of Sweden was never willing to write to the Grand Vizier.
2. [One of the two Polish Generals of the Crown.—J.]
3. [In France, *une peine infamante* entailed a loss of civil rights.—J.]
4. [King Charles XI.—J.]
5. [The text here is faulty, I think. Voltaire's anecdote of the boot in *Lion of the North*, Book 7, has nothing to do with this affair.—J.]

Part II, Chapter 1

1. Nordberg's report concerning the Grand Seignior's pretensions is just as false and just as puerile. He tells us that Sultan Achmet sent the czar peace conditions before commencing hostilities. These conditions were, according to Charles XII's confessor, that Peter must renounce his alliance with King Augustus, restore Stanislas to the throne, return Livonia to Charles, pay that monarch in cash for what he had taken from him at Poltava, and demolish Saint Petersburg. This document was forged by one Brazey, the penurious author of a sheet entitled *Satirical, Historical and Comical Memoirs.* Such was Nordberg's source. It would seem that Charles XII's confessor was not his confidant.

2. [I.e., the Crimea.—J.]

3. It is very odd that so many authors confuse Wallachia with Moldavia.

4. Or Lapouchin.

5. [She was originally called Martha. Cf. *Lion of the North,* Book 5.—J.]

6. Peter the Great's journal.

7. [Odoacer: first barbarian ruler of Italy after the fall of the Empire (434?–93); Theodoric: king of the Ostrogoths (454?–526).—J.]

8. [Actually Constantine Brancovan (1654–1714).—J.]

9. [I.e., the Patriarch.—J.]

10. [Voltaire calls it the *Sireth.*—J.]

11. [I assume this means the rest of the army, or at least of the rearguard, not just the 400; Voltaire simply says, "On se forma avec célérité."—J.]

12. [The Kehaya was the lieutenant of the Grand Vizier.—J.]

13. P. 177 of Peter the Great's journal.

14. [The sequin was a gold coin used in Italy and Turkey.—J.]

15. [Voltaire says *Falksen.* Faleshty is about forty miles north-northeast of Jassy.—J.]

16. [Prince Menshikov was said to have started his career as a street vender of pastries in Moscow.—J.]

17. [Achmet III's mother.—J.]

18. [The Battle of Bender and its aftermath are fully described in *Lion of the North.*—J.]

Part II, Chapter 2

1. [Of Poland, presumably.—J.]

2. [A Turkish official.—J.]

3. [Voltaire doesn't say sixty million *what:* presumably francs.—J.]

Part II, Chapter 3

1. [In 1648.—J.]

2. [The Treaty of Osnabrück is part of the Peace of Westphalia.—J.]

3. [Friedrich Christian Weber, Hanoverian ambassador to Russia.—J.]

4. [The Aulic Council was a supreme court in the Holy Roman Empire.—J.]

5. [Voltaire uses the two French verbs *baiser* and *embrasser;* both mean "to kiss," but the latter can also mean "embrace".—J.]

Part II, Chapter 4

1. [George I, reigned 1714–27.—J.]

2. I think it incumbent upon me to leave King Stanislas's declaration exactly as he made it, word for word. There are some grammatical errors: "Je me déclare de sacrifier" is not French, but the document is all the more authentic for this, and none the less worthy of respect.

3. [The French crown (écu) was worth three francs (livres)—J.]

4. [I.e., instead of the same number of potential mutineers.—J.]

5. [The incident is recounted in *Peter the Great,* Part I, ch. 15, not in *Lion of the North.*—J.]

6. In his history the chaplain and confessor Nordberg calmly states that General Stenbock only set fire to the town because he had no wagons to take away the goods and chattels.

7. [The Cimbrians were an ancient barbarian people destroyed by Marius in 101 B.C. Neustria was a kingdom of the northwestern Franks during the Merovingian period.—J.]

8. Pronounced *Gueurtz* in French.

9. [Baron von Görtz was in fact beheaded in Stockholm almost immediately after the death of Charles XII in 1718.—J.]

10. Secret memoirs of Bassevitz.

11. Stenbock's memoirs.

12. [I.e., the Aegean.—J.]

13. [Voltaire says *Borgo* and *Abo;* Borgå is about thirty miles northeast of Helsingfors; Turku, formerly Åbo, is about ninety miles west-northwest of Helsingfors.—J.]

Part II, Chapter 5

1. [Vaasa is in fact some 200 miles north-northwest of Helsingfors.—J.]

2. [Praams are flat-bottomed boats.—J.]

3. [Also known as the battle of Cape Hango (see Grey, pp 333–34).—J.]

4. [Voltaire calls him *Cha-Ussin.*—J.]

Part II, Chapter 6

1. [The Treaty of Nystadt, August 30, 1721.—J.]

Part II, Chapter 7

1. [I.e., Charles-Leopold of Mecklenburg; see preceding chapter.—J.]

2. [Voltaire naturally uses the French equivalent, *veau.*—J.]

3. [The last serious outbreak of civil war in France directly caused by the nobility occurred during the minority of Louis XIV—who never forgot the traumatic experiences he underwent as a result—in the so-called Fronde (1648–53). Louis's policy was always to keep the nobles as far as possible under his thumb and under his eye at Versailles.—J.]

4. [*Abbé,* even before Voltaire's time, had acquired the second and humbler connotation more or less equivalent to the English *Reverend.* Voltaire could never resist a gibe—even (or perhaps especially) an unfair one—at the expense of the clergy.—J.]

5. [Signed in 1678–79, 1697, and 1713, respectively.—J.]

Part II, Chapter 8

1. [Mostly *Scottish* Jacobites, in fact, though there were some English too.—J.]

2. [Philippe, duke of Orleans, regent from 1715 to 1723.—J.]

3. [I.e., during the long and bloody War of the Spanish Succession, 1701–14, in which England and her allies had fought to prevent Philippe d'Anjou from succeeding to the Spanish throne.—J.]

4. [Voltaire was just twenty-two in 1716.—J.]

5. [Elbeuf is a little under ten miles south of Rouen, Gournay-en-Bray some thirty miles east of the same city. The ceremonial escort was accordingly thirty-five miles southwest of the czar's party, which was twenty-odd miles closer to Paris and Versailles than they.—J.]

6. [Louis XV was only seven years old at the time.—J.]

7. [Holy Roman Emperors in, respectively, 1347–78, 1412–37, and 1519–56.—J.]

8. ["It gains strength by going (on its course)." Virgil, *Aeneid* 4. 175. Said of Fame.—J.]
9. [Henry IV died in 1610.—J.]

Part II, Chapter 9

1. [In the time of the Emperor Constantine the Great, i.e., early fourth century A.D.—J.]
2. [Unlike the Protestant Anglicans, the French Gallicans had remained in communion with Rome, though frequently taking a rather independent line.—J.]
3. [In fact, the Drunken Synod long antedated Peter's trip to Paris, Zotov's appointment as prince-pope dating back to 1698 (see de Jonge, p. 135; Massie, p. 120), so it is a little unfair to lay the whole thing at the Sorbonne's door.—J.]
4. [Frederick William I, 1713–40.—J.]

Part II, Chapter 10

1. [Voltaire has *Théodore ou Theodorouna.*—J.]
2. [An ironic reference to the full-bearded Muscovites of the old school, Peter's bitterest opponents inside Russia, priests and laymen alike.—J.]
3. [The late Princess Charlotte was Charles VI's sister-in-law, the Empress's sister.—J.]
4. [The initial inquiries after Alexei's return were made in Moscow, and many of his associates were executed there. In March, Peter took Alexei to Saint Petersburg, where his trial was held and he died. Cf. Grey, pp. 365–68; Massie, pp. 693–710.—J.]
5. This was the son of the empress Catherine, who died on April 15, 1719.
6. [An Austrian Imperial official. In typically cavalier fashion, Voltaire transforms *Pleyer* to *Beyer.*—J.]
7. [The Convent of Suzdal Pokrovsky.—J.]
8. [The prince's personal servant, according to Grey, pp. 364–65.—J.]
9. [Maria was Peter's half-sister by Czar Alexei's first wife (i.e., Sophia's sister).—J.]
10. [Count von Schönborn was the Austrian Imperial vice-chancellor.—J.]
11. [Prince Eugene of Savoy, 1663–1736, distinguished Austrian general and associate of the duke of Marlborough during the War of the Spanish Succession.—J.]
12. [Alexei was twenty-eight at the time.—J.]
13. [I have not included this document.—J.]
14. [Manlius Torquatus, Roman Consul in 340 B.C., had his own son beheaded—though he had been victorious in a single combat before a battle—for disobeying orders.—J.]
15. [Don Carlos, 1545–68, apparently somewhat deranged son of Philip II of Spain. His father had him imprisoned in 1568 and he died shortly thereafter. It was rumored that his father had him poisoned.—J.]
16. [This all sounds as if Peter did not actually intend to execute Alexei, but merely to put the fear of God into him.—J.]
17. [The word is ambiguous, no doubt deliberately so.—J.]
18. [The cause of Alexei's death remains uncertain; Massie (p. 707) and de Jonge (p. 214) both suggest that the forty strokes of the knout Alexei had undergone during questioning may have been (to say the least) a contributing factor.—J.]

Part II, Chapter 11

1. [*Une industrie encouragée* is a state-aided industry.—J.]
2. [A mark is about eight ounces.—J.]
3. [Bunting is a thin woolen cloth, chiefly used to make flags, etc.—J.]

Part II, Chapter 12

1. [I.e., the old Russian dream of gaining access to the Mediterranean.—J.]
2. [A caste of Hindu merchants and traders.—J.]
3. [The Treaty of Nerchinsk, 1689. Peter's half-sister Sophia was then virtual ruler of Russia, Peter (17) and Ivan being co-czars. "Our system of reckoning dates": i.e., not according to the Chinese calendar.—J.]
4. [Mongolia.—J.]
5. [Theodosius I, "the Great," Byzantine emperor, reigned 379–95.—J.]
6. [Not very specific, but everything else in this chapter points to the year 1718; at any rate, once Saint Petersburg was firmly established as Peter's new capital.—J.]

Part II, Chapter 13

1. [The first revised legal code in Muscovy since 1550.—J.]
2. [Cf. Part I, ch. 1, describing the various administrative districts.—J.]
3. [A euphemism for bribes.—J.]
4. [The French term *maître (général) des requêtes* literally means *master of requests* or *petitions*.—J.]
5. [Elizabeth Petrovna, later Elizabeth I, reigned 1741–62. She was thus still on the throne when the first edition of *Peter the Great* was being published.—J.]

Part II, Chapter 14

1. [Prokopovich was archbishop of Pleskov (Pskov) at this time, but became archbishop of Novgorod in 1724.—J.]
2. [I.e., the Holy Roman Empire.—J.]
3. [See Part II, chapter 7, n. 4. The clerical collar was the distinguishing mark of the *abbé*.—J.]
4. [Saint Basil the Great, bishop of Caesarea in the fourth century.—J.]
5. [No. 139 (by Richard Steele), dated August 9, 1711, on "The Love of Glory."—J.]
6. [*La Mère Sotte* (The Foolish Mother) is a *sotie*—a kind of satirical farce—by Pierre Gringore (d. 1538). It was written in 1512 to satirize Holy Mother Church, or, more properly, its bellicose head, Pope Julius II, with whom King Louis XII was engaged in various unseemly and disedifying disputes.—J.]

Part II, Chapter 15

1. [General Jacob Bruce was born in Moscow, though of Scottish parentage. He had commanded Peter's artillery at Poltava. Count Andrei Osterman (1686–1747) directed foreign affairs under Catherine I and remained powerful until Elizabeth I came to the throne, when he was sent to Siberia.—J.]
2. [According to Grey (pp. 483–84), this was not Rehnskjöld, but Vice Admiral Ehrenskjöld, captured by the czar at the Battle of Hango.—J.]
3. [The controversy over Charles XII's death is still by no means settled, despite several exhumations of the king's skull—one at least as recent as 1917—and exhaustive ballistic tests. The leading authority on Charles, Prof. Ragnhild M. Hatton, believes the "random shot" theory to be the correct one (Hatton, *Charles XII of Sweden* [London: Weybright & Talley, 1968], pp. 500–

509). However, assassination from a much closer range than the walls of Fredrikshald makes just as good sense, particularly in view of the suspicious haste with which Charles's brother-in-law and successor, the duke of Hesse-Cassel, moved to block the possible succession of the legitimate heir, Charles's nephew, the young duke of Holstein.—J.]

4. [At the Battle of Cape Passero (southeastern tip of Sicily), in 1718, by Admiral George Byng.—J.]

5. [Gold medals would themselves seem to be tokens of honor.—J.]

6. [As Frederick I.—J.]

7. [There is no mention of a first landing, except for Peter's.—J.]

8. [Possibly Naissaar, a small Estonian island northwest of Tallinn.—J.]

9. [Voltaire uses the old name, *Oesel*.—J.]

10. [The Church of the Holy Trinity in Saint Petersburg, according to Grey, p. 380.—J.]

Part II, Chapter 16

1. [If this is an allusion to the Treaty of Nerchinsk, Voltaire is a trifle off course. First of all, *Sophia* negotiated the treaty, though doubtless the co-czars Ivan and Peter signed it. Secondly, Russia had to pull out of a large area of Chinese territory.—J.]

2. [The Thirty Years' War, 1618–48; the Fronde, or civil disturbances caused by the last outburst of the feudal-minded French nobility during the minority of Louis XIV, between 1648 and 1653; the Saint Bartholomew's Day Massacre (of French Protestants—the Huguenots—by Catholic extremists), in 1572, at the peak of the Wars of Religion in France; Charles VI of France, known variously as *the Mad* or *the Well-Beloved*, reigned 1380–1422, while John II (the Good) was king of France from 1350 to 1364—i.e., both monarchs had to endure the worst disasters suffered by France during the Hundred Years' War; the English Civil Wars between the Royalist and Parliamentarian factions, personified by King Charles I and Oliver Cromwell respectively, lasted from 1642 to 1646 and 1648 to 1652; the Tartar domination of Russia lasted from the early thirteenth century right down to the close of the fifteenth (1223–1480), while their incursions into China continued for centuries.—J.]

3. [The Albani had nothing to do with modern Albania; they were tribesmen living south of the Caucasus.—J.]

4. [Mir Vais was chief of the Ghilzai Afghans and father of Mir Mahmud. He died in 1715.—J.]

5. [The Ghebers, like the Parsis, were Zoroastrian fire-worshippers.—J.]

6. [Who were, needless to say, Muslims.—J.]

7. [Voltaire doesn't say which grandson, Peter II or Peter III; see Note on Peter's Successors.—J.]

8. [Voltaire calls it *Andréhof*.—J.]

9. [Hyrcania was an ancient province of Asia southeast of the Caspian.—J.]

10. [*The New Columbia Encyclopedia*, ed. William H. Harris and Judith S. Levey (New York and London: Columbia University Press, 1975), says the city was founded "at Iron Gates (called Caspian or Albanian Gates by ancients), a defile between Caucasus and Caspian, on a major commercial route."—J.]

11. [The Caucasian Wall (or Alexander's Wall) was built by the Persians in the sixth century.—J.]

12. [Voltaire follows his usual practice of calling the Don the *Tanaïs*. The river Cyrus is now the Kura River, which in fact flows some 100 miles to the southwest of the city of Derbent.—J.]

13. [Darius III, king of Persia, died 330 B.C.—J.]

14. [Ashraf succeeded Mir Mahmud in 1725.—J.]

15. [Quli Khan, who eventually assumed the title of Nadir Shah in 1736, was an Afshar tribal chieftain.—J.]

Part II, Chapter 17

1. [The verbs *couronner* and *sacrer* used by Voltaire are as good as synonymous.—J.]
2. [Anna Ivanovna married the duke of Courland in 1710. Her husband died two months later.—J.]
3. [All Byzantine emperors.—J.]
4. Memoirs of Count von Bassevitz.
5. [William Mons, brother of Anna Mons, Peter's former mistress.—J.]
6. [Count von Bassevitz, according to Grey, p. 490, n. 25.—J.]
7. Count Bassevitz's manuscript memoirs.
8. [March 10/21: old/new style date.—J.]
9. [And by his younger daughters by Catherine, Elizabeth and Natalya, who were of course further down in the order of succession than Peter and Anna.—J.]
10. [Presumably the Fortress of Saints Peter and Paul.—J.]
11. [Feofan Prokopovich. Though Voltaire calls him archbishop of Pleskov below, he had actually become archbishop of Novgorod in 1724.—J.]
12. [Alexei Makarov, Peter's trusted cabinet secretary.—J.]
13. [See Note on Peter's Successors.—J.]
14. [A rather obvious, if well-deserved, animadversion on Charles XII, whose entire career was spent trying to excel Julius Caesar and Alexander the Great.—J.]
15. [An error: Anna *Ivanovna* was the czarina.—J.]
16. [Again, Voltaire omits Peter's male heirs, Peter II, Ivan VI, and Peter III, as negligible.—J.]

Letter to Shuvalov

1. [Count Ivan Ivanovich Shuvalov, Empress Elizabeth's favorite and Voltaire's Russian correspondent *extraordinaire*, 1727–97.—J.]
2. [Voltaire himself, who, from 1754 to 1760, passed his summers near Geneva, Switzerland, at a residence called Les Délices.—J.]
3. [Horace *Ars poetica* ll. 323–24. Citation in full reads: "Graïs ingenium, Graïs dedit ore rotundo/Musa loqui . . ." ("To the Greeks the Muse gave [native wit, to the Greeks she gave] speech in well-rounded phrase . . ." (*Ars poetica,* trans, H. Rushton Fairclough. Loeb Classical Library. Cambridge, Mass.: Harvard University Press; London: Heinemann, 1961 [1926]).—J.]
4. [Or Oirats, inhabitants of the Altai Mountains.—J.]
5. [Koko Nor, now Chinese *Ch'ing hai Hu*, is a lake northeast of Tibet, in the province of Tsinghai or Ching-hai.—J.]
6. [Cf. Samuel Johnson's remarks on the lack of trees in Scotland, in the *Journey to the Western Islands of Scotland,* and James Boswell's explanation of those remarks, in the *Journal of a Tour to the Hebrides with Samuel Johnson, LL.D.* The two appear in a single volume, edited R. W. Chapman (London: Oxford University Press, 1961); see, e.g., pp. 9–10 (Johnson), 202–3 (Boswell).—J.]
7. [Volhynia was a medieval Russian principality; Podolia (now Podolsk, in western Ukraine) was part of the medieval kingdom of Poland.—J.]
8. [Voltaire has *Kiow ou Kioff.*—J.]
9. [I use *Ivan Vasilievich.*—J.]
10. [Ivan the Terrible.—J.]
11. [Lord Carlisle was King Charles II's ambassador to Muscovy. Voltaire is right in saying there was never an Ambassador Bèze; his name was Sir Jerome *Bowes.*—J.]
12. [Photius, Patriarch of Constantinople, died in 891; Princess Olga, consort of Rurik the Great's son Igor, was converted to Christianity in 955.—J.]

13. [The French wrote this kind of history far more recently than a thousand years ago—more like 250, in fact. Cf., *inter alia,* Jean Lemaire de Belge's *Les Illustrations de Gaule et Singularités de Troie,* the first volume of which appeared in 1511.—J.]

14. [Unlike Antenor, Hector, Francus, Polimenes, et al., these are all historical characters of the early Merovingian period in France. See Augustin Thierry's *Récits des temps mérovingiens,* available in English as *Tales of the Early Franks,* trans. M. F. O. Jenkins (University, Ala.: University of Alabama Press, 1977).—J.]

Index